The Devils Messages

LANGUAGE AND CONTESTED SPACE IN 20TH CENTURY AMERICA

By Thomas Aiello
Valdosta State University

cognella™
academic publishing

Bassim Hamadeh, CEO and Publisher
Michael Simpson, Vice President of Acquisitions
Jamie Giganti, Managing Editor
Jess Busch, Graphic Design Supervisor
David Miano, Acquisitions Editor
Jessica Knott, Senior Project Editor
Luiz Ferreira, Licensing Associate

First published in the United States of America in 2014 by Cognella, Inc.

Printed in the United States of America

ISBN: 978-1-62131-565-0 (pbk)/ 978-1-62131-566-7 (br)

www.cognella.com   800-200-3908

Contents

Acknowledgments

T he author would like to thank Mary Farmer-Kaiser for her help, as well as Brent Riffel, a great friend and writing partner who coauthored "The Anhedonic Among the Camellias." In addition, the reviewers of *Inscribed, Crossroads, Virginia Magazine of History and Biography, Americana: A Journal of American Popular Culture, The McNeese Review, Film History, Interactions, The Journal of Popular Culture, Cinemascope,* and *Flow* provided valuable advice and help in crafting many of these essays, and the publishers of those journals kindly provided permission to reprint modified versions of the originals. The author would also like to thank Carol Fuller, Pete Aiello, and Dixie Milner.

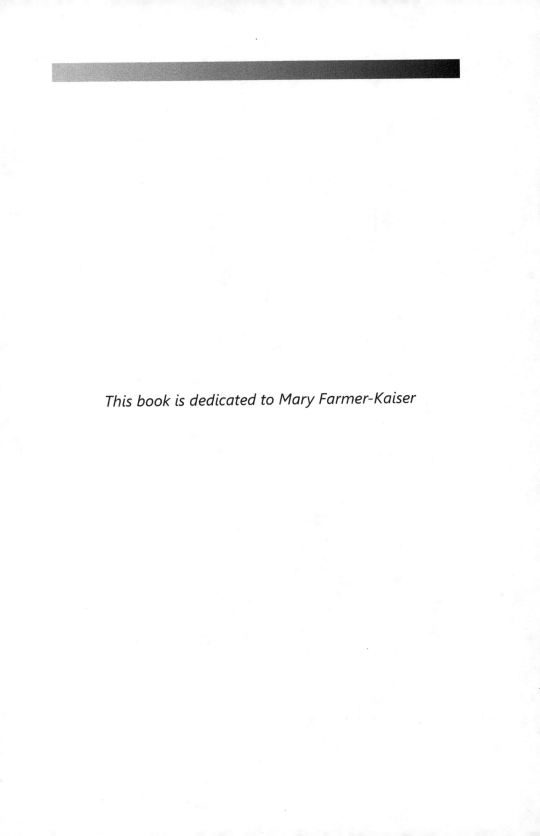

This book is dedicated to Mary Farmer-Kaiser

Introduction

When the elevator came to life, the ropes vibrated as they began to move, some up, some down, pushed as they were by the motor to which they were attached by way of the motor gear reducer. It was the classical apparatus of pulleys that conquered Newton's gravity, alternating its rebuke with a well-placed counterweight, but it was that gear system— its two perpendicular rotational axes gauging both speed and the rotation plane, thereby optimizing torque—that allowed the entire system to make that mysterious transition from electrical power to mechanical power. It was, in other words, a humming, creaking demonstration of the reconciliation of difference providing the fuel for a system in motion. Electrical power to mechanical. Newtonian physics to engineering. To wit:

$$P = \frac{IV}{\sqrt{2}}$$

with V standing in for the voltage, I over the square root of 2 being the electrical current source, and the resulting power transferred thusly:

$$P = T\varpi$$

power being equal to the torque (T) multiplied times the rotational speed (ϖ).

But there was more reconciliation at work. I stood there, pacing, tapping my fingers against the wall behind me, fed in my frustration by general impatience, not desperate for the elevator to arrive because of any baseline need, but rather desperate for the sake of desperation, because in those waking moments between already-completed action (parking the car, walking with purpose into the building, keeping my head down the whole way, watching the cracks in the sidewalk slide quickly below my feet and into oblivion before reaching the door, opening it, and making the necessary gestures to bring the elevator to life) and potential-future action (shuffling a stack of meaningless papers in my office on the fifth floor, meeting with a student about an inevitably late assignment, due no doubt to an inevitably dire medical situation or dead grandparent, or making a fresh pot of coffee), the expectation of potential colors all judgments of the present and leaves nothing but the residue of creeping discontent. And I stared at the bank of two elevators in front of me. Before the pulleys began their work, before the gears began turning, before the energy left its static state, a control system dictated by a series of computer chips chose which of the two elevators could do the job of carrying me to my office most efficiently. It reconciled the state of both contraptions, whose seeming equality belied the functional, relational inequality that allowed one to be better suited to the needs of the building, the electric company, and me.

The algorithm for any control system that makes choices for elevators must accommodate five possible states of elevator being. An elevator can 1) add a passenger riding up or 2) riding down. It can 3) add multiple passengers from multiple floors each riding in the same direction. More rarely, it can 4) add multiple passengers from multiple floors, some riding up and others riding down. Or, finally, an elevator can 5) serve a specific point-to-point function, where it travels from one inception floor to one destination floor without waiting for passengers at any subsequent middling stops.

It is, in other words, yet another reconciliation game, as the system itself uses the algorithm to choose the definition of 'elevatorness' that best suits everyone's needs.

So the story of my elevator ride is the story of difference, inequality, and reconciliation. It is the story of contested definitions, where choices based on the perceived best version of those definitions wins the day and drives the system to action. This collection of essays tells much the same story.

But I'm getting ahead of myself. The definition problems that fuel the mechanisms of elevator travel also provided personal validation that morning. To alert the bank of elevators to my presence, I had to do more than just push the button featuring the stylized arrow pointing north. I was also required to swipe my faculty identification card through a reader that determined my eligibility to ride. In the bygone days of the 1990s and early 2000s, the elevator control system responded to anyone's touch, allowed all to enter its doors, creaking and unvarnished as they might be. But the crush of students who thrust themselves into the metal boxes every morning, hoping to avoid the catastrophe of actually experiencing the aerobic exercise of stair-climbing, felled the vibrating ropes, the metallurgy and pulleys, and continually generated OUT OF ORDER signs, which appeared seemingly out of nowhere and forced us all to make the hike. To solve the problem, administration officials deemed that only those employed by the university or those students with the physical inability to climb would be allowed to ride. And so, there was, through all the other relational definition games that commenced after I arrived at the elevator doors, a definition of my own I had to provide. The nature of the system itself forced me to define myself against the other potential riders in the building.

Of course, as the doors opened and I entered the contraption, students walked in behind me, predictably fat, predictably clutching their cellular phones, hoping I wouldn't tell them to leave. They were desperate to save themselves a few steps, but they were also contesting the way the elevator defined them. They were making a status argument, challenging the words by which the elevator knew how to define them.

The essays in this collection describe similar, pivotal moments—elevator moments—in twentieth century America, moments where definitions break down, where meaning is contested, and the system is spurred to life as a result. We would be hard-pressed to call this motion progress, in the traditional sense. The elevator, after all, has five different situational states of being, none better or worse than the other. The fifth floor, despite my partiality to it, is not functionally superior to any of its counterparts. When people enter the elevator doors, they choose a floor based on their own personal whims. This is not Newtonian physics. This is Darwinian randomness. And like the biologist's finches, the elevator responds to situational realities. In human relations, those situational realities are created by shifts in meaning, by the cross-currents of language, which ultimately drive the system—not forward, perhaps, but into a new state of being, for better or worse, depending on one's own needs or beliefs.

Along these lines, for example, Frank R. Ankersmit, borrowing from Nietzsche's conceptualization of the vulnerability of traditional frameworks of causality and Wittgenstein's suggestion of inherent untruth in the product of reason, has argued that historical interpretations only gain their identity through recognition of other interpretations. In effect, "they are what they are only on the basis of what they are *not.*" The past in all its uncertain totality can be viewed as a linguistic edifice with the same properties as any other text. Definitional difference and contested meanings, it seems, drive the study of history itself.

Of course, that leads us just one logical step down the causal chain to someone like Jean Baudrillard, who argues that the grammar of the modern age leads to a simulated reality. Images have been over-represented, and therefore only refer to other representations. These images become referenced in response to signifiers, and representations that represent representations are not based in reality, thereby creating a false world of nothing but baseless symbols. Every one of our language games, he seems to be saying, is played on a field of sand. Still, even when we allow such contemplations to lead us down the slippery slope of postmodernism, we are left with definitions and difference. We are left with stakes games and meaning contests, even though folks like Baudrillard would argue that in the end, such contests lead to no meaning at all.

These essays, at any rate, still find meaning in the endeavor, though I would be lying if I claimed that the work of Ankersmit, Baudrillard, and their ilk didn't serve as at least a subtle, waterlogged theoretical underpinning to their authorship.

It was they who were on my mind as I finally entered the elevator, pushed FIVE, and set a new algorithm in motion. I rode up, listening to the clicks and hum of the gears, of the process, until the doors opened again, leading me out into the hallway that would take me to my office. Professor X was there, and he glared as he walked past me. Professor X, in the cliquish manner of many academics, hates my guts. It's partially professional jealousy, as all academic backbiting certainly is, even my own. It's partly because I often conduct myself in the grand manner of a ten-year-old. But even more than that, Professor X doesn't like me because he doesn't agree with my conception of history. An historian, according to him, writes about one tiny, spatially and temporally localized phenomenon, then spends the rest of his or her life parsing out its intricacies, imprisoning him or herself with the chains of that original choice of youth. Aiello, I imagine him arguing to any and all who will listen, has no spatially and temporally localized compartment. He writes about whatever suits his fancy. There is no unifying theme. No fundamental core.

As bothersome as his unkindness has been, it isn't the glares that disturb me most. It is instead his assumption about my work. "But wait!" I silently screamed as I made my way past him, down the hall to my waiting office, "There *is* a theme! There *is* a fundamental core!"

This collection is an attempt to scream less silently. The fundamental core of twentieth century American cultural history is the elevator moment. Breakdowns in the meaning of words or concepts—those moments when we talk past each other, even when we use the same terms—create a new historical reality from the rubble, whether that new reality can properly be called progress or not. It is, I suppose, the Hegelian dialectic in microcosm, minus the Enlightenment faith in the forward march of humanity. When our definitions, our language, fail us, the game isn't always zero sum, but it is always a game, and the winners ultimately become incumbents in the next, ever-waiting game.

The first essay, "Accumulated Grief" describes a curious coincidence in 1919, when two southern men—one rich, one poor; one rural, one urban—murdered their wives before killing themselves on the same night.

The second, "Jim Crow Ordained," examines religious and racial difference during the Civil Rights Movement. Religion remained the single most significant organizing principle of the civil rights struggle for the repeal of Jim Crow legislation, and southern civil rights religious leaders constantly referenced the Bible to justify their cause and convince their oppressors of wrongdoing. The oppressors, however, steeped their segregationist message and policy in the same Bible used by Martin Luther King, Jr. Both groups felt vindicated by similar faiths, causing each to perceive the "dark side" of its belief system. Vindication of one position was the necessary denunciation of the other, which created a southern imbalance and a dispossession of both whites and blacks.

Those arguments sounded similar in the realm of art. In the Spring of 1950, the Virginia Museum of Fine Arts in Richmond held "American Painting, 1950." It was the museum's seventh biennial exhibition of contemporary painting. Willem DeKooning, Arshile Gorky, Edward Hopper, Jackson Pollock and many others exhibited at the show. So too did Hyman Bloom and Stuart Davis. The third essay, "The Champion and the Corpse," describes the outrage two paintings in particular sparked in the Richmond community, which interpreted the exhibition as yet another intrusion by northern intellectuals into their preferred society. That intrusion of the unfamiliar formed the core of the Virginia outrage. For the citizens of Richmond, the biennial constituted a threat to their understood norms of both art and society. Many of them charged the painters with communism. Not coincidentally, the fourth essay, "Constructing 'Godless Communism,'" describes American Christianity throughout the early Cold War, as it pitted itself as both the primary target of communist annihilation and the most effective weapon against the atheistic scourge—against "godless communism." Throughout the post-war years of the Second Red Scare, "godless communism," along with similar linguistic variations, rooted itself as a functional epithet and cautionary tale to a reluctant America in a changing global environment. As the communist threat to the American way of life grew, so its godless materialism continued to threaten a Christianity increasingly tied to America's self-image. It was a metaphor of good versus evil, and a reinforcement of the notion of American divine right. That metaphor, however, became a definition, creating a patriotic American culture inextricably bound to religious faith.

Madalyn Murray was a more immediate threat to that faith. *Murray v. Curlett* removed the Lord's Prayer and Bible reading from public schools in 1963. The prevailing national discourse that emerged during the following school year represented a relatively united organization against the ruling, based primarily on moral, rather than legal, grounds. "*Murray v. Curlett* and the American Mind" examines the popular response to Supreme Court action, specifically focusing on the methods used by the majority to manipulate public sentiment for the purpose of counteracting judicial decrees. Public sentiment was set to boil two years later in Selma, Alabama. On Tuesday, March 9, 1965, Martin Luther King, Jr. walked across the Edmund Pettus Bridge. He sang songs along the way. As he reached the other side of the Alabama River, he spoke to police officers, arrayed to block the bridge's exit. He knelt in prayer, then stood up again. He turned around and walked back across the bridge to a nearby church. Hundreds of people trailed behind him, almost all expecting to continue walking to Montgomery, unaware that their leader struck a secret agreement to turn the marchers around. As "Hercules, the Tortoise, and the Edmund Pettus Bridge" argues, historical interpretations of the stunted "middle passage" between Bloody Sunday and the Selma to Montgomery voting rights march have dissected political backroom dealings and police strategies to subdue the marchers and save face from public embarrassment. Each evaluation also includes a description of the event itself. Those descriptions, however, tell just as much as the intended historical accoutrements. The language employed in various historical descriptions creates a sort of Zeno's paradox: the description of someone's motion causes the recipient of the description to doubt its very possibility. It creates a false impression, or in the case of different histories, creates a variety of impressions presenting themselves as empirical fact. Using five samples describing the march, this essay demonstrates the inconsistencies between the accounts, arguing that they are technically and functionally different.

In 1966, a year following Selma, Otto Preminger arrived in Baton Rouge, Louisiana to make his film *Hurry Sundown*. Members of the cast received death threats. Black actors and crew members were disallowed in certain restaurants and hotels. Others required advance permission before the integrated cast could bed down for the night. The seventh essay, *"Hurry Sundown,"* acknowledges that the film itself was a critical flop. Its production serves as one in a long line of examples of white Hollywood's clumsy, ham-handed, stereotypical treatment of race before the final fall of the Production Code. But it also demonstrates the South's continued racial intransigence, even as the sixties moved into their twilight and there was real money to be made from location filming. The white citizens of Louisiana weren't upset at the Civil Rights stances of black actors in the show. And they weren't upset that the film was portraying southern farm society as a cutthroat business wedded to class and race. Instead, the white citizens of Louisiana narrowed the focus of their ire to the simple fact of integration. And so the filmed representation of class unity across racial lines met its match in the lived presence of a racial reality that seemed to disregard class altogether.

The eighth essay, "Scrabble Tiles Can Help Decipher the Devil's Messages," examines Maria Monk's *Awful Disclosures of the Hotel Dieu Nunnery of Montreal* (1836) and Ira Levin's *Rosemary's Baby* (1967). Though published 131 years apart, the books carried many similarities that contributed to their popularity. They both featured a heroine who entered a dark, mysterious, labyrinthine house. Both heroines were subject to the horror of the "evil" taking place in each building. But the largest difference was that the early nineteenth century secret evildoers were Catholics, the late twentieth century secret evildoers were Satanists. The anti-immigrant sentiment of the early 1800s made people far more disposed to fear the Catholics, while the ultra-religious Cold War climate of the late 1960s was far more concerned with the prospect of "evil." So there were different forms of distrust—the first afraid that Catholic immigrants would infiltrate the country and erode the bedrock Protestant foundations of the nation, the second afraid that communists would infiltrate the country and destroy the Christian democracy they so cherished.

"The Man Plague," the collection's ninth essay, evaluates the words and meanings of popular music. In 1982, disco was at its low ebb, but the style and energy of the music had made its way into the broader popular music scene. That year, an unlikely hit made the transition from San Francisco dance clubs to the American mainstream. "It's Raining Men," written by Paul Jabara and Paul Schaeffer, and performed by The Weather Girls, became a popular hit for Columbia Records and was nominated for a Grammy Award. But it provided its listeners, whether wittingly or unwittingly, with stark and disturbing religious imagery rooted in the historical tradition of Christian theology. It was, through the hustles and shakes, the lights and mirrors, a radical reinterpretation of the Lucifer myth. "The Anhedonic Among the Camellias: Woody Allen and Reflective Love," co-authored with Brent Riffel, evaluates Woody Allen's cinematic treatment of love, which argues that the experience is an ineffective but ultimately worthwhile palliative for anhedonia—the inability to experience pleasure or romantic fulfillment. Love, for Allen, is essentially unattainable, or at least incapable of bringing happiness, but it remains the best coping strategy at our disposal, and thus remains a worthwhile endeavor.

The eleventh essay, "Denmark Vesey and Historical Context," describes the historical debate prompted by Michael Johnson's 2001 *William & Mary Quarterly* article, which declared the Denmark Vesey slave conspiracy to be, in actuality, a conspiracy of white magistrates to keep the South Carolina populace on its guard. The immediate responses in the journal's following issue seemed to defend against Johnson's charges, prompting historians of slavery and slave conspiracies to take sides. But the defenses never engaged Johnson's argument. Douglas Egerton, Edward A. Pearson, and David Robertson misapplied historical tenets to create influential responses, but in so doing exemplified the fallacy of false constants. The often helpful insistence on historiography and context, in this instance, led to unhelpful arguments. "The Linguistics of Taste," the twelfth essay, evaluates another unhelpful argument—the misuse of the term "taste" by two American beer brands. It argues that the campaigns are both different and more destructive than the usual deception in advertising. Finally, "Meta-Interloping and the New Double Consciousness: Traducing the Interdisciplinary Veil" describes the experience of being the only historian at Cornell University's School of Criticism and Theory. In so doing, it attempts to plot out the space between history and theory, historians and theoreticians.

The essays move chronologically, but they are by no means comprehensive. The evolution of American history tracks along myriad similar disputes. Instead, each is exemplary of historical points where disagreements over language create contested space. Some of those spaces are large—civil rights, Christianity, the Cold War. Others are smaller, more limited examples of similar problems.

As I returned to the elevators later that afternoon, I was confronted again with one of those limited examples. An elevator moment. I swiped my card, defined myself, then waited as the voltage joined the current source, as the torque multiplied times the rotational speed, creating the power transferred through the gears. Professor X was nowhere to be seen. But the reconciliation of difference, in each of its mechanical forms, continued unabated. Then the elevator doors opened.

Citations

"Accumulated Grief" originally appeared in *Inscribed* 1 (January/February 2006): 22-25; "Jim Crow Ordained: White and Black Christianity in the Civil Rights South" originally appeared in *Crossroads: A Southern Culture Annual*, edited by Ted Olson, 107-119. Atlanta: Mercer University Press, 2006; "The Champion and the Corpse: Art and Identity in Richmond, 1950" originally appeared in *Virginia Magazine of History and Biography* 117 (Spring 2009): 32-59 and won the 2009 William M.E. Rachal Award; "Constructing 'Godless Communism': Religion, Politics, and Popular Culture, 1954-1960" originally appeared in *Americana: The Journal of American Popular Culture* 4 (Spring 2005): http://www.americanpopularculture.com/journal/articles/spring_2005/aiello.htm; REPRINTED IN: *Americana: Readings in American Popular Culture* (Los Angeles: Press Americana, 2006): 253-263. This version has been modified to include Chicago Manual of Style endnotes. "*Murray v. Curlett* and the American Mind: Public Sentiment as Systematic Objectification, 1963-1964" originally appeared in *The McNeese Review* 43 (2005): 60-86; "*Hurry Sundown*: Otto Preminger, Baton Rouge, and Race, 1966-1967" originally appeared in *Film History: An International Journal* 21 (No. 4 2010): 394-410; "Scrabble Tiles Can Help Decipher the Devil's Messages: From Baby-Killing Nuns to Baby-Wanting Witches in American Fiction and Culture" originally appeared in *Interactions* 11 (Spring 2006): 1-9. This version, originally published with MLA internal notation, has been modified to include Chicago Manual of Style endnotes. "The Man Plague: Disco, the Lucifer Myth, and the Theology of 'It's Raining Men'" originally appeared in *The Journal of Popular Culture* 43 (October 2010): 926-941. This version, originally published with MLA internal notation, has been modified to include Chicago Manual of Style endnotes. "The Anhedonic Among the Camellias: Woody Allen and Reflective Love" originally appeared in *Cinemascope* 4 (January-April 2006): http://www.cinemascope.it/. "The Linguistics of Taste" originally published in Flow 4 (Issue 2 2006): http://jot.communication.utexas.edu/flow/?jot=view&id=1629.

Accumulated Grief

"It was the hand of God," said a beaming Alvin York, "that guided us all and brought about the victory." Tennessee's war hero stood confidently before howling New York reporters, each absorbed by the gravity of the man who single-handedly killed twenty Germans and helped usher in the Allies' victory in the Great War. He was smiling. "I feel a heap stronger spiritually than when I went away." It was the twenty-second of May, 1919.[1]

Meanwhile, W.K. Allsup, an unemployed carpet cleaner, lived and died in Birmingham, Alabama. As did his wife. Marion Padgett, a wealthy planter, lived and died in Nashville, Tennessee. As did his wife. "I don't approve of taking human life unless it's necessary," York said, "but I considered it necessary." Then he retired to his room in the Waldorf-Astoria. He received the Congressional Medal of Honor. He was a war hero. He was the pride of the South.

It had been some months since the late winter cold of Birmingham saw Allsup's hand unjustly taken from him. He lost it while working for the Frisco Railroad, and ever since, work had been hard to find. Ten-year-old Douglas, eight-year-old Jack, and five-year-old Irene would need food to eat and clothes to wear, but though the Earthquake Carpet Cleaning

Company gave the single-handed father a chance, it couldn't keep him employed. "You need two hands to clean carpets," they might have told him. "This is the *Earthquake* Carpet Cleaning Company, not just some Joes off the street."

And then there was Fannie. Even before the Earthquake and the Frisco, there was the earthquake of his separation from his wife. There was, it was remarked in hushed tones, domestic trouble. Allsup knew that he had been angry and destitute long before railroad work took his hand, but he remained appalled that he could fall farther down the well while his lawfully wedded wife began dressmaking in the house to support herself and the kids. "This isn't justice," he thought. "And now ... "

And now he was being sued for divorce on the grounds of cruelty and non-support. Cruelty? Wasn't he the one trying to make ends meet away from his family? Non-support? "I only have one hand!" he may have screamed into the hot May night. Fannie had the children. She had the house on South 27th and had even taken in boarders, J.D. Hayden and his son William, to bring in extra income. "I'm going to end it all," he told Fannie in one of many fits of desperate rage brought on by the accumulated grief of being working-class without work and being in love without the ability to demonstrate it properly.

Marion Padgett was one of the wealthiest farmers in middle Tennessee. It was that wealth, along with his valiant service to the Union during the Civil War, which gave him the social prominence he retained. It accumulated. It accumulated despite the incidents.

His wife had given him grief for more than his share of harvests. It accumulated, too, and soon a chancellor's injunction forced him to leave his own home—the home he built for himself with the currency of his prominence. She was the daughter of Hardin McDonald, another prominent farmer, and Padgett's second wife. Theirs was an alliance early on, but then there was one child seven years ago, and another five years ago, and resentment upon resentment upon resentment. It was early May when the former Miss McDonald sued for divorce.

The litany of reasons only accumulated. Marion treated his wife cruelly and inhumanly. He threatened her life and even attempted once to kill her. "It's best you stay away," said the chancellor in so many words, "at least until we straighten this out. We can't rightly have our war heroes and wealthy citizens killing their wives indiscriminately."

Padgett's farm spanned the borders of Overton and Pickett Counties. Three miles away lived a new generation's war hero, Alvin York.

While Alvin York slept comfortably in his room at the Waldorf-Astoria, 863 miles away W.K. Allsup climbed into a small lattice doorway on the back porch of what used to be his home, into a small pantry just off the dining room. He crept through a serving door, through the dining room and up the stairs with the utmost caution. Caution could have saved his marriage from collapse. Caution could have saved his hand from its untimely death. Nothing could stop the earthquake that was now plowing its way through the topography of his anguished mind.

At the top of the stairs, Allsup found the closet just across from his wife's bedroom—the closet just across from what used to be their bedroom, back when the children were just ideas, when he had two hands to hold her with, and when the world was more than a compendium of financial and emotional poverty. Before all this grief began to accumulate. He stood silently and stared at the quiet space, seeing it not as a bedroom but as a library of his former bliss. Then he removed his shoes to silence his footsteps and placed them behind the door, just as she might have always told him to do.

That morning, he came by in the light of day to beg for reconciliation. "These burdens have accumulated beyond my capacity to contain them," he said in one way or another. And she told him not to return. Fearing the worst, Fannie borrowed a shotgun from her boarder, William. "Just in case," she might have said, with a reassuring half-smile. "I won't need it, but I'd like to have it near me just the same." And William understood.

As Allsup stood there staring at what used to be, the clock spun 'round to 23 May in the quiet dark of night. He walked into the bedroom the two had shared. He stared at his sleeping wife. Fannie's thin neck and round face belied a peace her waking appearance hadn't shown in months. Her curly brown hair seemed to stay as patiently prepared as it was that troubled morning. And she was beautiful.

And he felt in his pocket for the 38-caliber pistol and the note that could never explain what he was about to do. He fired a bullet into the brain of his sleeping wife, killing her instantly, then pulled the gun to his own neck and fired again.

The children awoke. The Haydens awoke. "We rushed into the room," said J.B., "and there was Mrs. Allsup, on her left side, and Mr. Allsup lying on the floor with a bullet through his neck from the right side." The children, long since innocent, felt the press of the accumulated grief in the room. "I'm glad he is dead," said Douglas, "but mother—"

The note was still in the pocket of the motionless figure on the floor. It read: "I have found out much about my wife and I have decided to kill her and then myself. I want my brother in Montgomery to have Irene (which is a third child) and do what you think best about the boys. They are better off as it is."

"We are not better off as it is," was the message Marion Padgett had been receiving for weeks. Friday, the twenty-third, was to be his day in court and quite possibly the last day for the calm surrender of a familial bond. Surrender, however, was never a real option for a southerner who fought for the Union and a husband who threatened the life of his spouse. "This grief accumulates," he may have told himself, "but I won't let it break me."

He spent his Thursday afternoon in the company of a son from his first marriage. He felt calm in the midst of an environment not fraught with the complications of *I've-said-the-wrong-thing-one-too-many-times-and-I-know-it*. The burden of status and the burden of family must have melted away as he now saw the full-grown man across from him as a confidant rather than a colonial dependency. "These problems are nothing that squirrel hunting couldn't cure," he said. His son would have nodded knowingly, with a reassuring half-smile. "Yes," he might have responded, anticipating his father's next question, "you can take the shotgun."

And he did.

And he walked to the home he had been enjoined to leave such a short time ago, when all of his grief accumulated in his expulsion from the house that his hard work and reputation had conspired to bring him. His wife was asleep, resting for her day in court, when she would finally find recompense for the amputated plantation life that she never fully realized. She would find recompense for the civility she lost at the hands of her husband's Civil

War ghosts. Her surrender was still haunting the recesses of her sleeping mind when a shadow pulled its way across the bare walls of a bedroom long since devoid of passion. But now there was passion, even as she slept.

Marion may have hesitated just before he moved, as he glared at the womb that provided him two children. He may have thought about his long-gone military service and the sensation of the kill. He shot his wife through the belly. In her terrorized anguish in those waking moments before death, she would have stared up at her husband with empty eyes, her look feigning disdain as she rifled through her catalogue of *things-to-do-before-you-die.*

And then she died.

Padgett's exit was swift, as he ran quickly to his makeshift home in another building on the plantation grounds. After closing the door, he put two pillows at its base. He sat quietly with his back against the door. There was no catalogue for him to consult. The Bible and the War and the press of southern history declared that he was destined for Hell. "And Hell is where I'll go," he may have said, gritting his teeth with the force of Shiloh and the Tennessee State Bank. He was 762 miles from the war hero Alvin York. He put the gun's muzzle under his chin, then used a stick to finish what all of his accumulated grief began so long before.

Marion Padgett never returned from the grave—never haunted the memory of those who loathed and revered him in life. And yet he spoke. He said, "Look how money didn't matter when all my plans for myself were disrupted by unrequited love. Or by love whose requite I killed through my inability to demonstrate propriety. I was crushed by all this accumulated grief, as anyone else would be. And my money couldn't stop it. I could have been an unemployed carpet cleaner in Birmingham, Alabama, for that matter."

The unemployed carpet cleaner told of similar regrets in his preternatural absence from the world. "Coming to the big city was anathema for all I could have become, if I had just had two hands and a wife whose instincts were more like the South of our bygone days. Poverty is poverty, and it sinks into the fabrics that surround whatever small set of rooms you can find in the industrializing, urbanizing South. These burdens accumulate and make us who we are."

"And all of my grief," Padgett responded, "is a product of my fear: of being without, of change, of self-created loneliness, of not living up to the standards set by my accomplishments of long ago. These burdens accumulate and make us who we are—make us break in half no matter who we are."

Allsup: "And you don't have to tell me that justice is simply a fancy word for revenge, because I've known it every time it's crossed my lips. And our fear leads to grief, which carries through generations on the American notion that family is the most stable unit of social measure. It's given us all an unsteady foundation from the beginning. It has accumulated our grief."

"We're crippled by it. We shudder under its weight."

The next morning, the sun rose on four lifeless bodies and countless others bracing for another day. It rose on Alvin York in the luxury provided for those who kill by the rules laid down by those who have come before us.

At a banquet held in his honor that evening, York beamed to the crowd before him, unaware of the waiting tragedy just down the road from his farm. "I guess you all understand that I'm just a soldier and not a speaker. I'm just a soldier," he told them, but "I want you all to know that what you all have done for me is highly appreciated and I never shall forget it. Thank you very much."

Note

1. Sources for this account came from the *Nashville Tennessean, Birmingham News, Birmingham Age-Herald, New Orleans Item*, and Livingston, Tennessee *The Golden Age*, 23–28 May 1919.

Jim Crow Ordained

White and Black Christianity in the Civil Rights South

" **G**od wanted white people to live alone," urged the official newspaper of the White Citizens' Councils of America, instructing children of the late-1950s South. "And He wanted colored people to live alone ... The white men built America for you," it continued: "White men built the United States so they could make their rules ... God has made us different. And God knows best."[1] Religion held a dual role in American society. While churches maintained a vested interest in the status quo and a conservative bent towards traditional values, their general belief in divine justice and the fundamental goodness of man carried influence among social reformers and activists. Religion remained the single most significant organizing principle of the Civil Rights Movement, and southern civil rights leaders constantly referenced Biblical equality mandates to justify their cause and convince their oppressors of wrongdoing. The oppressors, however, steeped their segregationist message and policy in the very same Bible.[2]

Morality could be used as a source of rationalization, but also as a motivating force for the organization of action. Robert N. Bellah argued that tradition and practice created a de facto American civil religion that worked concurrently with, but apart from, actual religious communities.

Thomas Aiello, "Jim Crow Ordained: White and Black Christianity in the Civil Rights South," *Crossroads: A Southern Culture Annual*, ed. Ted Olson, pp. 107–119. Copyright © 2006 by Thomas Aiello. Reprinted with permission.

This civil religion set societal mores and gave Americans an idea of correct behavior. While the white and black religious communities diverged at the issue of race equality, for instance, both could acknowledge a correlation between church membership and community standing, or that general adherence to Biblical principles generally kept a proponent in line with American legal principles.[3]

The religious and social beliefs of US churchgoers, however, were not uniform. A 1963 survey conducted by the National Opinion Research Center demonstrated that white integrationist attitudes were most prominent in the moderate religionists, while opposition to the practice manifested itself most plainly in the polar extremes of religious dedication.[4] There has never been a constant American ethic. Civil rights activists and members of the White Citizens' Councils, for instance, certainly had varying "American dreams," and both groups extracted vindication from similar faiths, causing each to fully perceive the "dark side" of its belief system.[5] Vindication of one position was the necessary denunciation of the other. The Bible was essentially battling itself. Religion was a multipurpose weapon in these ideological struggles and lent legitimacy to a pervasive Protestant Americanism. The ability of the Bible to justify both Jim Crow and full equality demonstrated the problem of using such a malleable and cryptic document as a foundation for argument, but the collective faith of both races was not radically erased when shown through the looking glass.

Inherently, religious groups participating in the American civil rights debate clung to their Bibles as written documentation that God was on their side. The most common segregationist Biblical defense involved the story of Ham, cursed son of Noah, whose descendants settled in modern-day Ethiopia. Segregationists argued that since God cursed Ham, and Ham's descendants were black, then that curse became generationally and biologically adaptable to all proceeding manifestations of one singular black bloodline. Southern preachers such as Carey Daniel, of the First Baptist Church of West Dallas, Texas, proclaimed from the pulpit that the "nations" formed from these different tribes were actually "races" to be kept separate and distinct. Anti-segregationists argued that Biblical mandates for the restoration of world unity mitigated any claims to the story of Ham. Leviticus 19:18 required Biblical adherents to "Love your neighbor as yourself," and integrationist thinkers such as Daisuke Kitagawa, Executive Secretary of the Protestant Episcopal Church's Domestic Mission, argued that this mandate included both strangers and acquaintances.[6]

Segregationists also posed arguments based on the idea that God deemed the Hebrews His "chosen people," emphasizing the demonstration of a creational favoritism. The Apostle Paul, however, refuted any calls to Hebrew superiority or divine partisanship by claiming that his God was the God of everyone. "He made from one the whole human race to dwell on the entire surface of the earth," wrote Paul. Liberal integrationists understandably stressed this passage. The Bible's dual mandates allowed each group to ground its case in scripture and emphasized the inability of the book to base reasoned arguments for or against segregation. Paul's work often became the backbone of segregationist and integrationist argument. In his letter to the Galatians, Paul stated that all were God's children, but in his letter to the Ephesians, he encouraged slaves to serve their human masters as if they were serving Christ. Statements such as, "watch out for those who create dissensions and obstacles, in opposition to the teaching that you learned," offered fodder for the segregationists in the White Citizens' Council journal *The Citizen*, but could also theoretically represent the other side. God "is not the author of disorder, but of peace," offered additional seemingly innocuous advice that both groups, particularly the segregationists, recruited for their cause. These arguments and others stemmed from the same book, which ostensibly stemmed from the same author, but were inconsistent in their use and reuse for various ends. When God asked, "Are ye not like the Ethiopians to me, O people of Israel?" America awkwardly answered with contradictory responses.[7]

Sociological studies conducted in the 1940s and 50s generally described a church-attending community more opposed to integration than its non-attending counterparts. Thomas F. Pettigrew's 1959 analysis demonstrated a proportional relationship between church attendance and racial intolerance, but most concluded that the greatest level of tolerance existed at polar extremes—avid church attenders and non-attenders forming minorities of racial acceptance while the majority of churchgoers tended toward segregationist attitudes.[8] The church naturally developed an ideology based around the desires and feelings of the people committed to membership. The white southern Protestant church was an agent of the society at large, tied as much to community fellowship and social stability as it was to spiritual endeavor. Its rejection of integration was not simple hypocrisy, but a conscious choice of the civil religion.[9]

Religion was both a reason for and product of the prevailing culture. "Despite assertions in favor of compulsory integration," stated William Workman in his 1960 defense of segregated society, *The Case for the South*, "a massive wall of resistance has arisen within the framework of many of the churches themselves." Historian David L. Chappell has demonstrated in his *A Stone of Hope* that Workman's claim was largely bluster, but the Southern Baptist majority did prefer and work for segregation. A 1964 study demonstrated that a minister's social activism or lack thereof remained fundamentally proportional to the activity of his college-aged congregants. The Biblical literalism of conservative Protestantism promoted obedience and submission to religious as well as secular authority figures, thereby placing any thought of rejecting the established societal norms out of the realm of possibility. Therefore, belief in the Bible as the final word of the Lord had an inversely proportional relationship with the likelihood of Protestant Christians becoming involved in any form of social protest. Southern Baptist Pastor Wallie Amos Criswell, at a 1956 South Carolina Baptist Convention, referred to integrationist reformers as "infidels," and this conservatism in local church life trumped any progressive liberal leanings within groups such as the Southern Baptist Convention. As the Civil Rights Movement grew, white southern churches replaced rigid denials of strict segregation with vague references to abstract concepts of an integrated society at national conferences.[10]

D.M. Nelson, president of the Southern Baptist affiliated Mississippi College, argued in 1955 for segregation's Christian foundation and integration's communistic tendencies, declaring that "such a position is untenable and cannot be sustained either by the Word or the works of God." Eight years later, delegates to the 1963 Mississippi Baptist Convention refused to ratify a statement favoring universal good will. In response, a Nigerian missionary from the state, frustrated by domestic action, wrote the Convention a letter arguing that, "Communists do not need to work against the preaching of the Gospel here; you are doing it quite adequately."[11]

The religious activism moving through society in the late 1950s and early 1960s was not the religion familiar to conservative critics. Swedish sociologist Gunnar Myrdal argued that there existed a significant "American Dilemma," in which the practice of democracy did not match the commonly assumed ethic of equality and justice—the "ever-raging conflict" between the traditionally understood "American Creed, where the American thinks, talks, and acts under the influence of high national and Christian precepts," and the reality of "personal and local interests," "group prejudice against particular persons or types of people," and "all sorts of miscellaneous wants, impulses, and habits." White religious communities that failed to respond to civil rights imperatives could deflect guilt and take solace in the shared ideals of fellow congregants and the relative inaction of the ministerial community. "The moral struggle," wrote Myrdal, "goes on within people and not only between them." Meanwhile, segregationists went relatively unchecked, arguing that the North had more racial problems than the South, precisely due to the South's policies of segregation, and warning against "pseudo-Christian panaceas which produce only trouble." "Our neighbor's sin always looks larger than ours," declared Alabama Presbyterian minister John H. Knight in 1964, "especially if our neighbor lives in the South."[12]

White ministerial trepidation empowered black ministers to increased militancy, a point made plainly clear in Martin Luther King, Jr.'s Letter from Birmingham Jail. "In the midst of blatant injustices inflicted upon the Negro," wrote King, "I have watched white churches stand on the sideline and merely mouth pious irrelevancies and sanctimonious trivialities." Civil rights leaders and segregation defenders shared the common belief that God supported them and fully backed and encompassed their worldview but held differing conceptions of the religious endgame. One saw a pluralistic society of communal equality as a viable Christian desire, while the other's religion dictated an effort towards individual liberty and traditional values. Integration, then, became friend or foe dependent on the offering plate in which one dropped his or her donations.[13]

The leaders of the Civil Rights Movement did not emerge unanimously, and being a black minister did not automatically qualify one as a civil rights leader. Many preachers, such as Reverend W.J. Winston of Baltimore's

New Metropolitan Baptist Church, continued to support doctrines of patience, focusing their calls on heavenly equality and divine justice. Activist black theology, however, argued that equality could probably be attained on earth and that the unequal had a duty to fight for it. More reticent ministers responded by claiming that activist preachers in protests and jails did more harm to religious institutions than good. Martin Luther King, Jr., however, proved that ministers could make a successful transition into political activism, and that political issues could be cast in a moral and religious light. "First and foremost we are American citizens, and we are determined to apply our citizenship to the fullness of its means," said King in his first major civil rights address, December 1955, at Montgomery's Holt Street Baptist Church. As the oratory evolved and the speech progressed, King's message began to shift. "I want it to be known throughout Montgomery and throughout this nation that we are a Christian people," said King. "We believe in the teachings of Jesus. The only weapon we have in our hands this evening is the weapon of protest." He moved focus from legality to conscience. Of course, a declaration of principles by a minister did not necessarily come with a requirement that his congregation agree with him. African-American churchgoers responded by making decisions with the influence of clergy, but not solely with their mandate.[14]

"Any religion," argued King in 1958, "that professes to be concerned with the souls of men and is not concerned with the slums that damn them, the economic conditions that strangle them, and the social conditions that cripple them is a dry-as-dust religion." Liberation, in King's view, could only be achieved through suffering. "Unmerited suffering," wrote King in 1958, "is redemptive." Not only would suffering lead to black equality, subsequently erasing the inherent inferiority complex present in a dispossessed people, but it would attack the conscience of the white populace. He understood the necessity of self-respect often promoted by the Black Power movement, but maintained that bitterness only begat bitterness and led to unnecessary confrontation rather than to beneficial negotiation.[15]

The 1956 Religious Emphasis Week, a University of Mississippi tradition that featured speakers on religious topics from throughout the nation, disinvited Alvin Kershaw after the preacher noted his support for the NAACP and the principle of desegregation at a separate function. The lack of pluralism in Mississippi created a closed society that required religious organizations and representatives to accept, if not openly endorse, segregation. The crisis generated many editorials from local newspapers, reprinted in the Jackson *Clarion-Ledger*, arguing that only truly Christian ministers merited a place on the dais at Religious Emphasis Week, and truly Christian ministers realized that segregation was the product of Biblical mandate. One such editorial urged that only ministers "who know that segregation is of God" be invited to the annual program, while another compared inviting NAACP supporters to Ole Miss to "coddling a viper in your own bosom." When Morton King, Jr., chair of the Ole Miss Sociology and Anthropology Department, resigned in protest, and Duncan Gray, Jr., an Episcopal reverend in Oxford, acknowledged a silent religious community's role in propagating segregationist policy, the closed society interpreted a direct threat. Ole Miss never held Religious Emphasis Week again.[16]

Two years prior, in 1954, the Supreme Court desegregated America's schools with its *Brown* decision, and the Southern Baptist Convention responded with a recognition of the "Christian principles of equal justice and love for all men," along with a declaration of tacit support. Vigorous debate and much opposition ensued, and the majority of letters-to-the-editor in the various state Baptist newspapers such as the *Alabama Baptist* and *Mississippi Baptist* clearly described a local Christianity that did not recognize the decision as legitimate. The 1954 Georgia Baptist Convention successfully adopted a resolution endorsing the necessity of peace and a generic form of justice, but only after an extended floor fight. The year of the *Brown* decision also witnessed the southern branch of the Presbyterian Church and its Northern counterpart fail in an attempted merger. Racial politics hovered over the stalled negotiations. The debates over segregation never congealed into one consistent defense or damnation of the practice, behind religious arguments or otherwise. In the face of an active black religious community arguing desperately that the Bible mandated equality, white southern denominations reacted with either combative hyperbole or deafening silence.[17]

The white southern churches, as institutions, attempted to balance a devotion to principles and a budget that required local contributions.

In the end, the financial perpetuation of the physical organization won the day. Of course, there was never a formal segregation of southern Protestant churches. There was, in fact, no need. Each congregation was unrecognizable to the other. Segregation in housing only exacerbated this segregation in churches, because church attendance normally revolved around neighborhoods and social circles. Residential patterns formed not only along color lines, but, as a 1961 Canadian study demonstrated, along religious lines within that broader color category. Churches formed in neighborhoods, from groups of like-minded believers who sustained the church's existence through attendance and financial support. White southern ministers often turned from civil rights activism due to job security concerns or abandoned their pulpits in the face of a congregation hostile to integration. White civil rights activist Will Campbell quit his job as pastor of the Taylor Baptist Church in Taylor, Louisiana in 1954 when faced with a congregation vehemently opposed to integration.[18]

During the 1957 crisis over the desegregation of Central High School in Little Rock, local Protestant preachers acknowledged the right of Christians to disagree over the policy of integration and made public pleas for prayer. "Good Christians can honestly disagree on the question of segregation and integration," said one participant in a community-wide prayer service held in response to the Little Rock crisis. "But we can all join together in prayers for guidance, that peace may return to our city." In April, 1961, the Southern Baptist Theological Seminary in Louisville, Kentucky, invited Martin Luther King, Jr. to speak. Many churches throughout the South publicly disagreed with the seminary's actions, the loudest denunciations emanating from Alabama, where more than thirty churches withheld funding contributions from the college. Following the bombing of the Birmingham, Alabama Sixteenth Street Baptist Church, the Southern Baptist Convention's Executive Committee proposed a sympathy resolution encouraging Christian unity, but the Convention's participants soundly defeated the measure. The black church had become something that whites could no longer recognize as viable religion, so they treated the institution as yet another enemy target.[19]

After the 1968 assassination of Martin Luther King, Jr., the Southern Baptist Convention's Executive Committee drafted a "Statement Concerning the National Crisis," which, in part, acknowledged "our share of the responsibility" for the creation of the hostile environment that fostered the murder. No states in the Deep South reaffirmed the "Statement." Black churches were able to use the incident to draw the black community in and mitigate prior differences among factions and groups, whereas white church membership fluctuated throughout the period as the different sects continued to waffle on direct or indirect support or denial of segregation. This phenomenon led to a fundamental inability of white churches to muster support equal to their black counterparts and only sustained the devotional divide between the competing versions of religion and religious purpose.[20]

A study by the National Opinion Research Center published in 1954 indicated that white support for integration generally hovered between 40 and 50 percent, with younger adults (aged twenty-one to twenty-four) revealing the highest tendency toward acceptance of the practice and the elderly (age sixty-five and older) revealing the slightest. When divided regionally, however, the results indicated no white southern response rate above 20 percent. New findings by the same organization ten years later demonstrated an increase in both northern and southern support for integration, with southern numbers reaching as high as 35 percent approval in the twenty-five to forty-five-year age range.[21] Progress, it seemed, was slow but existent. An analysis of the findings of the National Opinion Research Center and corresponding Gallup Polls by sociologist Paul Sheatsley demonstrated that, as of 1963, a younger generation, whose formative years had witnessed *Brown* and its aftermath, made up the majority of civil rights proponents. A general acknowledgment of the natural inevitability of complete social integration, for instance, grew from an insubstantial minority in 1957 to approximately 83 percent six years later. A growing media in the 1950s and 60s ensured that civil rights gains and losses would reach the population, offering each American the option of evaluating the merits of segregation and integration arguments. In essence, the white newspapers accomplished what the white churches could, or would, not.[22]

Nancy Tatom Ammerman noted that many church membership lists dropped significantly during the Civil Rights Movement because of dissension among congregants and clergy. Some saw the movement as viable religious territory while some saw traditional southern religion as long-spoken on the issue. White southerners tried to squeeze everything possible from the old southern civil religion, while black southerners attempted to create a new civil religion within the black community to rally and organize adherents. Both religions dictated acceptable feelings and behavior to congregants increasingly wary of the religion practiced on the other side of the railroad tracks.[23] When a group presented foreign values from the same Biblical source, however, the exchange was not unlike an encounter with a non-believer. Each value system was unrecognizable to the other, and the coexistence of the two posed a fundamental threat to the existence of each. No Biblical analysis would ever allow the activist, equalitarian relativism of, say, Martin Luther King to accept that, "God wanted white people to live alone."

Notes

1. "A Manual for Southerners," *The Citizens' Council*, February 1957, 1, 4; James Silver, "Mississippi: The Closed Society," *Journal of Southern History* 30 (February 1964): 12.

2. The true role of religion in activist politics has been widely debated, with social theorists such as Gunnar Myrdal arguing that religion pacified black protest and focused black attention on otherworldly rather than immediate issues, while scholars such as Daniel Thompson emphasize the use of the black church as a vehicle of organization and social protest. Gary T. Marx, "Religion: Opiate or Inspiration of Civil Rights Militancy Among Negroes?" *American Sociological Review* 32 (February 1967): 64–65; Jane Cassels Record and Wilson Record, "Ideological Forces and the Negro Protest," *Annals of the American Academy of Political and Social Science* 357 (January 1965): 92; Frank S. Loescher, *The Protestant Church and the Negro: A Pattern of Segregation* (New York: Association Press, 1948; reprint, Westport, Conn: Negro Universities Press, 1971) 50 (page citations are to the reprint edition); Rodney Stark, "Class, Radicalism, and Religious Involvement," *American Sociological Review* 29 (October 1964): 698; Richard Rose, "On the Priorities of Citizenship in the Deep South and Northern Ireland," *Journal of Politics* 38 (May 1976): 258–59; Christopher Beckham, "The Paradox of Religious

Segregation: White and Black Baptists in Western Kentucky, 1855–1900," *Register of the Kentucky Historical Society* 97 (Summer 1999): 322.

3. Record, "Ideological Forces and the Negro Protest," 90; and Robert N. Bellah, "Civil Religion in America," *Daedalus* 96 (Winter 1967): 5. In this atmosphere, the church became the original and primary societal stratifier in post bellum America. Beckham, "The Paradox of Religious Segregation," 321–22.

4. In 1964, approximately 90 percent of African-Americans and 65 percent of whites were Protestant. Paul B. Sheatsley, "White Attitudes Toward the Negro," *Daedalus* 95 (Winter 1966): 228–29. Also see the chart on page 226; Norval Glenn, "Negro Religion and Negro Status in the United States," in *Religion, Culture and Society*, ed. Louis Schneider (New York: John Wiley & Sons, Inc., 1964) 623. Also see the table on page 624. Also see, http://norc.uchicago.edu.

5. The Citizens' Councils, though statistical minorities throughout the South, served as both mainstream symbols of white resistance and active defenders of the anti-integration ideology. Neil R. McMillen, *The Citizens' Council: Organized Resistance to the Second Reconstruction, 1954–64* (Urbana: University of Illinois Press, 1971) 159; Record, "Ideological Forces and the Negro Protest," 90–91.

6. In actuality the original story of Canaan did not even include a father named Ham. Ham's presence was a later editorial addition, which gave the false impression that the sons of Ham were born to be slaves. Andrew M. Manis, "'Dying From the Neck Up': Southern Baptist Resistance to the Civil Rights Movement," *Baptist History and Heritage* 34 (Winter 1999) Infotrac pdf file. Article A94160905, 1–10, http://web2.infotrac-custom.com/pdfserve/get_item/1/S1d1829w6_1/SB729_01.pdf, accessed 24 March 2003: 3 [hereinafter cited as Manis, "Dying From the Neck Up." Page numbers refer to pdf pages, rather than original bound journal pages.]; "Pastor Says 'Bible Orders Color Line,'" *The Citizens' Council*, May 1956, 4; R. Tandy McConnell, "Religion, Segregation, and the Ideology of Cooperation: A Southern Baptist Church Responds to the *Brown* Decision," *Southern Studies* 4 (Spring 1993): 22; I.A. Newby, "Epilogue: A Rebuttal to Segregationists," in *The Development of Segregationist Thought* (Homewood, IL: The Dorsey Press, 1968) 171; David L. Chappell, "Religious Ideas of the Segregationists," *Journal of American Studies* 32 (April 1998): 241, 244–45; Mother Kathryn Sullivan, "Sacred Scripture and Race," *Religious Education* 59 (January-February 1964): 11; Daisuke Kitagawa, "The Church and Race Relations in Biblical Perspective," *Religious Education* 59 (January-February 1964): 7, 8–9.

7. Deuteronomy 7:7, 10:14–15; Ezekiel 16:3–14; Acts 17:26–27; Galatians 3:26–28; Amos 9:7; Ephesians 6:5 NAB; Romans 16:17 NIV; Medford Evans, "A Methodist Declaration of Conscience On Racial Segregation," *The Citizen* 7 (January 1963): 12–13; Albert S. Thomas, "A Defense of the Christian South," in *Essays on Segregation*, ed. T. Robert Ingram (Houston: St. Thomas Press, 1960) 70–71; Henry T. Egger, "What Meaneth This: There is No Difference," in *Essays on Segregation* (Houston: St. Thomas Press, 1960) 27–29; John H. Knight, "The NCC's Delta Project—An Experiment In Revolution," *The Citizen* 8 (June 1964): 9; "Pastor Says 'Bible Orders Color Line,'" *The Citizens' Council*, May 1956, 4.

8. Elizabeth M. Eddy, "Student Perspectives on the Southern Church," *Phylon* 25 (Fourth Quarter 1964): 369. For examples of various American sociological studies, see Thomas F. Pettigrew, "Regional Differences in Anti-Negro Prejudice," *Journal of Abnormal and Social Psychology* 64 (July 1959): 28–36; Bruno Bettelheim and Morris Janowitz, "Ethnic Tolerance: A Function of Social and Personal Control," *American Journal of Sociology* 55 (September 1949): 137–45; Robert W. Friedrichs, "Christians and Residential Exclusion: An Empirical Study of a Northern Dilemma," *Journal of Social Issues* 15 (Number 4 1959): 14–23.

9. Samuel S. Hill, "Southern Protestantism and Racial Integration," *Religion in Life* 33 (Summer 1964): 426–27; David Edwin Harrell, *White Sects and Black Men in the Recent South* (Nashville: Vanderbilt University Press, 1971) ix–x, 3–4, 18, 47; Manis, "Dying From the Neck Up," 2, 7; Kenneth K. Bailey, *Southern White Protestantism in the Twentieth Century* (New York: Harper & Row, 1964) 162, 164–65.

10. Joseph H. Fichter, "American Religion and the Negro," *Daedalus* 94 (Fall 1965): 1094; William D. Workman, Jr., *The Case for the South* (New York: The Devin-Adair Company, 1960) 101; David L. Chappell, *A Stone of Hope: Prophetic Liberalism and the Death of Jim Crow* (Chapel Hill: University of North Carolina Press, 2004); James F. Findlay, "Religion and Politics in the Sixties: The Churches and the Civil Rights Act of 1964," *The Journal of American History* 77 (June 1990): 66; Senate, "Civil Rights Act of 1964," Richard Russell, 88th Cong., 2nd sess., *Congressional Record*, 110, pt. 11 (18 June 1964): 14300; Gordon F. DeJong and Joseph E. Faulkner, "The Church, Individual Religiosity, and Social Justice," *Sociological Analysis* 28 (Spring 1967): 35–36. Also see the charts on pages 40 and 41; Darren E. Sherkat and T. Jean Blocker, "The Political Development of Sixties' Activists: Identifying the Influence of Class, Gender and Socialization on Protest

Participation," *Social Forces* 72 (March 1994): 823, 833; Nancy Tatom Ammerman, *Bible Believers: Fundamentalists in the Modern World* (New Brunswick, NJ: Rutgers University Press, 1987) 188; David Stricklin, *A Genealogy of Dissent: Southern Baptist Protest in the Twentieth Century* (Lexington: The University Press of Kentucky, 1999) 164–65, 168–69; Charles W. Eagles, "The Closing of Mississippi Society: Will Campbell, *The $64,000 Question*, and Religious Emphasis Week At the University of Mississippi," *Journal of Southern History* 67 (May 2001): 335.

11. "Conflicting Views On Segregation," *The Citizens' Council*, October 1955, 4; Silver, "Mississippi: The Closed Society," 9; "Christian Love and Segregation," *The Citizens' Council*, August 1956, 1–2; "Pinkos In The Pulpit," *The Citizens' Council*, December 1956, 2; "Methodist Patriots Expose Pinks," *The Citizens' Council*, August, 1957, 1; Thomas R. Waring, "Aroused Churchmen Are Studying Leftist Trends," *The Citizen* 6 (April 1962): 11.

12. Homer H. Hyde, "By Their Fruits Ye Shall Know Them," *American Mercury* 94 (Summer 1962): 35–36; Homer H. Hyde, "By Their Fruits Ye Shall Know Them," *American Mercury* 94 (August 1962): 22; David L. Chappell, "The Divided Mind of the Southern Segregationists," *Georgia Historical Quarterly* 82 (Spring 1998): 50; Henry Clark, "Churchmen and Residential Desegregation," *Review of Religious Research* 5 (Spring 1964): 158, 161–62; Gunnar Myrdal, *An American Dilemma: The Negro Problem and Modern Democracy*, 20th Anniversary ed. (New York: Harper & Row, 1962) lxxii; Ernest Q. Campbell, "Moral Discomfort and Racial Segregation—An Example of the Myrdal Hypothesis," *Social Forces* 39 (March 1961): 228–29; Knight, "The NCC's Delta Project," 8.

13. Chappell, "Religious Ideas of the Segregationists," 240, 251; S. Jonathan Bass, ed., "A Documentary Edition of the 'Letter from Birmingham Jail,'" in *Blessed Are the Peacemakers: Martin Luther King Jr., Eight White Religious Leaders, and the "Letter from Birmingham Jail"* (Baton Rouge: Louisiana State University Press, 2001) 251; Andrew Michael Manis, *Black and White Baptists and Civil Rights, 1947–1957* (Athens: The University of Georgia Press, 1987) 106.

14. David Milobsky, "Power from the Pulpit: Baltimore's African-American Clergy, 1950–1970," *Maryland Historical Magazine* 89 (Fall 1994): 279–81; Joseph L. Scott, "Social Class Factors Underlying the Civil Rights Movement," *Phylon* 27 (Second Quarter 1966): 140. Also see the chart on page 140; Martin Luther King, Jr., "Speech by Martin Luther King, Jr., at Holt Street Baptist Church," in *The Eyes on the Prize Civil Rights Reader: Documents, Speeches, and Firsthand Accounts from*

the *Black Freedom Struggle, 1954–1990*, ed. Clayborne Carson, David J. Garrow, Gerald Hill, Vincent Harding, and Darlene Clark Hine (New York: Penguin Books, 1991) 48–49.

15. Martin Luther King, Jr., *Stride Toward Freedom: The Montgomery Story* (New York: Harper & Row, 1958) 28; William Augustus Banner, "An Ethical Basis for Racial Understanding," *Religious Education* 59 (January-February 1964): 18; Marc H. Tanenbaum, "The American Negro: Myths and Realities," *Religious Education* 59 (January-February 1964): 34.

16. Eagles, "The Closing of Mississippi Society," 348; Ernest M. Limbo, "Religion and the Closed Society: Religious Emphasis Week, 1956, At the University of Mississippi," *Journal of Mississippi History* 64 (Spring 2002): 2, 10, 15; Silver, "Mississippi: The Closed Society," 3, 7, 32.

17. Manis, "Dying From the Neck Up," 2; David M. Reimers, "The Race Problem and Presbyterian Union," *Church History* 31 (June 1962): 203; Benton Johnson, "Do Holiness Sects Socialize in Dominant Values?" *Social Forces* 39 (May 1961): 309–10; Joseph A. Tomberlin, "Florida Whites and the *Brown* Decision of 1954," *Florida Historical Quarterly* 51 (July 1972): 31; Chappell, "The Divided Mind of Southern Segregationists," 47–48.

18. The historical social situation of southern whites and blacks necessarily influenced the tendency of social reticence from white congregations and social activism from their black counterparts. Church segregation originally manifested itself through social mores, but as the twentieth century progressed, both white and black congregants began to recognize value in the operation of an independent religious body that offered the opportunity for free expression and a "home base" for organization and community activities. Glenn, "Negro Religion and Negro Status in the United States," 630; Hill, "Southern Protestantism and Racial Integration," 423; Ernest Q. Campbell and Thomas Pettigrew, "Racial and Moral Crisis: The Role of Little Rock Ministers," *American Journal of Sociology* 64 (March 1959): 509; David M. Reimers, *White Protestantism and the Negro* (New York: Oxford University Press, 1965) 158; James Reston, "The Churches, the Synagogues, and the March on Washington," *Religious Education* 59 (January-February 1964): 5; Fichter, "American Religion and the Negro," 1087, 1089; Thomas F. Pettigrew, "Wherein the Church Has Failed in Race," *Religious Education* 59 (January-February 1964): 64, 72–73; Liston Pope, "The Negro and Religion in America," *Review of Religious Research* 5 (Spring 1964): 148, 149; Peter Smith, "Anglo-American Religion and Hegemonic Change

in the World System, c. 1870–1980," *The British Journal of Sociology* 37 (March 1986): 99; Roland Gammon, "Why Are We Changing Our Churches?" *American Mercury* 86 (May 1958): 66; Gordon Darrock and Wilfred Marston, "Ethnic Differentiation: Ecological Aspects of a Multidimensional Concept," *International Migration Review* 4 (Autumn 1969): 79, 80, 90; Mark Newman, "Southern Baptists and Desegregation, 1945–1980," in *Southern Landscapes*, ed. Tony Badger, Walter Edgar, and Jan Nordby Gretlund (Tübingen: Stauffenburg-Verlag, 1996) 186, 188–89.

19. Campbell and Pettigrew, "Racial and Moral Crisis," 510–11; Mark Newman, "The Arkansas Baptist State Convention and Desegregation, 1954–1968," *Arkansas Historical Quarterly* 56 (Autumn 1997): 300–301; Bill J. Leonard, "A Theology for Racism: Southern Fundamentalists and the Civil Rights Movement," in *Southern Landscapes* (Tübingen: Stauffenburg-Verlag, 1996) 168; Fichter, "American Religion and the Negro," 1089; Manis, "Dying From the Neck Up," 5.

20. Manis, "Dying From the Neck Up," 5–6; Milbosky, "Power from the Pulpit," 285; Chappell, "Religious Ideas of the Segregationists," 259.

21. Herbert Hyman and Paul Sheatsley, "Attitudes Toward Desegregation," *Scientific American* 195 (December 1956): 38; Herbert Hyman and Paul Sheatsley, "Attitudes Toward Desegregation," *Scientific American* 211 (July 1964): 23.

22. Sheatsley, "White Attitudes Toward the Negro," 223. Also see the tables on pages 222 and 224; Ammerman, "The Civil Rights Movement and the Clergy in a Southern Community," 339.

23. Ammerman, "The Civil Rights Movement and the Clergy in a Southern Community," 339–40; Fichter, "American Religion and the Negro," 1086.

The Champion and the Corpse
Art and Identity in Richmond, 1950

T wo men, a Richmond doctor and a New York museum curator, strolled through the quiet halls of the Virginia Museum of Fine Arts (VMFA) in late April 1950, where they found an image of a bright and vibrant corpse, seemingly rotting in ribbons of technicolor paint. (Aline Loucheim, art critic for the *New York Times*, would describe the piece as the "miraculously painted iridescence of decay.") The doctor was skeptical of the work's value. He turned to the curator and asked, "What do you think of it as a cadaver?" The curator took the question in stride. The doctor was neither the first nor the last patron to voice his displeasure. He was patient but direct. "And what do *you* think of it as a picture?"[1]

The exchange took place at the beginning of the controversial VMFA exhibition "American Painting—1950," and it serves to encapsulate the complex negotiation that was the acculturative process of modern art's move into Richmond. There was southern skepticism of northern intrusion. There was doubt about the subject matter's appropriateness, as well as about its status as legitimate art. Additionally, Virginians expressed concerns that they would be the unwitting hostages of an elitist artistic intellectual community that had somehow lost its way. They grappled with the relationship between publicly funded exhibitions and publicly unpopular art. And, more broadly, they manifested a unique and particularly southern version of what Michael Kammen has termed "visual shock."[2]

In 1919, long before that shock would make itself manifest, John Barton Payne, former government official and head of the American Red Cross, donated his collection of art to the state of Virginia, thereby beginning the collection that would become the Virginia Museum of Fine Arts. The museum itself would come fifteen years later in 1934, the first state museum in the United States.[3] The VMFA had conducted a biennial event every two years beginning soon after its creation, starting in 1938, with a respite during World War II. It was designed to supply a survey of the current state of American painting to a Virginia population that might not otherwise be aware of any artistic evolution. Previous biennials were chosen by the museum director and a selection jury. The process, however, often came as a compromise. As a remedy, new museum director Leslie Cheek commissioned James Johnson Sweeney to select the representative paintings for the museum's 1950 seventh biennial, to direct the exhibition, and to make a series of lectures in Richmond and its surrounding areas as a Visiting Scholar with the Richmond Area University Center. The exhibit opened on 22 April.[4]

Sweeney was certainly qualified. The Brooklyn native studied at Georgetown before moving on to graduate work at Cambridge and the Sorbonne. He had served as both the director of the Department of Painting and Sculpture at the Museum of Modern Art and the vice president of the International Art Critics Association. He was the author of numerous books on various artists and artistic movements.[5]

"The poet," Sweeney argued in his catalogue-opening essay, "in dealing with his own time must see that language does not petrify in his hands. This is also the responsibility of the painter." Tradition, too, had its place, and the best art was a product of the tension between tradition and innovation.

> "A painting, like any other true work of art, is essentially a metaphor of structure. Relations are more real and important than the things they relate. And the work of art which introduces us through a metaphor in its own terms—line, color, and space, in

the case of painting—to a fresh, or at any rate unfamiliar, configuration of relationships in nature is a new 'noun,' an expansion of human expression."

Sweeney ended his catalogue essay with hope. "The road ahead," he wrote, "is clear."[6]

But the road ahead was anything but clear. Letters to the editors of local papers began soon after the exhibit's opening. "So-called modern art is not modern, and it assuredly is not art," wrote Richmond's W.C. Smith. "When the first little boy became angry with the first little girl, in some prehistoric age, the aggrieved party drew a picture expressing his emotion. And the picture was far more sincere and certainly as well executed as the monstrosities which are called modern art." This sentiment was echoed by fellow Richmond resident W. Clyde Maddox in a similar letter to the editor printed the same day.[7] And more would follow, propelled by a frustrated Richmond population.

The Richmond of 1950 had grown by almost twenty percent since 1940. The greater Richmond metropolitan area held more than three-hundred thousand residents, just under seventy-five percent of whom were white.[8] The median family income hovered around three thousand dollars per year, but far more families fell below that line than rose above it.[9] More than sixty percent of Richmond residents over twenty-five years old did not complete high school.[10] Despite its growth, Richmond appeared unready for a change in its definitions. "By tradition, inheritance, geography, and every intangible of the spirit," wrote James Jackson Kilpatrick, from Richmond, in his 1962 *The Southern Case for School Desegregation*, "Virginia is part of the South.

> "Richmond was for four years the capital of a *de facto* nation, the Confederate States of America; to this day, our children play soldier in the trenches and romp happily on the breastworks left from the bloody conflict in which the CSA were vanquished. The Confederacy, the War, the legacy of Lee—these play a role in Virginia's life that continues to mystify, to entrance, sometimes to

repel the visitor of the State. Virginia's 'Southerness' reaches to the bone and marrow of this metaphysical concept."[11]

Though there were a number of talented and well-known artists among the seventy-seven entries—Josef Albers, Isabel Bishop, Salvador Dali, Max Ernst, Arshile Gorky, Adolph Gottlieb, George Grosz, Edward Hopper, Willem de Kooning, John Marin, Robert Motherwell, Georgia O'Keefe, Jackson Pollock, Mark Rothko, Ben Shahn, Mark Tobey, and Andrew Wyeth among them—three in particular would stand out.[12]

Hyman Bloom, born in Lithuania in 1913 before coming to Boston at the age of seven, was influenced most directly by his Jewishness, and, consequently, the horrors of Nazi Germany. The two dominant themes of his work were religious scenes of synagogues and rabbis, and death scenes of mutilated dead bodies, considered to be inspired by the Holocaust. It was one of the latter that appeared at the Virginia biennial, a picture titled *Female Corpse, Back View*. "One feels in the presence of these 'mortality' images an insistent invitation to be horrified," said Hilton Kramer in a 1955 *Commentary* critique. "Bloom's whole effort here is toward upsetting our traditional expectations of beauty in a work of art."[13] The body pictured was decorated with vibrant color, with circles of red around the buttocks. White and brown wild strokes surrounded the slender arms and legs. A piece of the skull was cut away, revealing another swath of vibrant red. Pinks and yellows and blues combined on the corpse's back. The picture was morbid but paradoxically brightly colored.

And Bloom consistently denied that his corpses were Holocaust images. They were, in fact, intended as celebrations of life. "The paintings are emblems of metamorphosis," he argued, "as the living organisms which inhabit the body in death transform it into life in another form."[14] Bloom's corpse was one of three pictures based on a 1943 visit to Kenmore Hospital's morgue, in his hometown of Boston. Two years after the visit, Bloom painted *Severed Leg*, and *Female Corpse, Front View*. Two years after that, in 1947, he painted the work exhibited in the VMFA biennial.[15]

Bloom was a veteran of the WPA Art Program and an instructor at Harvard. Two years after the show, a young John Updike sat in Bloom's Advanced Composition class. "He moved about the classroom on shoes notable for the thickness and the silence of their soles," Updike later wrote. He noted that Bloom's "moldering rabbis and corpses were notable more for their lurid coloring than for their linear draftsmanship."[16]

These distinctions, however, would fall by the wayside in Richmond. There was, after all, a painting of a decomposing dead body on the wall of the people's gallery. The leader of the sentiment against Bloom's painting would be the same man who led the fight against all of the work at the biennial, Ross Valentine. An editorialist and art critic for the *Richmond Times-Dispatch*, Valentine believed that art was perfected during the Renaissance, and that all worthwhile art in 1950 did well to strive for a similar inspirational realism. Bloom's *Female Corpse* did not meet his criteria: "I maintain that an heroic oil painting of a female corpse stressing the decomposition of the bloated buttocks is nauseating, and should not be dignified by being exhibited in this Virginia temple of art," he wrote. "It is not art. It is either the pathetic handiwork of mild aberration, or the deliberate opus of a notoriety-seeking mountebank."[17]

Valentine was certain, however, that modern art was on its way out. Soon these artists would conform to more "wholesome, more honest standards," because there was a clear trend in that direction. And modern artists only followed trends. "Most of them," he wrote, "give their opinion not because of any conviction they may feel (their individual critical sense has been atrophied), but because they will always voice an opinion they feel is expected of them." The modernists were making a last, desperate stand. But their efforts would be futile. "A younger and wiser generation, less gullible and more critical, will throw off the shackles of Parisian depravity … 'Modern Art' (and I mean specifically the Hyman Bloom 'Female Corpse, Rear View' kind) will, like a slatternly strumpet, be abandoned by her followers, and will sit among the ashes of her mercenary past, mumbling and weeping into her absinthe."[18]

The museum itself then singled out two more of its selections when it awarded them John Barton Payne medals for artistic excellence. James Johnson Sweeney's first lecture in his Richmond Area University Center series was at the Virginia Museum of Fine Arts, and though its original intent was to announce the winners of the medals for the show's most spectacular entries, the *Times-Dispatch* presented him as the "big gun" of the modernists, imported from New York to beat back the legitimate doubts of Virginians. And those doubts, from Valentine and the public, were growing louder. Colonel Herbert Fitzroy, administrator of Richmond Area University Center, introduced Sweeney, exaggerating that the exhibition controversy "had shared the headlines in Richmond with atomic bombs and attacks on the Truman administration."[19]

Sweeney emphasized vitality and the virtue of expression in his speech, while nodding toward the Southerners' most cherished ideal. "Tradition," he argued, both to the crowd and—through the press—to Valentine, "is one of the artist's most valuable assets, but it must not be permitted to freeze out the vitality of current expression ... Today's painters respect art from the past and from abroad, but they no longer imitate. They try to produce something from it that will carry a fresh accent, a fresh way of organizing line, color, and space suggestions as well as emotional stimuli." Sweeney did not, the *Times-Dispatch* noted, mention Bloom's *Female Corpse, Back View.*[20]

The two medal winners were *De Mains Pales Aux Cieux Lasses* (*Pale Hands to the Tired Sky*) by Yves Tanguy, and *Little Giant Still Life* by Stuart Davis. A French native, Tanguy came to America in 1939 and made his home in Connecticut. He was never formally trained, a fact that surely didn't surprise many of the exhibition patrons, but the controversy surrounding his work would prove minimal compared to its medal-winning counterpart (to say nothing of Bloom's *Corpse*). Sweeney's explanation of the virtues of *Pale Hands* was minimal, and prompted no angry response. "Tanguy's composition gives an example of perfect control," he said. "Every color, every shape, every empty space is in perfect harmony."[21]

Response to Sweeney's other selection, however, would be both prompt and angry, descending upon a painting and an artist with a distinguished pedigree. Davis based *Little Giant Still Life* on an advertisement for Champion sparkplugs (known as "Little Giant" batteries, thereby giving the painting its title). He claimed to have chosen the logo not for its stimulating prospects, but because of "the challenge of the lack of interest."[22] "The word 'champion,' is clearly the subject matter of the painting," wrote Davis, "and that was derived quite casually and spontaneously from a book of paper matches ... and it was the challenge of the lack of interest in this case, rather than the direct stimulus of a subject."[23] Born in 1898, Davis studied with Robert Henri in "Ash Can" Philadelphia before taking the modern turn. His father had been the art director for the *Philadelphia Press*, giving him entrée into the circles of Henri, John Sloan, George Luks, and others. His first and most important encounter with modern art was the 1913 Armory Show, though his own break with social semi-realism did not come until the 1920s. In 1950, he worked as an instructor at the New School for Social Research in New York.[24]

The word 'champion' dominated the 33 by 43 inch *Little Giant Still Life*, standing in red letters on a white background. A blue field surrounded the white, framed by a magenta swath. Playful yellow marks decorated the far left of the magenta frame. A green vertical bar rested just to the left of the champion's 'c,' balanced by a green 'x' running through the word's 'n.' Three blue vertical lines cut through the 'h,' 'p,' and 'o.' A rare appreciative visitor to the Virginia gallery, Mrs. J.B. Jackson, enjoyed the work's "carnival spirit. It's like the little shows that used to come up in the country on a hot summer day. I can feel the big banners, the balloons, the painted wagons, the bright poster colors and giant letters that built up each performance as the biggest and best."[25]

Sweeney, in his explanation of his choice, would again focus on the painting's combination of the traditional and the innovative. He described *Little Giant Still Life* as "out of the folk vision of our contemporary industrialized world." It was "puckish in the manner of Huck Finn; strident, yet soft; rough cast, but gentle; apparently casual, but pictorially subtle." Sweeney also noted that "it takes a poet of our industrial world to turn signboard material into a lyric."[26]

But patrons would not be so inspired. Richmond's R.D. Lucas was more than willing to bow to the experience of Sweeney and others, particularly on the matter of Davis's *Little Giant Still Life*, but their validation didn't help him make heads or tails of the work. "I know," he wrote, "that this is a most excellent example of art, because three New York experts have come right out and said so; but it's one of those congenitally mute pictures that cannot speak for themselves. So its artistic value is as far out of reach as treasure at the bottom of the ocean."[27] Lucas's criticism, however, was mild compared to that of Valentine.

The *Times-Dispatch* art critic reproduced a quote from London's *Punch* magazine suggesting that modern artists striving for originality should "take a subject no more unusual than a beautiful woman and paint her as well as he knew how—a procedure which had commended itself to the most excellent masters."[28] Valentine was convinced that something was wrong with Davis himself. "Having studied published reproductions of Mr. Davis's earlier *pre-fauve*, intelligible paintings, I am convinced that (when he painted *those*) he knew what he was doing." Now, though, Davis was not only degenerate in form, but degenerate in morality. Valentine accused the painter of hiding the word "shit" upside down in the painting.[29] The accusation was unfounded, and his effort at deriding the work brought a strong defense from the editors of *Art Digest*. The magazine defended *Little Giant Still Life* as a worthy award-winner at the Virginia biennial, but avoided specific evaluation of the painting in favor of denouncing its foremost detractor. Valentine, "an art critic of sorts," wasn't engaged in valid art criticism. Rather, he wrote "abusive riposte[s]" that passed for intelligent discourse. The issue included a painting by Davis on its cover.[30] Alfred H. Barr, director of museum collections for the Museum of Modern Art, also responded to Valentine's charge of "shit" being hidden in Davis's painting: "I suppose that we New Yorkers are not ordinarily considered to be innocents, yet neither Rene d'Harnoncourt, who has been involved in some debate with 'Ross Valentine,' nor James Johnson Sweeney, who selected the picture for the museum, nor the artist who painted the picture, nor the writer of this letter were able themselves to find any such word even after careful examination. 'Ross Valentine' must be gifted with a peculiarly prurient imagination."[31]

Rene D'Harnoncourt, director of New York's Museum of Modern Art, defended *Little Giant Still Life* as "distinguished," and described Valentine's assertions as "absurd and reprehensible."[32] D'Harnoncourt was decidedly correct in his assessment. Valentine's claim that Davis's work somehow distorted his own view of art was itself an argument for the painting's distinguished quality. He was fallaciously arguing that innovation had to conform to a fixed set of guidelines. As such, he had backed the Hercules of Zeno's paradox, ever unable to move past the tortoise in front of him. Conformity precluded innovation. Far from silencing the issue, however,

D'Harnoncourt only fired Valentine and his readership even further. "If I detest 'modern' art's vulgarities and distortions," wrote Valentine, "and resent their being compared favorably to the upward-strivings of creative genius like Michelangelo's, it is because I feel very strongly about what amounts to sacrilege by implication. As usual, I cannot help but consider Stuart Davis's 'Champion' as typical of such cynical daubs."[33] It was, for Valentine's adherents, a "glorified piece of sign painting" and a "contaminated altar of the vulgar."[34]

Upon his death, John Barton Payne endowed the museum based on his original collection to purchase additional works. Adding fuel to the interpretive fire, on 24 May, the accessions committee announced that *Little Giant Still Life* would be the museum's purchase from the Payne endowment, at a price of two thousand dollars (the actual purchase price was $3,400). Though many of the Richmond letter-writers railed against the purchase and the show as products of state action, the Payne endowment included no state money. The VMFA, in fact, did not and does not use government funding for art acquisitions. But the controversy had been raging over the painting for weeks, and the decision to purchase by Leslie Cheek—himself a southerner from Nashville—and the accessions committee, most of whom were Virginians, took a tremendous amount of courage. Davis said that the work was his best to date.[35]

Valentine disagreed. He created a story based on the Sherlock Holmes mysteries of Arthur Conan Doyle. The beleaguered Holmes, in Valentine's tale, was charged with the duty of discovering just what Davis's *Little Giant Still Life* was. "Tell me what it means, Mr. Holmes!" demanded his employer. "It must mean something, else they wouldn't have bought it, would they? Or can this be a conspiracy against the sanity of the people of Virginia." Finally, though, Holmes had his answer. It was all too obvious. "Don't you see?" he asked his audience. "'The breakfast of champions! It is, my dear sir—a sign advertising *Wheaties!*"[36]

As the controversy raged in Virginia, museums to the north banded together to endorse the modern art project and to defend freedom of expression. New York's Museum of Modern Art and Whitney Museum combined with Boston's Institute of Contemporary Art. Rene D'Harnoncourt, MoMA's director, was the lead signatory.[37] "We believe that the so-called 'unintelligibility' of some modern art is an inevitable result of its exploration of new frontiers. Like the scientist's innovations, the procedures of the artist are often not readily understood and make him an easy target for reactionary attack." The group rejected the idea that art deviating from any pre-conceived norm was somehow un-American. Their goal was to protect innovation from unfounded and often careless attacks.[38]

Two years later, the VMFA loaned *Little Giant Still Life* to the Venice International Exhibition of Contemporary Paintings, sparking Valentine and his acolytes to revive their criticism. His northern counterparts, though, also had more to say. In his 1952 rebuttal of Valentine, d'Harnoncourt argued that "people who cannot see the difference between good and bad modern art and who deny that modern masterpieces have any merit, are unconsciously admitting to a lack of aesthetic sensitivity which is needed for the full appreciation of both modern art and the art of the old masters." He noted that Valentine seemed preternaturally opposed to the modern era itself. "He calls it a half century of fiscal alcoholism and confusion and accuses it of having brought us such heterogeneous evils as 'the spectacle of a mock United Nations,' Adolf Hitler, and perverted 'demonic ingenuity' used for destructive purposes."[39]

Valentine responded to d'Harnoncourt by calling on religion. "As in science," he wrote, "the upward-striving instinct of man demands that art, also, be not exempt from 'moral obligation' in the pursuit of achievements that, to use an old-fashioned phrase, should be 'pleasing in the sight of God.'" Valentine explained that the best art celebrated God's work, and that of all the arts, modernist painting fell farthest from that ideal. Ergo, it couldn't be good.[40]

It was Valentine's readers, however, who produced the most telling criticism of the show. For letter writers to editors of the local papers, this was an unwelcome imposition on local values brought by elitist New Yorkers who thought they knew best—an imposition very familiar to a Jim Crow society fighting a growing tide of civil rights agitation. This was not a society that accepted radical change without a fight.

And they fought their art battles in much the same way that they would fight their segregation battles. George E. Barksdale, for example, didn't like the painting, but his criticism, tellingly, went to the government. "That a museum supported by a State should be used apparently as an agency of the galleries in New York (for I noticed that most of the paintings shown were lent by them as shown by the labels) is just past belief!" This wasn't just the fault of irresponsible or degenerate artists. And it wasn't just Sweeney's poor selection. Agents of the museum were agents of Virginia, and they had allowed and encouraged New York galleries to dictate what counted as legitimate art.[41]

This emphasis on the need for southerness as an arbiter of art legitimacy wasn't new. Richmonders had made the argument before. In 1937, the Treasury Section of Painting and Sculpture hired Paul Cadmus and Jared French to paint a mural for the Richmond Parcel Post Building. Cadmus chose a scene depicting Pocahontas saving John Smith, while French covered the Civil War subject of Jeb Stuart's maneuver around George McClelland. Both pictures included—at different stages of their development—depictions of nude males, and Cadmus's nudity lasted until after the installation. But southerners had no real problem with "savages" being depicted savagely. Instead they turned their attention to French, who, even after he covered his nudes, insulted southern sensibility by depicting Confederate soldiers with modernist brush strokes. Richmond fumed. The United Daughters of the Confederacy pronounced the mural an insult. The southern soldiers, they argued, looked like Yankees. "I think," said B. A. Blenner, UDC president, "that the Confederate period should not be depicted unless the pictures are painted by southern artists who know the spirit and traditions of the South."[42]

But the anger of Richmond wasn't relegated to those in the North. Local portraitist Hugo Stevens expressed similar dismay at the "chamber of horrors (miscalled 'American Painting, 1950')," producing a decidedly political critique of the event. He described the "wails of anguish coming from the apologists of this cult of the ugly, who must sense that their days are numbered and that the long-suffering Joe Doakes, who pays the taxes, is getting good and mad at supporting such trash. In time it will come out that the whole field of modern art is rotten with parlor pinks and Reds."[43]

The communist talk proved popular. Again, much like Civil Rights organizations would find themselves singled out by threatened southerners as possible harbingers of commie infiltration, so too would artistic innovators. "Elevating a befuddled modernism," wrote Frederick William Sievers, "is not unlike the vacuous boast that communism is the only form of pure democracy. Some sort of hypnosis seems to overwhelm the converts of each."[44] Virginia Parsons, of New Rochelle, New York, understood the Virginians' disgust, and wrote a letter of encouragement to the *Times-Dispatch*. "If only the financial supporters of this museum could realize," she wrote, "the irreparable damage they are doing to American culture!" Another writer, an anonymous Roanoke resident, worried that "this wretched evil of modern art is one of the most fearful influences we have to put up with in America."[45]

Of course, the similarity in the messages of the angry art patrons of 1950 and those of angry segregationists of the later years of the decade doesn't necessarily indicate that those of the former were portents of the latter. They were symptoms, not warnings. Those disappointed in the linguistic turn of Davis's 'Champion' or the serrated buttocks of Bloom's 'Corpse' weren't necessarily racists. They weren't hardening attitudes that would reemerge through the decade to stifle Civil Rights agitation. Rather, they were demonstrating an attitude that was already hardened—that had been there since the arrival of Ulysses Grant and would last through the arrival of Martin Luther King. The threatening similarity of the exhibition and, say, segregation, was change. And white southerners responded in similar ways to that threat, despite its different forms.[46]

Mrs. Ora Rupprecht of Baltimore also felt threatened by the exhibit. "People who appreciate truth and beauty have always found them in nature, religion, art and music. In these unsettled times they look to them for a balm to the spirit and for inspiration to help promote a more settled and reasonable world. How can people find courage, cultural beauty, or anything but confusion in the modern pictures?" If the project of modern art distracted viewers from truth and beauty and inspiration, then it was more trouble than it was worth. Rupprecht continued, "They are taking advantage of the gullibility, acceptance and encouragement of a fad by that portion of the public always ready to follow a new idea, without ever looking for merit in the idea."[47]

Those who did find merit in the modernist project were far fewer in number, and usually defended it in guarded prose. "How else except by looking at new art can people judge its worth for themselves instead on accepting judgments passed on to them by others?" asked Raymond B. Pinchbeck, Dean of Richmond College. Pinchbeck called on "free speech," announcing that though he personally found the show repugnant, he respected the artists' right to create and display their wares. Letter-writer Louis W. Ballou of Richmond defended the show, reminding his fellow patrons that both painting and taste were the product of personal choice. "Sometimes [painting] is not easily understood because of lack of education, proper training or through pure prejudice." But it was William Bevilaqua of Richmond who defended the show most scathingly. He satirically argued that blood tests and written exams should be required of artists before they were allowed to exhibit their wares. Perhaps a poll of what people want to see should be taken. Then artists could cater more specifically to individual audiences. "And as for those who refuse to conform," he wrote, "why, lynch them!"[48]

But the would-be art lynchers were not to be outdone. An editorial in the *Richmond News Leader* again took up Valentine's cause in 1952. It described the story of customs officials in Los Angeles, who mistook a Matisse for packing material. An art dealer had to explain their mistake. The *News Leader* clearly sided with the customs officials. "Art, in our humble, browbeaten nation, ought to be some manifestation of beauty." The paper argued that art did well to evoke emotion, but that the emotion had to be something more than "the irritable thought that junior could do better."[49] The editor established a double standard. Art must evoke emotion, but it must be a recognizable, approved emotion that isn't threatening to the audience. Again, this insistence on recognizability as a prerequisite for acceptance, on the synonymous equation of foreignness and threat, appears in Virginia history (and white southern history) from Civil War to Civil Rights, in venues far afield of the museum floor.

Of course, this phenomenon wasn't limited to southerners. Historian Michael Kammen has noted that the bulk of negative reactions to modernism in the first half of the 1950s "equated modernism with disorder, a source of uncertainty and hence bewilderment." The most famous example of this awe came at the 1913 International Exhibition of Modern Art—the notorious Armory Show—where modern European art made its American debut. Those who found the work baffling or distasteful interpreted it as a threat, an unwelcome European invasion that had missed the artistic point at best, presented innocent Americans with obscenity, at worst.[50] Like the Richmond show, it was a foreign imposition, and that foreignness helped define the critique.

In Virginia, Yankees were the foreigners. Letter-writer Hugo Stevens, for example, told a similar tale to that of the Matisse mistake, emphasizing the gullibility of northern muckety-mucks. "A friend of ours (who wanted to show them up, by the way) won a second prize at the Detroit Museum with an old blotter from his office desk, framed and called 'The Lancers!' And the joke was on the modern experts, who raved about it, using fancy words like 'nuances.'"[51] Valentine chimed in on this count as well. "Swami Sweeney," he noted in 1952, "is a Brooklynite."[52]

But it wasn't just the Brooklynites. And for all of Richmond's outrage at the 1950 biennial, another segment of the Virginia population had consistently worked to bring innovative new art by white and black painters to the state. The same accessions committee that purchased *Little Giant Still Life* had already purchased works by African-American artists Leslie Garland Bolling, Jacob Lawrence, and George H. Benjamin Johnson. The year following the biennial, 1951, the committee approved the purchase of a Benjamin Wigfall painting. Members of the committee had a far broader art education than most, but they, like each letter-writer to the *Richmond Times-Dispatch* and *Richmond News Leader*, were southerners. Were Virginians. Their work to enrich a public museum, particularly one that the public did not want "enriched," demonstrates that an anti-progressive attitude was not entirely uniform.[53]

The year prior to the 1950 biennial, Cheek again riled the public by bringing an exhibition of Alexander Calder's mobiles to the museum. The Richmond population was baffled, and Valentine was again angry. The idea of such "aberrations" having a place of honor in the museum "causes me to react like a cayuse to the prick of a burr on a saddle sore." He decried "the *deliberate* return to the primitive" as "a revolt against the mental discipline required to interpret an increasingly complex civilization."[54]

But Cheek had also been responsible for "Healy's Sitters: or, A Portrait Panorama of the Victorian Age," which ran just before the American

Painting biennial. The exhibition was a catalogue of the nineteenth-century portraits of George Healy, "America's first international portraitist." A variety of American statesmen were included, as were many Civil War generals. Included in the "Healy's Sitters" exhibit was a canvas titled, *The Peacemakers*. Grant, Sherman, Lincoln, and Admiral David Dixon Porter sat at a shipyard near Richmond. Robert E. Lee and P.G.T. Beauregard also took places of honor. "General Lee is in a dominating position," noted the *New York Times*, "but Northern and Southern heroes are not segregated in the display."[55] It was this that Virginia museum patrons found appealing. Civil War portraits had the bravery, grandeur, and realism that proper art required. And they were, above all, familiar.

Cheek also oversaw acquisitions of paintings by Titian and Tintoretto, Rembrandt and Rubens, and the George Washington portraits of Julius Brutus Stearns. He successfully fought for a one million dollar appropriation to build two new wings for the museum. (Valentine, however, was quick to point out that the appropriation was one million dollars of taxpayer money, and that if taxpayers were doling out to support a "fine" arts museum, the displays should categorically be "fine.") The year of the biennial, the museum's endowment never reached $250,000. Under Cheek's leadership, its endowment topped $4 million by 1955.[56]

There was never any poll of the Richmond population as to whether or not it was majority pro or anti-modern art, but the majority of letters to the editors of Richmond papers were clearly anti. Local letter-writer Florence Dickinson Stearns argued that the vast majority were against the biennial, but that fear of being thought classless or uneducated kept them from some form of protest.[57] That fear, however, did not keep them away from the museum itself. "Visitors to the museum," reported the *Times-Dispatch*, "invariably ask, in the manner of whodunit detectives, 'Where's the corpse?'" Their anger led to curiosity. During the 1949–1950 fiscal year, 203,236 people participated statewide in one or another museum activity. 52,258 attended the VMFA itself. More and more people were angry, but more and more people were paying attention. Even Valentine was pleased about the attendance. Not only had the furor sparked an interest in art, but "it has given some of us something to talk about besides atom bombs, hidden treason, deficit embezzlement and other historical obscenities in an age that has, I am afraid, become hardened to obscenities."[58]

Like the Confederates of Healy's portraits and segregationists on the Civil Rights barricades, however, Valentine's protests in the "Battle of Richmond" would eventually fall to the "obscenities" they tried to destroy. Angry Virginians of 1950 would shudder to know that today the museum still retains Davis's *Little Giant*, but also work by Franz Kline, George Segal, Andy Warhol, and Jasper Johns.[59]

They still shudder. A 1999 Canal Walk mural project that featured Robert E. Lee and other famous Virginians sparked outrage from Richmond's black community. In 2003, a new statue of Abraham Lincoln at Richmond's Tredegar Iron Works sparked similar racially motivated anger from the Sons of Confederate Veterans. But these later controversies concerned the racial politics left by the legacy of the Civil Rights Movement. They weren't, like Richmond's 1950 controversy, about a perceived imposition from a threatening outsider. They weren't even about art. Neither the mural nor the statue came under scrutiny for miscasting or distorting an otherwise beautiful image. Instead, art became a battleground for policy disputes within the Richmond community.[60]

In 1950, art itself was the dispute. Modern art was at best a sacrilegious mistake, at worst a Trojan horse carrying with it the New York intellectual establishment. But despite the various controversies that still occasionally appear, twenty-first century Virginians have largely divested themselves of those mid-century fears. As eventual familiarity helped ease the process of white Virginia's reintegration into the Union, and as eventual familiarity helped ease the process of black Virginia's integration into public schools, eventual familiarity demonstrated its power to tame the profane images of 1950. When they became familiar, they ceased to be threats.

Notes

1. *New York Times*, 30 April 1950, II, p. 8.

2. Though Kammen's 2006 *Visual Shock: A History of Art Controversies In American Culture* does not reference the 1950 Virginia Museum of Fine Arts Biennial, it

references many other art exhibitions in a near-exhaustive analysis of America's relationship with its art. Kammen interprets art controversies as signposts of broader social and cultural shifts that fundamentally change American expectations about what art should be. They are, therefore, avenues through which to engage cycles of social turmoil. Michael Kammen, *Visual Shock: A History of Art Controversies in American Culture* (New York, 2006), pp. xi–xii, 351–357.

3. The Virginia Museum of Fine Arts was the Virginia's oldest state-owned art museum. Anne B. Barriault, *Selections: Virginia Museum of Fine Arts* (Richmond, 1997), pp. vii–viii; and Louis D. Rubin, Jr., "Art Row In Virginia," *Baltimore Evening Sun*, Curatorial Administration, Virginia Museum of Fine Arts.

4. Cheek came to the VMFA in 1948 from the Baltimore Museum of Fine Arts. He had also served as associate editor of *The Architectural Forum*, as a faculty member of the history department at The College of William and Mary, and as the founder of that university's Department of Fine Arts. *New York Times*, 30 April 1950, II, p. 8; Rubin, "Art Row In Virginia"; Elizabeth L. O'Leary, Associate Curator of American Art, Virginia Museum of Fine Art, email correspondence, in possession of the author; Liza Kirwin, "Regional Reports: Southeast," *Archives of American Art Journal* 33 (1993): 34–35; and *American Painting, 1950* (Richmond, 1950). The exhibition catalogue does not include page numbers, so none are included in these notes. For a thorough biography of Leslie Cheek and his myriad exploits with the Virginia Museum of Fine Arts, see Parke Rouse, Jr., *Living by Design: Leslie Cheek and the Arts* (Williamsburg, 1985).

5. *American Painting, 1950.* For a selection of Sweeney's work prior to 1950, see James Johnson Sweeney, *Henry Moore* (New York, 1947); James Johnson Sweeney, *Joan Miro* (New York, 1941); James Johnson Sweeney, *Marc Chagall* (New York, 1946); James Johnson Sweeney, and *Stuart Davis* (New York, 1945).

6. *American Painting, 1950.*

7. W.C. Smith, "The Graphic Garbage That Passes as Modern Art," *Richmond Times-Dispatch*, 6 May 1950, p. 6.

8. The total black population of greater metropolitan Richmond was 87,087, or 26.5%. All tabulations made by the author based on census data. "Table 12—Summary of Population Characteristics, for Counties and Independent Cities," *Census of Population: 1950*, Vol. II, *Characteristics of the Population*, Part 46, *Virginia* (Washington DC, 1952), pp. 46–30; and "Table 34—General Characteristics of the Population, for Standard Metropolitan Areas, Urbanized Areas, and Urban

Places of 10,000 or More: 1950," *Census of Population: 1950*, Vol. II, *Characteristics of the Population*, Part 46, *Virginia* (Washington DC, 1952), pp. 46–54.

9. The median income of families and individuals was $2,555. When families were considered by themselves, the number rose to $3,283. "Table 37—Income in 1949 of Families and Unrelated Individuals, For Standard Metropolitan Areas, Urbanized Areas, and Urban Places of 10,000 or More: 1950," *Census of Population: 1950*, Vol. II, *Characteristics of the Population*, Part 46, *Virginia* (Washington DC, 1952), pp. 46–62. With that money, the average total retail sales per Richmond household was $2,127. *The New Dominion* (Richmond, 1949), p. 24.

10. 60,980 men had less than four years of high school, 64.2% of the total; 65,125 women had less than four years, 60.7% of the total. 126,105 of 202,365 adults over the age of twenty-five had less than four years of high school. All tabulations made by the author based on census data. "Table 34—General Characteristics of the Population, for Standard Metropolitan Areas, Urbanized Areas, and Urban Places of 10,000 or More: 1950," pp. 46–54.

11. James Jackson Kilpatrick, *The Southern Case for School Desegregation* (Richmond, 1962), pp. 7–8.

12. *American Painting, 1950.*

13. Hilton Kramer, "Bloom and Levine: The Hazards of Modern Painting: Two Jewish Artists from Boston," *Commentary* 19 (1955): 583, 586–587; and Dorothy C. Miller, ed., *Americans, 1942: 18 Artists from 9 States* (New York, 1942), p. 18.

14. Quoted in Isabelle Dervaux, "Color and Ecstasy in the Art of Hyman Bloom," in *Color and Ecstasy: The Art of Hyman Bloom*, ed. Isabelle Dervaux (New York, 2002), p. 21. Interestingly, in the sentence just prior to his statement about transformation, Bloom (seemingly contradictorily) states, "The bodies are emblems in which the process of decay symbolizes the corruption of society and of the human spirit." Dorothy Abbott Thompson, however, does not read contradiction. She argues instead that Bloom saw the meaning of his pictures "on many levels." Dorothy Abbott Thompson, *The Spirits of Hyman Bloom: The Sources of His Imagery* (New York, 1996), p. 35.

15. Dervaux, "Color and Ecstasy in the Art of Hyman Bloom," pp. 18–19; and Thompson, *The Spirits of Hyman Bloom: The Sources of His Imagery*, pp. 35–36.

16. John Updike, "Hyman Bloom," in *Color and Ecstasy: The Art of Hyman Bloom*, ed. Isabelle Dervaux (New York, 2002), p. 11; and *Americans, 1942*, p. 18. For more

on Bloom, see Linda Conti, ed., *Hyman Bloom: Paintings and Drawings* (Durham, NH, 1992).

17. Ross Valentine, "'Modern Art' on Its Last Legs," *Richmond Times-Dispatch*, 30 April 1950, p. 2-D. Bloom did have one documented supporter among the visitors to the museum. A Mrs. Flave Tyson told the *Richmond Times-Dispatch* that she disapproved of modern art, but strikingly found *Female Corpse, Back View* the most successful of the collection. "I can understand," she said, "how an artist haunted by an image would have to put it on canvas for release." "Modern Art Stirs Controversy at Virginia Museum," *Richmond News Leader*, 3 May 1950, Curatorial Administration, Virginia Museum of Fine Arts.

18. Whether or not the error was intentional, when mentioning Bloom's work by its full name, Valentine referred to the painting as *Female Corpse, Rear View* (instead of *Back View*). Valentine, "'Modern Art' on Its Last Legs," VMFA. After *Female Corpse, Back View* finished receiving its lashings in Virginia, the painting went to a summer exhibition of postwar paintings at the University of Michigan were it was received with far greater sympathy. Frederick S. Wight, *Hyman Bloom* (Boston, 1954), p. 12.

19. "Museum to List Winning Art in Exhibition," *Richmond Times-Dispatch*, 4 May 1950, p. 2; and "Sweeney Picks Payne Medal Winners," *Richmond Times-Dispatch*, 6 May 1950, p. 2.

20. "Sweeney Picks Payne Medal Winners"; and "Sweeney Tells of Paintings at Museum," *Richmond News Leader*, 6 May 1950, Curatorial Administration, Virginia Museum of Fine Arts.

21. "Sweeney Tells of Paintings At Museum"; and "Sweeney Picks Payne Medal Winners."

22. H.H. Arnason, "Introduction," in *Stuart Davis Memorial Exhibition, 1894–1964* (Washington DC, 1965), 34; Patricia Hills, *Stuart Davis* (New York, 1996), p. 128; and "Stuart Davis to Alfred Barr," 3 November 1952, in Diane Kelder, ed., *Stuart Davis: A Documentary Monograph* (New York, 1971), p. 100.

23. Stuart Davis, "Visa (1952)," in *Stuart Davis*, ed. Diane Kelder (New York, 1971), p. 100.

24. "Painting in Sweeney Collection Bought by Virginia Art Museum," *Richmond Times-Dispatch*, 24 May 1950, p. 7.

25. "Sweeney Tells Of Paintings at Museum."

26. "Sweeney Picks Payne Medal Winners"; "Sweeney Tells of Paintings at Museum"; "Donald Burgess Shows Drawings," *New York Times*, 6 May 1950, p. 13.

27. R.D. Lucas, "Sure, It May Be Art, But—What Does It Mean? He Asks," *Richmond Times-Dispatch*, 12 March 1952, p. 14.

28. Ross Valentine, "'Modern Art' on Its Last Legs."

29. The italics are Valentine's. "Well, They Asked for It," *Richmond Times-Dispatch*, 21 March 1952, p. 14.

30. The cover art was *Owh! In San Paõ*. The editorial was the first substantive writing in the issue. "Editorial," *Art Digest*, 15 March 1952, pp. 3, 5.

31. Alfred H. Barr, Jr., "Fails to Find the World In 'Champion' Painting," *Richmond Times-Dispatch*, 21 March 1952, p. 14.

32. Rene d'Harnoncourt, "What d'Harnoncourt Thinks of 'Little Giant Still Life,'" *Richmond Times-Dispatch*, 9 March 1952, p. 2B.

33. Ross Valentine, "A Question for Mr. D'Harnoncourt," *Richmond Times-Dispatch*, 21 February 1952, p. 16.

34. Florence Dickinson Stearns, "Sees Nothing 'Distinguished' About 'Champion' Painting," *Richmond Times-Dispatch*, 13 March 1952, p. 14; and F. William Sievers, "Ross Valentine's 'Service' is Attacking Modern Art," *Richmond Times-Dispatch*, 2 March 1952, p. 2B.

35. "Museum to List Winning Art In Exhibition"; "Painting in Sweeney Collection Bought by Virginia Art Museum"; Parke Rouse, Jr., *Living by Design*, p. 109; and Elizabeth L. O'Leary, Associate Curator of American Art, Virginia Museum of Fine Art, email correspondence, in possession of the author.

36. Ross Valentine, "The Case of the Little Giant," *Richmond Times-Dispatch*, 28 May 1950, p. 2D.

37. Other signatories were Alfred H. Barr, collections director, and Andrew C. Ritchie, director of painting and sculpture, both of MoMA; Hermon More and Lloyd Goodrich, director and associate director of the Whitney; and James S. Plaut and Frederick S. Wight, director and education director of the Boston Institute. *New York Times*, 28 March 1950, pp. 33, 35.

38. *New York Times*, 28 March 1950, pp. 20, 33, 35.

39. Ross Valentine, "There Are Honest Modern Artists," *Richmond Times-Dispatch*, Curatorial Administration, Virginia Museum of Fine Arts; and Rene D'Harnoncourt, "'Unpulverized' d'Harnoncourt Answers Critic," *Richmond Times-Dispatch*, 20 February 1952, p. 14.

40. Ross Valentine, "A Question for Mr. d'Harnoncourt." At the same time, on 9 April, someone pulled a Degas brush drawing, *The Mounted Jockey*, from the wall of the museum, took it into the bathroom, removed it from the frame, and took the $3,500 painting from the museum. *New York Times*, 10 April 1952, p. 31.

41. This skepticism and disappointment with the government was and would continue to be a hallmark of segregationist thought, as well. "That is the way the anti-Christ seeks to displace Christ," argued T. Robert Ingram in a 1962 editorial, "by promising and working for one world government under man." Segregationists placed the onus of coercion on government intervention and claimed that the different races simply belonged apart. Outside agitators and governmental officials were impinging on personal freedom. "In the final analysis," wrote William Workman, in his 1960 *The Case for the South*, "the burden of performance rests upon the individual, and his prospects for success vary in direct ratio to his ability, his ambition, his industry, and his determination to overcome obstacles." When the government got in the way, individuals suffered, whether that interference was in Civil Rights legislation or art hanging in the public museum. George E. Barksdale, "'Disgusting' Exhibition," *Richmond Times-Dispatch*, 6 May 1950, p. 6; Homer H. Hyde, "By Their Fruits Ye Shall Know Them," *American Mercury* 94 (1962): 22; T. Robert Ingram, "Why Integration Is Un-Christian!" *The Citizen* 6 (1962): 9; I.A. Newby, "Introduction," in *The Development of Segregationist Thought*, ed. I.A. Newby (Homewood, IL, 1968), p. 16; David L. Chappell, "The Divided Mind of the Southern Segregationists," *Georgia Historical Quarterly* 82 (1998): 50; and William D. Workman, Jr., *The Case for the South* (New York, 1960), p. 158. For an in-depth treatment of white Virginia's full relationship with Jim Crow, from its nineteenth-century birth until its post-Civil Rights death, see J. Douglas Smith, *Managing White Supremacy: Race, Politics, and Citizenship in Jim Crow Virginia* (Chapel Hill, 2002).

42. Karal Ann Marling, *Wall-to-Wall America: A Cultural History of Post-Office Murals in the Great Depression* (Minneapolis, 1982), pp. 282–289. Quote from the *Richmond News Leader*, 31 October 1939, quoted in Marling, *Wall-to-Wall America*, p. 288.

43. Hugo Stevens, "When Will This 'Travesty On Art' End? He Asks," *Richmond Times Dispatch*, 7 May 1950, p. 3D.

44. Sievers was a Richmond sculptor who made his reputation crafting the Virginia Confederate monuments at Gettysburg and Vicksburg. His reaction, like that of

Stevens, is understandable. Not only are these artists responding to an aesthetic with which they disagree, but they are also arguing for their professional lives. Our art, they seem to be saying, is still viable. Dorothy B. Gilbert, ed., *Who's Who in American Art* (New York, 1953), p. 388.

45. This resort to communist name-calling would continue to be familiar. Segregationists deemed attempts at achieving social change as "radical" and radicalism as fundamentally communistic—just as disgruntled southern museum visitors similarly deemed attempts at artistic change. Many found the communist epithet a useful arguing tool. That said, such charges weren't solely a southern phenomenon. Communism was more than just a foil for southern anger. Michael Kammen notes that the potential threat from modern art had been equated with the potential threat from Bolshevism, ever since the post-World War I Red Scare. Sievers, "Ross Valentine's 'Service' In Attacking Modern Art"; Virginia Parsons, "'Super Doodling' and 'Shrieking Distortions,'" *Richmond Times-Dispatch*, 11 May 1950, p. 18; Rubin, "Art Row In Virginia"; and Kammen, *Visual Shock*, pp. 92–93, 103.

46. Stanley Cohen has described similar moments as "moral panics," when a society that sees itself in crisis mitigates the pending disaster by defining itself against a supposed evil. It is a beast particularly fed by the nation's newspapers and other media outlets, who sell copies with lurid headlines while damning the intrusion from the editorial page. (Of course, these "moral panics" have run far afield of art, and newspaper participation in the proliferation of such events dates at the very least to the 1880s and the birth of yellow journalism.) Stanley Cohen, *Folk Devils and Moral Panics: The Creation of the Mods and the Rockers*, Third Edition (New York, 2002), pp. 1–3.

47. Ora Rupprecht, "Hopes Modern Art Soon Will Come to a 'Dead End,'" *Richmond Times-Dispatch*, 7 May 1950, p. 3D.

48. "Modern Art Stirs Controversy at Virginia Museum"; Louis W. Ballou, "View Art With 'Open Mind' and 'Thirst for Knowledge,'" *Richmond Times-Dispatch*, 6 May 1950, p. 6; and William Bevilaqua, "Tongue-In-Cheek Proposal For Blood Tests for Artists," *Richmond Times-Dispatch*, 11 May 1950, p. 18.

49. "But Is It Art?" *Richmond News Leader*, 20 May 1952, Curatorial Administration, Virginia Museum of Fine Arts.

50. Aside from New York—host of the Armory Show—Kammen mentions Hartford, Boston, Philadelphia, Chicago, and other northern venues as places that made a

slow and difficult transition to accepting modern art. Kammen, *Visual Shock*, pp. 88, 90, 93–95, 102.

51. Stevens, "When Will This 'Travesty On Art' End? He Asks."

52. Valentine, "There Are Honest Modern Artists."

53. Elizabeth L. O'Leary, Associate Curator of American Art, Virginia Museum of Fine Art, email correspondence, in possession of the author.

54. The italics are Valentine's. In 1951, Cheek would sign, along with his fellow Trustees of the American Federation of Arts, a petition in defense of the Metropolitan Museum of Art's "American Sculpture, 1951" exhibition. Rubin, "Art Row In Virginia"; and "American Sculpture, 1951," *College Art Journal* 11 (1952): 287–288.

55. The exhibition ran from 24 January to 5 March, 1950. During the revived feud in 1952, the VMFA was holding an exhibition titled "Furniture of the Old South, 1640–1820." *Healy's Sitters: or, A Portrait Panorama of the Victorian Age* (Richmond, 1950), pp. 5, 68–70, 76; *New York Times*, 25 January 1950, p. 25; and "Antiquarian Society to Meet," *Richmond Times-Dispatch*, 19 February 1952, p. 16.

56. In 1953, Cheek designed Richmond's Artmobile, "a mobile exhibition gallery developed by the Virginia Museum of Fine Arts as the most recent feature in its state-wide educational program." Cheek would retire from the museum in 1968. Rubin, "Art Row In Virginia"; Valentine, "'Modern Art' on Its Last Legs"; Muriel B. Christison, "The Artmobile: A New Experiment in Education," *College Art Journal* 13 (1954): 295; Rouse, *Living by Design*, 107, 167–169; and David S. Hudson, "The Virginia Museum Artmobiles," *Art Journal* 25 (1966): 258.

57. Stearnes, "Sees Nothing 'Distinguished' About 'Champion' Painting."

58. Rubin, "Art Row In Virginia"; "Sweeney Tells of Paintings At Museum"; and Valentine, "'Modern Art' on Its Last Legs."

59. Barriault, *Selections: Virginia Museum of Fine Arts*, pp. 93, 110–112, 115–116.

60. Kammen, *Visual Shock*, pp. 147–148, 45–46.

Constructing "Godless Communism"

Religion, Politics, and Popular Culture, 1954–1960

James W. Fifield, minister of the First Congregational Church of Los Angeles, recalled in 1954 that a man once speaking with John Dewey commented, "Mr. Dewey, I don't see how you can believe all this collectivist thinking and all these collectivist things and still call yourself a Christian," to which Dewey responded, "I don't." Although Dewey eschewed religious supernaturalism, he embraced a pragmatic vision that allowed any new experience in hopes that it could make the world somehow better. He argued for social improvement, so long as, on the way, it did not become detrimental to the concept of freedom or personal liberty. "It is this *active* relation between ideal and actual to which I would give the name 'God,'" wrote Dewey in his 1934 treatise *A Common Faith*.[1]

Conservative thinkers twenty years later, however, remained skeptical of Dewey's pragmatic educational models, increasingly concerned that they prepared American children for globalization. Pragmatism left little room for the idea of a preordained universe, and globalization signaled the possibility of economic and political ties to nations neither capitalist nor religious. Mid-twentieth century America clung to the Manifest Destiny of earlier generations, claiming a superiority and godliness diametrically opposed to Communist claims of superiority and god*less*ness. American

Thomas Aiello, "Constructing 'Godless Communism': Religion, Politics, and Popular Culture, 1954–1960," *Americana: The Journal of American Popular Culture* (1900 to Present), vol. 4, issue 1. Copyright © 2005 by Americana: The Institute for the Study of American Popular Culture. Reprinted with permission.

religiosity tempered and shaped American anticommunism, creating the pervasive sentiment that the United States engaged in a religious battle with a religious foe, rather than a political battle with a collectivist answer to capitalism. This American pietism shaped the American character. It defined Americanism. But a definition of Americanism that categorically included religious belief dispossessed a disbelieving minority in a nation whose First Amendment had consistently been interpreted as offering freedom of and from religion.

Throughout the nation's history, majority opinion tended to substitute for truth—such was the nature of democracy. An outspoken and proactive electorate ensured that prevailing public opinion essentially became the American Way. That public's opinions were subjective perceptions spread through the media outlets of cultural discourse. National images and patriotic feelings necessarily tainted any decision maker's self-perception, as well as his or her received image of a presumed national foe. The American perception of the Soviet Union in the 1950s found a base in atheism, totalitarianism, and communism. It fostered a public belief that no nation could positively engage with a counterpart perceived by so many as evil. Popular Christianity became the zenith of popular culture.[2]

That counterpart survived throughout the 1950s and 60s, ensuring that the domestic discourse would turn primarily on U.S.-Soviet relations. Internal security would be paramount. The House Un-American Activities Committee (HUAC) began its search for potentially subversive individuals and organizations in 1938, and by 1954, the Congressional interrogators reached the zenith of their power. In the Senate, the Government Operations Committee, chaired by Wisconsin Republican Senator Joseph McCarthy, expanded its investigatory scope from simple concern with government waste. The Permanent Subcommittee on Investigations hunted Communist infiltration in the executive branch, stretching the limits of its authority and eventually culminating in McCarthy's 1954 Congressional censure. That censure and the continued inquiries of the House Un-American Activities Committee only heightened a popular paranoia steadily accumulating throughout the first post-war decade. There was a clear enemy, and Communists became scapegoats for American trepidation. American Christianity throughout the Cold War decades pitted itself as both the primary target of Communist annihilation and the most effective weapon against the atheistic scourge.[3]

American claims that Communist philosophy was fundamentally atheistic had obvious merit. Communist thinkers from Marx to Lenin to Trotsky to Stalin advocated an abandonment of a religion they felt to be superstitious and unproductive. Thus mid-century Americans referred to "godless communism."[4] Throughout the post-war years of the Second Red Scare, "godless communism," along with similar variations, rooted itself as a functional epithet and cautionary tale to a reluctant America in a changing global environment. As the Communist threat to the American way of life grew, so its godless materialism continued to threaten a Christianity increasingly tied to America's self-image. The choice between Americanism and Communism was vital, without room for compromise.

President Dwight D. Eisenhower began attending church regularly in the 1950s. Former President Herbert Hoover called Communism "human slavery." Walter R. Courtenay, minister of the First Presbyterian Church of Nashville, Tennessee, insisted in 1957 he "would personally rather see [his] nation die cleanly under the H-bomb than rot away under Socialism." When Brooklyn clergyman William Howard Melish suggested in 1954 that Christianity and Communism could coexist, he was immediately labeled a Communist. For the majority of Americans, the idea that a Christian could be a Communist became almost universally inconceivable. The paranoia associated with Soviet policy and global change subtly shifted to fear and hatred of atheistic philosophy—the godlessness of "godless communism." Excoriating Russia's lack of faith and emphasizing a more semantically potent "godless communism" label, United States political and religious leaders gave the populace a simple yet profound point of divergence from the confusing glob of collectivist policy they were supposed to despise. It was a metaphor of good versus evil, and a reinforcement of the notion of American divine right. That metaphor, however, became definition, thus defining American disbelievers out of their citizenship.[5]

American church membership, approximately 49 percent of the population in 1940 irrespective of denomination, increased to 65 percent by 1970, pushed in part by the absolutist rhetoric of Cold War American politicians and evangelicals. Due to an economic climate that caused many to move and an overall growth in church construction, large numbers of Americans throughout the 1950s began changing church membership, either shifting denominations within Protestant Christianity or simply transferring membership to a new house of worship. The growth of American religious participation was a response to Communism's unqualified rejection of God, according to commentators such as Billy Graham, igniting a virtual revival and an increasing resort to the Bible for battle with the Communist foe.[6]

Evangelists such as Graham fueled the revival spirit in America. The minister was a popular voice for fundamentalist, nationalistic conservatism, arguing that Christian salvation was the only vaccine against Communism.[7] "The greatest and most effective weapon against Communism today," wrote Graham in 1954, "is to be born again Christian." He encouraged a new religious turn in America, as he portrayed Communism as Satanic, an anti-Christian religion competing with Christianity for American souls. Individual atonement with God by each loyal citizen was necessary. The only way for America to combat Communism was through faith, prayer, and religious revival. America without the Bible could not survive.[8]

Billy James Hargis, another conservative fundamentalist evangelist, also saw a vital need for American biblicism, warning from the pages of II Timothy that "the time will come when people will not tolerate sound doctrine." "For there have been some intruders," Hargis recalled from the book of Jude in 1957, "who long ago were designated for this condemnation, godless persons, who pervert the grace of our God into licentiousness and who deny our only Master and Lord, Jesus Christ." In this formulaic evangelical conception, any Biblical reference to evil was a *de facto* reference to Communism.[9]

"Ye shall know them by their fruits," offered the most common preparatory encouragement for the American religious community. "Prove all things," wrote the apostle Paul, "hold fast that which is good." Verses such as these argued that Biblical knowledge was the best defense against Communism. Paul's letter to the Romans taught that renewing one's heart and mind with God protected against evil. His first letter to the Corinthians reminded Americans that understanding the duality of man offered a weapon against Communist tactics. While progressive ministers such as theologian Reinhold Niebuhr and Episcopal Bishop G. Bromley Oxnam quoted Acts 4:32–37 as an example that early Christians were themselves communistic, if not simply communal, religious patriots responded with Jesus' parables of the "talents" and "pounds." Christ, they said, believed in private property. In an article published in the January 1964 edition of the *American Mercury*, conservative theologian T. Robert Ingram utilized the Bible's ninth commandment, which warns against bearing false witness, to argue for the necessity of full disclosure of Communist suspicions by the general religious public. When Paul's second letter to the Corinthians warned of false prophets, it warned of Communist infiltration of liberal, socially conscious clergy.[10]

The most commonly referenced scriptural reference for the supposed capricious nature of liberal ministers was the story of Jesus and the moneychangers. In this tale, Jesus entered the temple of Jerusalem, and upon seeing merchants selling goods on holy ground, drove them away, chiding them for turning a religious place into "a den of thieves." Conservative ministers, calling on the story, argued that socially active clergy were using their temples for something other than prayer—turning themselves into makeshift moneychangers in the house of the Lord. With a growing clerical correlation between social activism and Communist affiliation, more conservative houses of worship became closed sanctums rather than tools of community improvement.[11]

Despite the differences in activist and fundamentalist dogma, U.S. religious leaders used the Bible to convince Americans that their freedom, liberty, and citizenship were inextricably tied to Christian faith. Often, ministers ignored Jesus' command to "stop judging and you will not be judged. Stop condemning and you will not be condemned," as a simple matter of political expediency. The growing threat of a "godless communist" menace pushed many Christian teachers toward a different passage from the Sermon on the Mount as a bedrock of moral instruction, carefully reminding America that "no man can serve two masters."[12]

The American reliance on religion for ideological legitimacy blended the Christian and patriotic ideals, making Christianity a prerequisite for patriotic citizenship. Louisiana Representative George Long portrayed the battle between capitalism and communism as a battle between fear of men and faith in men, referring to Christianity as "our religion" and claiming it as the primary reason for public education and other public services. "We are richly endowed with a spiritual treasure," said Minnesota Senator Hubert Humphrey in 1959, "that can, and does, give us overwhelming strength in any contest between totalitarianism and freedom." Louis Rabaut of Michigan claimed from the House floor that Communism was antithetical to the American way of life on the basis of its lack of religion, citing that Christianity was the fundamental element of Americanism. Rabaut noted that America was "a Christian nation which believes in God; a nation founded upon and imbued with a fundamental faith in our Creator," while "communism, with all that it stands for, is an odious and abhorrent monster." Judging Russian action by American moral standards led to stereotyping and overemphasized a sense of U.S. superiority. "You can no more talk Communists out of Government," cried the pages of the *American Mercury*, demonstrating the stark U.S. caricature of its foreign foe, "than you could talk an onrushing lion out of molesting you."[13]

Pundits contradictorily used freedom as the principal argument against a communist ethos, then told their audiences how to exercise that freedom. Television fueled a growing consumer culture in the 1950s and 1960s, and, when combined with "majority rule," encouraged conformity and made dissenting choices reactionary responses to the American will. The dissenting choice to disbelieve was tied to Communism in the American mind, for "Communism is the deadly foe of belief in God and of all organized religion," according to former President Truman in 1953.[14] Freedom of religion was *de facto* freedom not to ascribe to religion, but governmental verdicts such as the Supreme Court's incremental removal of public school prayer became interpreted publicly as a tacit approval of anti-religious attitudes.

American practice and tradition made it a Christian nation, so went the prevailing belief, despite judicial First Amendment interpretations. In making the argument that the fight against Communism was the fight to preserve Christian civilization, many forgot that totalitarianism disrupted the entire world—a world in which the majority of the citizens were not Christian. Commentator Max Eastman, though in the minority among conservative thinkers, argued that Christianity's focus on heavenly rewards and forgiveness made it less able to maintain the ruthlessness required to fight Soviet Communism. Eastman portrayed the battle against totalitarian Communism as a worldwide necessity, and wrote in 1964 that, "to regard it as a Christian struggle seems to me parochial and self-defeating."[15]

Of course, Communist paranoia did not exist in a vacuum, and the nuclear threat and the fear it provoked were both palpable and legitimate. That fear spawned a turn against reform, as liberality became both the model cause and symptom of postwar change in the conservative mind. It fueled racial unrest, a burgeoning women's movement that challenged traditional female roles, and a growing nuclear threat from a godless Communist menace. The national racial unease—and its particularly violent form in the American South—was similar to a subtler conservative reaction to feminism. Emerging from a violent, world-changing conflict in which women answered a national call to leave the home for the sake of the country's economic and military viability, a society wary of change countered attempts to sustain that progress with a maternal, subservient image of womanhood. "Over and over women heard in voices of tradition and of Freudian sophistication that they could desire no greater destiny than to glory in their own femininity," wrote Betty Friedan in 1963. "A thousand expert voices applauded their femininity, their adjustment, their new maturity." The nation that had required so much wartime domestic change of its citizens attempted to redirect its energies on regaining an idealistic prewar society exemplified by the potency of a uniform, homogenized, white, Christian male. This backlash stifled groups representative of change—be they atheistic, black, or female—creating a situation where legitimate fears fed irrational hostility to activism.[16]

The intellectual group under some of the most intense scrutiny by anti-communist Americans were liberal theologians, principal among them Reinhold Niebuhr. Prior to, during, and after the Second World War, Niebuhr took the lead among American theologians in attempting to construct a new, progressive religious counter to Marxist conceptions of religion, history, and social change for the working poor. His theology allowed liberal social theory to coexist with more traditional forms of belief. It was anti-communist in that he argued against the presence of a utopia and the human need to achieve it. Along with his brother,

H. Richard Niebuhr and fellow theologian Paul Tillich, who argued for a change in traditional Protestantism to confront the challenge of collectivization, Reinhold Niebuhr became a relative celebrity. The popular media portrayed the thinkers as divine authorities as America searched for anti-communist justification through religious leaders. Paul Tillich appeared on the cover of *Time* magazine in 1959, the accompanying article lauding the philosopher as an intellectual giant and declaring his theology as an "edifice ... densely packed and neatly shaped against the erosion of intellectual wind and wave."[17]

But all was not praise. Conservative pundits labeled Niebuhr a Communist in the pages of the *American Mercury* for his liberal theology, his "malodorous materialistic philosophy ... poisoning the mainstream of dogmatic theological teachings in our country for four decades." Union Theological Seminary, Niebuhr's principal institution, endured a variety of communist-tinged epithets for its social activism. "Niebuhr," chided the *American Mercury*, "is one of a coterie of intellectual mediocrities centering at Union whose pernicious influence has spread like a pestilential stream along the conduits of denomination control." In 1958, the Seminary opposed the continuation of rigid hostility to Communism, both politically and religiously, instigating a flood of fundamentalist response.[18]

Fundamentalist discontent over Niebuhr and Union highlighted the struggle between traditionalism and progressivism in U.S. Christendom, the former represented by evangelicals emphasizing God's salvation of the righteous, the latter represented by activist ministers emphasizing God's benevolence in social causes. Conservative theologians such as Graham and Hargis stressed the moral evils of Communism. Every conflict was a battle between good and evil, between the Godly and the damned. "Either Communism must die, or Christianity must die," wrote Reverend Graham in 1954, "because it is actually a battle between Christ and anti-Christ." Conversely, the religious progressives of Union by no means approved of Communism, but stressed that building a socially conscious infrastructure was America's best defense against the Red Menace. Activism was the extension of religious belief. This seemed logical enough. But groups bearing names such as Christian Crusade, the Christian Anti-Communist Crusade, and the National Association for Evangelicals used patriotism as an arguing tactic replacing logic. The groups combined political and ecumenical rhetoric to the point of creating an overgrown right-wing perversion of Christianity. The National Association for Evangelicals, which carried over ten million members in the 1950s, consistently tied its message of salvation to strong denunciations of the Red Menace, emphasizing the Christian duty to "safeguard free enterprise from perversion." The Christian Anti-Communist Crusade, led by Fred Schwartz, did the same. By 1961, Schwartz's Crusade earned over a million dollars annually, promoting the belief that no bilateral negotiation could exist with Communism. The anti-morality of the Reds, for Schwartz, suggested that "the battle against Communism is the battle for God." Billy James Hargis's Christian Crusade reached millions each month through print and radio, and earned over a million dollars annually. Hargis consistently referred to the free enterprise system as a fundamentally Christian entity. It was Hargis's hope that "the atheistic regimes in Communist lands might fall and Christian governments might rise in their place"—"Christian" blatantly replacing more common modifiers such as "democratic," "popular," or "elected."[19]

These groups secularized the Christian battle. They did not attack Communists as the mortal enemy of Christian faith, they attacked them as representations of that mortal enemy—Satan. They attacked the secular manifestation, whether wittingly or unwittingly, instead of the religious one. When Fred Schwartz declared that "Stalin is the fulfillment of Communism," or Billy Graham described Communism as "Satan's religion," each created a broad caricature—a metaphor that everyone could understand. Leaders such as Schwartz, Graham, and Hargis took relative American pietism and made it absolute. They offered totalitarianism to guard against totalitarianism.[20]

Virulent anti-atheist, anti-communist rhetoric, however, was not just a feature of the fundamentalist fringe. Frederick Brown Harris, chaplain of the Senate in 1954, referred to "atheistic world communism" as the "most monstrous mass of organized evil that history has known," claiming that the philosophy was "lower in its practice than primitive, cannibalistic tribes. Even they," wrote Harris, "will not turn on their own." Senator Richard Nixon, former member of the House Un-American Activities Committee, equated Communism with pure evil, arguing in 1952 that the only way to combat "the netherworld of deceit, subversion, and espionage which is the Communist conspiracy" was Christian religious faith—"a faith based not on materialism but on a recognition of God." Nixon asserted that Western-style freedom was impossible without Biblical Christianity.[21]

Archbishop Richard Cushing enunciated a common Christian belief (and a common propaganda tactic) when he wrote in 1958 that the primary goal of Communism was the worldwide dismantling of all religious institutions, establishing "an enforced atheism for all men through what the Communists call 'dialectical and historical *materialism*.'" "What does 'dialectical *materialism*' mean?" asked Cushing. "It is the enunciation of *atheism* as Communism's world outlook—that there is no God or soul or world of the spirit." The *American Mercury* made the argument that faith in God was the principal point of separation between humans and animals and that anyone who did not believe in God was fundamentally animalistic and untrustworthy. "We can love and trust our fellow man only because we know him to possess certain qualities transcendent to his animal nature," explained the October 1963 *American Mercury*. "Take away this divine spark and you are up against a dangerous beast."[22]

Demonizing opponents was a recurring practice throughout the Cold War period. Regardless of logical merit, attacks on the godlessness of Communism habitually referred to Satan and the Antichrist.[23] The only tactic more frequent was the call to patriotism. Pundits assured Americans that the founding fathers, despite their political differences, all shared a similar belief in God. Billy Graham equated the Constitution's relation to the United States with the Bible's relation to Christianity—both documents acting as time-tested arbiters of time-tested entities.[24]

Communism, commented Idaho Senator Henry Dworshak, only found sustenance through revolution. Capitalism found sustenance through belief in God, so destroying capitalism through revolution would subsequently destroy God. Citizens of the United States had to remain eternally vigilant against godlessness. J. Edgar Hoover wrote that the American ideal, from its inception, based itself on a fundamental belief in God. "It is time for all of us," declared the FBI Director, "to reacquaint ourselves with our historical treasures and the moral values which inspired our forefathers to lead our country to the pinnacle of world leadership." As the arguments mounted, the full citizenship of the disbelieving minority became more and more tenuous.[25]

"Communism, like homicide, must be met with direct action," wrote conservative commentator and former HUAC investigator J. B. Matthews. In August 1954, passage of the Communist Control Bill deprived the Communist Party of any legal rights and forced any party member to register with the government. The House Un-American Activities Committee received only one negative response to its 1954 appropriation, and the full house overwhelmingly endorsed the Communist Control Bill. Conservative politicians and commentators alike justified HUAC's appropriation as necessary for national and philosophical survival in the face of a clear and present danger. "The Soviet threat is real, a non-controversial assumption shared by the entire spectrum of non-Communist opinion in this country," wrote William F. Buckley, arguing for the Committee's validity eight years later in 1962. Liberal attacks on the committee appeared periodically through the 1950s and 60s, making the general case that abusing individual rights for the sake of an intangible national ideal was itself an un-American activity. They were, of course, unsuccessful. "This annual assault has come to be expected by the Committee," taunted the pages of the *American Mercury*. "The Left Wing clique tries to cut the Committee appropriation to the bone ... [but] the position of this courageous committee seems reasonably secure."[26]

HUAC scrutinized propaganda exporters such as Voice of America and the National Book Committee, but it also investigated activist churches as suspected importers. Methodist Bishop G. Bromley Oxnam's prominent role in the World Council of Churches exacerbated suspicions about his loyalty. His HUAC testimony, however, reaffirmed his belief in moral absolutes. American rights were a gift from God, not the state, a result of the country's divine parentage. The state simply facilitated God's plan. "I reject Communism," Oxnam told the committee, "first, because of its atheism." Another activist minister, Martin Luther King, Jr., admired Communism's attempt to redress the underprivileged, but could not support the atheism inherent in Marxist doctrine. He insisted on the addition of the word "Christian" to the title of the Southern Leadership

Conference, formerly the Southern Negro Leaders Conference, so as to deflect charges of Communism.[27]

Intellectuals beyond the ecumenical fraternity were also suspect. A 1956 study in the *American Sociological Review* showed an academic community troubled by a reduction in its freedom through the decade. Espousing atheism, wrote J. Edgar Hoover, did not necessarily create a Communist intellectual, but it paved the way for Communism and influenced younger Americans to become Communists. "Their pernicious doctrine of materialism," he wrote of the atheist community, "fed to young Americans as something new and modern, readies the minds of our youth to accept the immoral, atheistic system of thought we know as communism." Following Hoover's logic, noncommunist atheists and intellectuals needed to be stopped, as well. "Reactionary politicians have managed to instill suspicion of all intellectual efforts into the public," Albert Einstein declared in 1953, "by dangling before their eyes a danger from without."[28]

The culture of suspicion, however, received a blow on 17 June 1957, known to anti-communists as "Red Monday." A series of three Supreme Court decisions in *Watkins v. United States*, *Sweezy v. New Hampshire*, and *Yates v. United States* set new federal and state standards for just cause in investigations and inquiries. The Court's ruling in *Yates* established that Communist Party membership was not advocacy of governmental overthrow. "The distinction between advocacy of abstract doctrine and advocacy directed at promoting unlawful action," wrote Justice John Harlan, author of the majority opinion in *Yates*, "is one that has been consistently recognized in the opinions of this Court."[29]

The Court's *Yates*, *Watkins*, and *Sweezy* decisions, while discouraging to anti-communist America, did not receive the amount of violent criticism that *Brown v. Board of Education* and the Court's other education decisions received. It was the teaching system that could make good children into atheists. The United States remained suspicious of its children's education, whether in the form of Dewey's pragmatism or UNESCO's globalism. The United Nations Educational, Scientific, and Cultural Organization frightened many parents by offering a secular education program to American children. Secularism was atheism by any other name. "UNESCO," wrote a contributing editor of the *American Mercury*, "is the nearest thing to a 'managed' world culture that has emerged in this confused postwar world." Veterans' organizations such as the American Legion and Veterans of Foreign Wars took a primary role in advocating religious belief as patriotic duty and denouncing UNESCO as an atheistic organization.[30]

In 1956, New Jersey attempted unsuccessfully to remove religious references from school Christmas celebrations to comply with the state's anti-discrimination laws. The barrage of parental denunciations that followed prompted an investigation into the motives of the school super-intendent who initiated the change. Fear that secular education would become atheistic indoctrination, however, was not confined to New Jersey. J. Edgar Hoover assailed its inherent atheism. Belief in God, according to Hoover, was the foundation of free inquiry, Christian faith the only avenue to American happiness and success. The foremost duty of any patriotic parent was to bring children to church. "The parents of America can strike a telling blow against the forces which contribute to our juvenile delin-quency," wrote Hoover, "if our mothers and fathers will take their children to Sunday School and church regularly." Religious practice would ensure that children would grow up properly American.[31]

A study of college students at Dartmouth College and the University of Michigan in the early 50s and late 60s demonstrated a sharp decline in students' willingness to curtail the civil rights of suspected Communists. In the study, religiosity directly related to a student's fear of Communism and willingness to suspend individual freedoms. Religious orthodoxy heightened the possibility of support for social constraints and concern about Communist infiltration. Similar studies acquired similar results, pitting American godliness against the blanket assumption of "godless communism." As the 1950s turned into the 1960s, the belief that collectiv-ism and Christianity could not coexist remained.[32]

Churches throughout the decade had varying reactions to Soviet po-litical ideology. A 1954 Roper study showed that the Methodist church, a member of the National Council of Churches, was the least likely among Protestant groups to support Joseph McCarthy and his subcom-mittee. The Baptist World Alliance came under anti-communist scrutiny for the appearance of globalism, while Pentecostals adhered to a more personal theology, effectively removing them from the political discourse.

The Presbyterian Church publicly rejected McCarthyism as a violation of civil liberties. "The shrine of conscience and private judgment," declared the General Council of the Presbyterian Church, U.S.A. in 1953, "which God alone has a right to enter, is being violated." Any religious debate on the finer points of political philosophy, however, could congeal at a mutual disapproval of the menace of atheism.[33]

The nation's virulent anticommunism during the 1950s and 1960s could have been a product of political manipulation, or American politicians could have simply responded to a national consensus left over from the First Red Scare after World War I. Either way, the virtual anticommunist consensus existed, and the commonly held American view of Communism included a lack of Christian faith. By the time the cultural climate allowed dissent on Soviet policy, atheism had established itself as the one touchstone of agreement to an otherwise divided nation. Belief in America meant a belief in the God who created it, thus defining out an atheistic minority from full citizenship. Americans were loyal believers. And despite John Dewey's essential contributions to the philosophy of education, no loyal American parents would have let him near their child's classroom.

Notes

1. James W. Fifield, "Freedom Under God," *American Mercury* 78 (June 1954): 51; William G. McLoughlin, "Pietism and the American Character," *American Quarterly* 17 (Summer 1965): 163, 174, 185; John Dewey, *A Common Faith* (New Haven: Yale University Press, 1934), 51; "The Children's Crusades," *American Mercury* 91 (August 1960): 108; Rick Nutt, "For Truth and Liberty: Presbyterians and McCarthyism," *Journal of Presbyterian History* 78 (Spring 2000): 52; Arthur K. Davis, "Some Sources of American Hostility to Russia," *American Journal of Sociology* 53 (November 1947): 176; and Kenneth D. Wald, "The Religious Dimension of American Anti-Communism," *Journal of Church and State* 36 (Summer 1994): 484.

2. This study concerns the creation of a domestic mindset—a cultural creation. Certainly, foreign policymakers had more on their minds than religion, as a policy

of containment was understandably based far more on strategic maneuvering to protect U.S. interests. (The prospect of a godless world couldn't have gone unnoticed in the State Department, but such is far from the purview of this work.)

3. By the Communist model, religion was simply a collection of superstitions that took time and energy from true progress. The Soviet Union was not necessarily anti-Christian, it was post-Christian, meaning that communism—created by Marx, who left the Christianity of his youth for Hegelian atheism—drew influence from a Christianity that was there first. The state did not remove God, it replaced him. *New York Times*, 11 November 1953, 20; Read Bain, "What Is This Crisis?" *Philosophy of Science* 20 (January 1953): 26; Ralph K. White, "Social Science Research in the Soviet Bloc," *Public Opinion Quarterly* 28 (Spring 1964): 21–22; H.M. Waddams, "Communism and the Churches," *International Affairs* 25 (July 1949): 295; Richard M. Fried, *Nightmare In Red: The McCarthy Era in Perspective* (New York: Oxford University Press, 1990), 9; Donald A. Ritchie, "Introduction," in *Executive Sessions of the Senate Permanent Subcommittee on Investigations of the Committee on Government Operations*, Vol. 1, 83rd Cong., 1st sess., 1953 (made public January 2003), xiii, http://www.access.gpo.gov/congress/senate/senate12cp107.html, accessed 13 May 2003; M.J. Heale, *American Anticommunism: Combating the Enemy Within, 1830–1970* (Baltimore: The Johns Hopkins University Press, 1990), 178–179; and Talcott Parsons, "McCarthyism as Social Strain," in *The Meaning of McCarthyism*, ed. Earl Latham (Boston: D.C. Heath and Company, 1965): 87.

4. The U.S.S.R., however, conducted public opinion research through the Public Opinion Institute, as did Soviet Bloc countries such as Poland. One such Polish poll indicated a vast majority of religious citizens, although the government was ostensibly atheistic. This demonstrated, if nothing else, the ability of Polish citizens to speak relatively freely about their beliefs. According to the Communist model, religion was simply a collection of superstitions that took time and energy from true progress. The Soviet Union was not necessarily anti-Christian, it was post-Christian, meaning that communism—created by Marx, who left the Christianity of his youth for Hegelian atheism—drew influence from a Christianity that was there first. The state did not remove God, it replaced him.

5. Fried, *Nightmare in Red*, 5; *New York Times*, 22 August 1956, 15; Milton Miles Lory, "Masks of Subversion," *American Mercury* 85 (September 1957): 115; and

Cedric Belfrage, *The American Inquisition, 1945–1960* (Indianapolis: The Bobbs-Merrill Company, Inc., 1973), 224.

6. Peter Smith, "Anglo-American Religion and Hegemonic Change in the World System, c. 1870–1980," *The British Journal of Sociology* 37 (March 1986): 99; Roland Gammon, "Why Are We Changing Our Churches?" *American Mercury* 86 (May 1958): 66; Jerry F. Beavan, "100 Years From Fulton Street," *American Mercury* 84 (June 1957): 26–27; and *New York Times*, 17 June 1959, 3.

7. As of 1957, 85 percent of the American population could positively identify Billy Graham and his religious affiliation. "Billy Graham—Survey #583-K, Question #25a, 2 June 1957," in *The Gallup Poll: Public Opinion, 1935–1971*, vol. 2, *1949–1958*, ed. George H. Gallup (New York: Random House, 1972), 1490–1491.

8. Billy Graham, "Satan's Religion," *American Mercury* 79 (August 1954): 42; J.M. Stickley, "There Was a Man Sent from God," *American Mercury* 79 (October 1954): 22; Billy Graham, "Our World in Chaos: The Cause and Cure," *American Mercury* 83 (July 1956): 21; Billy Graham, "A Christian America," *American Mercury* 80 (March 1955): 69–71, 72; and Billy Graham, "Our Bible," *American Mercury* 81 (December 1955): 124.

9. Billy James Hargis, "*Communist America … Must It Be?*" *Mid-Eighties Update* (Green Forest, AR: New Leaf Press, 1986), 189; Pete White, "Bibles From the Sky!" *American Mercury* 84 (April 1957): 89; and II Timothy 4:3, Jude 4, NAB.

10. "The community of believers was of one heart and mind, and no one claimed that any of his possessions was his own, but they had everything in common … Those who owned property or houses would sell them, bring the proceeds of the sale … and they were distributed to each according to need." Acts 5:32–35; and William Ward Ayer, "Communism Against Christianity," *American Mercury* 87 (September 1958): 105, 106. Jesus' parable of the talents demonstrates the advantageous nature of investing. "Should you not then have put my money in the bank so that I could have got it back with interest on my return?" Matthew 25:14–30 NAB. The parable of the pounds is remarkably similar. "I tell you, to everyone who has, more will be given, but from the one who has not, even what he has will be taken away." Luke 19:12–27 NAB. The ninth commandment states, "You shall not bear false witness against your neighbor." Exodus 20:16 NAB; T. Robert Ingram, "The World Under God's Law," *American Mercury* 96 (January 1964): 51–55; and Ayer, "Communism Against Christianity," 103. Paul's letter to the Corinthians states,

"Such people are false apostles, deceitful workers, who masquerade as apostles of Christ." II Corinthians 11:13–15 NAB.

11. The force of the story lies in Jesus' resort to violence, actually overturning the tables of dove salesmen. Very similar versions of the story appear in Mark 11:15–18 and John 2:13–16 NAB. J.A. Lovell, "Jesus and the Money Changers," *American Mercury* 91 (December 1960): 122–123.

12. "Termites of the Cross," 26; Luke 6:37 NAB; and Matthew 6:24 KJV.

13. Wald, "The Religious Dimension of American Anti-Communism," 487, 500, 501; House, "America's Challenge Today," Extension of Remarks of Hon. George S. Long of Louisiana, 83rd Cong., 1st sess., *Congressional Record*, 100, pt. 11 (10 August 1954): 13977, 13979; Read Bain, "What Is This Crisis?" *Philosophy of Science* 20 (January 1953): 22; Senate, "The Struggle for the Minds of Men," Hubert Humphrey, 85th Cong., 2nd sess., *Congressional Record*, 104, pt. 12 (5 August 1958): 16194–16195; Senate, "Eastertime and the American Will for Peace," Hubert Humphrey, 86th Cong., 1st sess., *Congressional Record*, 105, pt. 4 (20 March 1959): 5346; House, "New Atheistic Drive Sweeps Soviet," Hale Boggs, 84th Cong., 1st sess., *Congressional Record*, 101, pt. 2 (10 February 1955): 1421–1423; House, "Address by Hon. John W. McCormack, of Massachusetts, Upon the Presentation to Him of the Bellarmine Medal, Bellarmine College, Louisville, Ky., May 13, 1957," Extension of Remarks of Hon. James J. Delaney, 85th Cong., 1st sess., *Congressional Record*, 103, pt. 6 (29 May 1957): 8115; House, "Communism: A Threat to Freedom," Extension of Remarks of Hon. Louis C. Rabaut, 86th Cong., 2nd sess., *Congressional Record* 106, pt. 14 (1 September 1960): 19391–19392; Davis, "Some Sources of American Hostility to Russia," 175; and Reginald Aldo, "The American Universities and Senator McCarthy," *American Mercury* 79 (December 1954): 140.

14. *New York Times*, 11 November 1953, 20.

15. Max Eastman, "Am I Conservative?" *National Review*, 28 January 1964, 57; and Willmoore Kendall and George W. Carey, "Towards a Definition of 'Conservatism,'" *The Journal of Politics* 26 (May 1964): 413, 417, 419–420.

16. David Halberstam, *The Fifties* (New York: Villard Books, 1993), 25, 429–430, 677–678; Joanne Meyerowitz, "Competing Images of Women in Postwar Mass Culture," in *Major Problems in American Women's History*, ed. Mary Beth Norton and Ruth M. Alexander (Lexington, Mass.: D.C. Heath and Company, 1996), 421, 424–426; Betty Friedan, *The Feminine Mystique*, Tenth Anniversary Edition

(New York: Dell Publishing Co., 1974), 11; and Laura McEnaney, "Atomic Age Motherhood: Maternalism and Militarism in the 1950s," in *Women's America: Refocusing the Past*, ed. Linda K. Kerber and Jane Sherron De Hart (New York: Oxford University Press, 2000), 448–449.

17. Kenneth O'Reilly, "Liberal Values, the Cold War, and American Intellectuals: The Trauma of the Alger Hiss Case, 1950–1978," in *Beyond the Hiss Case: The FBI, Congress, and the Cold War*, ed. Athan G. Theoharis (Philadelphia: Temple University Press, 1982), 317; Robert Banks, "The Intellectual Encounter between Christianity and Marxism: A Contribution to the Pre-History of a Dialogue," *Journal of Contemporary History* 11 (July 1976): 323–324; McLoughlin, "Pietism and the American Character," 172; Salo W. Baron, "Impact of Wars on Religion," *Political Science Quarterly* 67 (December 1952): 552; Fried, *Nightmare in Red*, 65; Martin E. Marty, "Reinhold Niebuhr and the Irony of American History: A Retrospective," *The History Teacher* 26 (February 1993): 162; Paul J. Tillich, "Protestantism in the Present World-Situation," *American Journal of Sociology* 43 (September 1937): 236–237; and "To Be or Not to Be," *Time*, 16 March 1959, 46.

18. John Benedict, "What Religion Does Reinhold Niebuhr Peddle?" *American Mercury* 89 (October 1959): 18, 20–26; August W. Brustat, "Enemies of the Cross," *American Mercury* 85 (July 1957): 128; John Clarence Petrie, "The Making of a Left Wing Parson," *American Mercury* 88 (January 1959): 87; "De-Christianizing Christianity," *American Mercury* 87 (October 1958): 96; and J.B. Matthews, "Christ and Communism," *American Mercury* 88 (May 1959): 121–122.

19. Wald, "The Religious Dimension of American Anti-Communism," 488–489; *New York Times*, 29 July 1953, 22, 12 October 1953, 24; Billy James Hargis, "The Printed Record of the National Council of Churches," *American Mercury* 91 (August 1960): 145; Galston, "Public Morality and Religion in the Liberal State," 811; Peel, "The Wackacobi: Extremists of Our Own Times," 572, 574; Heale, *American Anticommunism*, 171, 199; Warren Lang Vinz, *Pulpit Politics: Faces of American Protestant Nationalism in the Twentieth Century* (Albany: State University of New York Press, 1997), 10–11; Chip Berlet and Matthew N. Lyons, *Right-Wing Populism in America: Too Close for Comfort* (New York: The Guilford Press, 2000), 201; Fred C. Schwartz, "Communism—Murder Made Moral," *American Mercury* 84 (April 1957): 92, 96–97; Donald Janson and Bernard Eismann, *The Far Right* (New York: McGraw-Hill Book Company, Inc., 1963), 56, 62–63; Billy James Hargis, "A Christian Ambassador Surveys the Divided World," *American Mercury*

85 (October 1957): 141–143; Warren Lang Vinz, "A Comparison Between Elements of Protestant Fundamentalism and McCarthyism," (Ph.D. diss., University of Utah, 1968), 97; Seymour Martin Lipset and Earl Raab, *The Politics of Unreason: Right Wing Extremism in America, 1790–1970* (New York: Harper & Row, 1970), 273; and John Harold Redekop, *The American Far Right: A Case Study of Billy James Hargis and Christian Crusade* (Grand Rapids, MI: William B. Eerdmans Publishing Company, 1968), 61–62.

20. J. Roger Lyons, *Godless Communism* (St. Louis: Queen's Work, 1938), 1–3, 14; Howard Elinson, "The Implications of Pentecostal Religion for Intellectualism, Politics, and Race Relations," *American Journal of Sociology* 70 (January 1965): 412; McLoughlin, "Pietism and the American Character," 174; Kenneth Goff, "Red Invasion of the Church," *American Mercury* 91 (August 1960): 31; Schwartz, "Communism—Murder Made Moral," 94; and Graham, "Satan's Religion," 41.

21. Willmoore Kendall, "McCarthyism: The *Pons Asinorum* of American Conservatism," in *The Meaning of McCarthyism*, ed. Earl Latham (Boston: D.C. Heath and Company, 1965), 42–43; Senate, "Spires of the Spirit-The Truce of the Bear," Matthew Neely, 83rd Cong., 1st sess., *Congressional Record*, 100, pt. 2 (1 March 1954): 2390; and Richard Nixon, "Plea for an Anti-Communist Faith," in *Thirty Years of Treason: Excerpts from Hearings before the House Committee on Un-American Activities, 1938–1968*, ed. Eric Bentley (New York: The Viking Press, 1971), 570.

22. The italics are Cushing's. Senate, "Christianity Today," Styles Bridges, 87th Cong., 1st sess., *Congressional Record*, 107, pt. 2 (24 February 1961): 2644–2647; J. Edgar Hoover, "The American Ideal," *American Mercury* 85 (October 1957): 102; "Termites of the Cross: Part V, The Disciples of Judas," *American Mercury* 90 (January 1960): 65; Richard J. Cushing, "The Godlessness of Communism," *American Mercury* 86 (March 1958): 32–34; Leopold Braun, "Russian Youth Wants Religion," *American Mercury* 86 (January 1958): 114–115; James W. McClain, "What Is Your Faith-Quotient?" *American Mercury* 80 (February 1955): 131–132; J. Howard Pew, "We Must Not Appeal From God to Caesar," *American Mercury* 85 (December 1957): 102–103; T. Robert Ingram, "The World Under God's Law," *American Mercury* 95 (October 1963): 62; Fifield, "Freedom Under God," 46, 49–50; and Hollington K. Tong, "The Plight of Christianity in China," *American Mercury* 87 (November 1958): 46, 49.

23. Duncan Aikman, "Devil Words: A Political Weapon," *American Mercury* 82 (February 1956): 5, 7, 10; Gene, Birkeland, "Deliver Us From Evil," *American Mercury* 88 (March 1959): 93–96; Fulton J. Sheen, "World Battles Demonic Forces," *American Mercury* 91 (November 1960): 99–100; Ezra Taft Benson, "Is There a Threat to the American Way of Life?" *American Mercury* 94 (March 1962): 50–53; T. Robert Ingram, "You and Your Constitution's First Amendment," *American Mercury* 95 (January 1963): 46; and T. Robert Ingram, "The World Under God's Law," *American Mercury* 95 (July 1963): 44.

24. Henry G. Riter, "The American Concept," *American Mercury* 81 (August 1955): 18; Lory, "Masks of Subversion," 115; Pew, "We Must Not Appeal From God to Caesar," 101; Hoover, "The Deadly Menace of Pseudo Liberals," 11; Graham, "Satan's Religion," 45; Graham, "A Christian America," 68; and Graham, "Our Bible," 123, 125.

25. Senate, "The Christian and the Challenge of Communism," Henry Dworshak, 87th Cong., 1st sess., *Congressional Record*, 107, pt. 10 (29 July 1961): 14007; Hoover, "The American Ideal," 100; and Hoover, "The Deadly Menace of Pseudo Liberals," 8.

26. J.B. Matthews, "An Anti-Communist's Guide to Action," *American Mercury* 78 (May 1954): 21. The Communist Control Bill received two negative House votes while passing unanimously in the Senate. Heale, *American Anticommunism*, 182; and William F. Buckley, Jr., "A New Look at a Controversial Committee," *National Review*, 16 January 1962, 15, 17, 19. While Protestant and Catholic support was strong, Jewish representatives tended to oppose the committee. Lewis A. Kaplan, "The House Un-American Activities Committee and its Opponents: A Study in Congressional Dissonance," *The Journal of Politics* 30 (August 1968): 649–650, 656, 661, see also Table 5, p. 656, and Table 9, p. 661; Sheldon Hackney, "Southern Violence," *The American Historical Review* 74 (February 1969): 924; and Hubert W. Stanley, "Who Wants to Abolish HUAC?" *American Mercury* 90 (June 1960): 89.

27. Eugene W. Castle, "Ambassadors of Anti-Americanism: How the U.S.A. Has Suffered from Our Efforts to Sell 'Culture' Abroad," *American Mercury* 82 (February 1956): 85–87; *New York Times*, 8 May 1953, 12, 22 July 1953, 5, 9 November 1953, 6, 7 February 1954, 46, 6 August 1954, 1, 11; Vinz, "A Comparison Between Elements of Protestant Fundamentalism and McCarthyism," 159; Fried, *Nightmare In Red*, 173; and G. Bromley Oxnam, "Testimony of a Bishop," in *Thirty Years of Treason: Excerpts from Hearings before*

the House Committee on Un-American Activities, 1938–1968, ed. Eric Bentley (New York: The Viking Press, 1971), 671–672.

28. "The Climate of Opinion and the State of Academic Freedom," *American Sociological Review* 21 (June 1956): 354, 357, see also Table 2, p. 354, Table 3, p. 355, and Table 5, p. 356; Aldo, "The American Universities and Senator McCarthy," 140–141; Hoover, "God and Country or Communism?" 13; John T. Flynn, "Socialism and Our Colleges," *American Mercury* 80 (April 1955): 106–107; Fred Schwarz, "The Five Basic Steps to Communism," *American Mercury* 84 (February 1957): 144; Lory, "Masks of Subversion," 112–113; *New York Times*, 26 May 1958, 32; and Albert Einstein, "A Letter from Albert Einstein," in *Thirty Years of Treason: Excerpts from Hearings before the House Committee on Un-American Activities, 1938–1968*, ed. Eric Bentley (New York: The Viking Press, 1971), 668.

29. *Watkins v. United States*, 354 US 178 (1957), http://laws.findlaw.com/us/354/178.html, accessed 20 June 2003; and *Sweezy v. New Hampshire*, 354 US 234 (1957), http://laws.findlaw.com/us/354/234.html, accessed 20 June 2003. *Watkins* hinged on the Due Process Clause of the Fifth Amendment, while *Sweezy* applied the Fourteenth. *Yates v. United States*, 354 US 298 (1957), http://laws.findlaw.com/us/354/298.html, accessed 20 June 2003.

30. Harold Lord Varney, "UNESCO: UN's Brainwashing Apparatus," *American Mercury* 78 (February 1954): 3–5; Harvin Moore, Jr., "UNESCO: 3¢ Worth of Poison," *American Mercury* 81 (August 1955): 151, 154; Burns, "Flight from Reason," 10; Karl Hess, "Your Checklist On the UN: The Truth About This International Organization," *American Mercury* 82 (March 1956): 8, 14, 16; J.A. Lovell, "The Godless United Nations," *American Mercury* 89 (August 1959): 20–22; *New York Times*, 29 June 1952, 1, 27, 13 October 1955, 1, 18, 26 November 1965, 14; Heale, *American Anticommunism*, 173; and George E. Stratemeyer, "Fourteen Commandments for America Today," *American Mercury* 80 (May 1955): 40.

31. "Why Take Christ out of Christmas?" *American Mercury* 85 (December 1957): 115–116; *New York Times*, 14 November 1954, 75; J. Edgar Hoover, "Man's First Need," *American Mercury* 80 (March 1955): 47; and J. Edgar Hoover, "Should I Force My Child?" *American Mercury* 86 (February 1958): 19.

32. Dean R. Hoge, "College Students' Value Patterns in the 1950s and 1960s," *Sociology of Education* 44 (Spring 1971): 182–184, 189, see also Table 6, p. 183 and Table 8, p. 190; Stormer, *None Dare Call It Treason*, 124–125; and Richard H. Pells, *The*

Liberal Mind in a Conservative Age: American Intellectuals in the 1940s and 1950s (New York: Harper & Row, 1985), 350–351.

33. Lipset, *The Politics of Unreason*, 230; Mrs. William W. McClaugherty, "A Methodist Speaks Out," *American Mercury* 87 (August 1958): 88; Kenneth W. Ryker, "Do the Reds Speak Through the Methodist Church?" *American Mercury* 91 (December 1960): 128–131; Carl McIntire, "Communist Influence in the Baptist World Alliance," *American Mercury* 91 (October 1960): 93–95; Elinson, "The Implications of Pentecostal Religion for Intellectualism, Politics, and Race Relations," 403; and Nutt, "For Truth and Liberty," 53, 64–65.

Murray v. Curlett and the American Mind

Public Sentiment as Systematic Objectification, 1963–1964

W hen the United States Supreme Court decided *School District of Abington Township v. Schempp* in conjunction with *Murray v. Curlett* in June 1963, effectively removing the Lord's Prayer and compulsory Bible reading from public schools, Horace Mann had been dead for more than one hundred years. John Dewey had been dead for eleven. A desperate majority of national representatives, Christian religious leaders, and pundits claimed God would be next. A significant and vocal minority of the American populace, however, supported the high court's ruling and summoned Mann's Twelfth Annual Report of 1848 and Dewey's philosophy of progressive education as cornerstones for their concurrence.[1]

The arguments for and against school prayer and Bible reading in 1963, regardless of individual merit, represented an attempt to organize, both personally and collectively, the judicial vindication of unbelief and the perceived threat it posed. The prevailing popular ethic, flush with a white Protestant Christianity that had weathered the deism of its forebears, entrenched itself as a significant component of an American ideal—sanctioned by Congress in a 1954 joint resolution inserting "under God" into the Pledge of Allegiance and a similar 1956 mandate that "In God We Trust" become the country's official motto.[2] Any challenge to that ideal,

Thomas Aiello, "Murray v. Curlett and the American Mind: Public Sentiment as Systematic Objectification, 1963–1964," *The McNeese Review*, vol. 43, pp. 60–86. Copyright © 2005 by Thomas Aiello. Reprinted with permission.

especially in the form of outspoken atheist petitioner Madalyn Murray, was an argument against the contradiction between American "equality" and modern middle-class religious categories—an atheist, no matter how hard she tried, could never be a Baptist. Or, more precisely, an atheist could never comply with the various codes and customs expected to accompany the Baptist label.

An atheist, in most cases, still can't. The affluence of the ideal created a systematic organizational dispossession of those who did not display the proper labels. The logic of the system was self-defeating—"Americanism" was universal, personal, and tethered to the whim of the majority. These concepts were (and still are) bedrock elements of society, but none can coexist. Any qualifier on universality or equality immediately bankrupts both ideas. Nowhere were those qualifiers so rampant as in the popularity of popular Christianity. The objectification of those who did not meet those qualifiers was a result of the system itself. It created a popular mind that based its ideas about equality on the non-universal elements of "Americanism." So when the Supreme Court rendered its *Murray v. Curlett* decision, the emerging national discourse represented a relatively united organization against the ruling based primarily on moral, rather than legal, grounds.

Organizational dispossession, however, was not always blatant. Every American was theoretically free to choose methods of belief or disbelief and to make pragmatic judgments based on response to national events. Therefore, when a palpable discourse of popular belief maintained the cultural limelight in the year following the Court's *Murray* decision, every recipient of information became a *de facto* participant—a participation only aided by a vitriolic and pervasive "godless Communist" rhetoric still resonating from the Congressional walls of the former House Un-American Activities Committee.

Murray v. Curlett stood as significant—*to* a discourse of disbelief and *from* the concurrently decided *School District of Abington Township v. Schempp*—primarily due to petitioner Madalyn Murray, whose boisterous manner and outspoken atheism made her an American pariah and lent the general public a unified perception of what it was to disbelieve. The soft-spoken Unitarian Schempp family of Pennsylvania did not present the threat to religious values offered by Murray. Moreover, the *Murray* decision overturned the ruling of a Maryland appellate court, directly stymieing state will and lending the verdict a tone of imposition not present in its affirmed Pennsylvania cohort. Certainly, the opinion for both cases remained the same, decided as they were in unison, but *Murray* continued a perceived trend of national interference with state governmental will, exacerbated by the decade-long national civil rights crisis initiated by the Court's *Brown* decision, another denial of state policy. *Murray* (and *Brown*) reconciled contradictions within that ideological system, bringing latent popular tendencies away from universality to the fore. In addressing *Schempp*, the Court essentially acknowledged that the Pennsylvania state court made the correct decision. Both, however, gave many the impression that something had been stolen from believers.[3]

In the immediate aftermath of the Court's 1963 ruling, various arguments abounded either for or against the Supreme Court's theft of the Lord's Prayer and Bible reading from public schools, whether judicial, philosophical, or popular. The prevailing societal attitude, along with briefs, arguments, decisions, reactions, and the actual human participants, encompassed the entirety of what Americans constructed as a "court case." The attendant features and personalities of *Murray v. Curlett* led to a public assessment of the Court's decision as an infringement upon the historical values of the majority for the sake of minority rights. The backlash present in the response of the religious majority contributed to the overriding goal of the American discourse to subjugate the minority by defining "Will of God" as "Majority Rule."

Of course, the Supreme Court's *Schempp* and *Murray* decision prompted more popular debate than blind public outrage throughout the subsequent school year. While the majority of the population approved of public recitation of the Lord's Prayer and Bible verses, prior case law lent the Court's verdict a perception of inevitability. Slight variations in precedent over time, beginning in the 1940s, gradually formed and finalized new public conceptions. The justices recognized the necessity of deciding another public school establishment case and granted certiorari to *Schempp* and *Murray* primarily to clarify the obscure language of prior decisions.[4]

As early as 1817, the first legal challenges to American establishment of religion emerged, involving protests, usually unsuccessful, against Sabbath laws. Between the 1830s and 1870s, heavy Catholic and Jewish immigration led to the first substantial arguments against public school Bible reading, and most states outlawed public funding for parochial education by the early 1880s. The public school religion cases that directly led to *Murray*, however, began in 1940 with *Cantwell v. Connecticut*, in which the Court first incorporated the Fourteenth Amendment with the First by requiring states to protect religious freedom.[5]

Following *Cantwell*, the Supreme Court decided a series of cases throughout the 1940s, 50s, and early 1960s, that created a solid foundation for the 1963 *Murray* decision, essentially developing the Court's interpretation of "freedom of religion" to include "freedom from religion." In 1943, the Court's decision in *West Virginia State Board of Education v. Barnett* established that the Fourteenth Amendment protected citizens from states in upholding the right of Jehovah's Witnesses to abstain from saluting and pledging allegiance to the American Flag, a practice the group believed to be a sign of devotion to a graven image. *Barnett* overturned the Court's decision in a similar Pennsylvania case, *Minersville School District v. Gobits*, three years prior, the same year as the *Cantwell* decision, demonstrating an interpretational progression that was certainly not strictly linear.[6] Four years later in *Everson v. Board of Education*, the Court ruled five to four that although the Establishment Clause was applicable to the states by the Fourteenth Amendment, parochial schools could still use public funds to bus children in need, further illustrating the continuing judicial struggle with the dichotomy between "freedom from" and "freedom of" public school religion.[7] In the 1948 session following *Everson*, the Court established in *McCollum v. Board of Education* that schools could not excuse students from general classroom activity for the purpose of religious instruction on public school grounds, but *Zorach v. Clauson*, decided in 1952, deemed the excusal constitutional if the parochial teaching took place away from school premises. Again, *McCollum* and *Zorach* indicated a nonlinear evolution, demonstrating a considered, incremental process that allowed for caveats such as *Zorach* even as the judicial interpretation moved toward support for the disbelieving minority. Even in the *Zorach* decision, the theists, not the atheists, required the excusal.[8] The Court's 1961 decision in *Torcaso v. Watkins*, which removed any devotional oath to a supreme being as a license requirement for notary publics, mandated that government could not aid religion over non-religion or God-based religions over other forms of belief. This distinction was crucial, for it revealed a notable policy shift from a Court that had traditionally viewed non-establishment as the government's inability to aid one religion over another.[9] Each incremental decision was vital to the Court's eventual 1963 *Murray* ruling, but none played the prominent role of *Engel v. Vitale*, decided during the preceding 1962 session.

On 25 June 1962, the Supreme Court held six to one in *Engel v. Vitale* that a 1951 prayer composed by the New York Board of Regents presented an unconstitutional establishment of religion in public schools. The state never mandated the prayer and never kept records as to the prayer's use or disuse, however, because the state's Commissioner of Education, James Allen, feared violating the Constitution. *Engel v. Vitale*'s petitioners, five Long Island parents, all but one of whom claimed religious faith, argued that a constitutional violation had occurred. The subsequent ruling enflamed the passions of the American public and made the Court's *Murray* decision the following year a virtual inevitability. New York Republican Representative Frank Becker, voicing the majority's frustration with *Engel*, called the Court's decision, "the most tragic in the history of the United States." *The Pilot*, a Boston Catholic newspaper, called the verdict "a stupid decision, a doctrinaire decision, a decision that spits in the face of our history, our tradition and our heritage as a religious people." While courtroom attendance had been sparse for *Engel*'s oral arguments, the uproar following the Court's decision created a full house during the next session's *Schempp* and *Murray* arguments.[10]

The 1962 *Murray* argument had its genesis in a 1905 mandate by the Baltimore school district that required either the reading of one Bible chapter or recitation of the Lord's Prayer at the inception of each school day. Fifty-six years later, thirty-seven states and forty-one percent of public school districts required or allowed the Lord's Prayer or Bible reading in classes. Indeed, a 1961 survey demonstrated that the number of religious requirements in public schools rose dramatically in the southern and eastern regions of the country. During this same time, eighty-three differ-ent religious denominations featured membership lists of more than fifty thousand worshipers, and a sectionally divided yet overwhelmingly reli-gious nation annually spent twice as much on church construction as it did on hospital construction.[11] In early-1960s Baltimore, William J. Murray, son of Madalyn Murray and the petitioner of standing, suffered continual verbal and physical assault after his mother's initial protest of the school board's Bible reading or Lord's Prayer participation requirement. The school district responded to Murray's objection by amending its policy to allow the option of excusal—essentially stating that William Murray, or any other dissenting student, could leave the classroom during the Bible chapter or Lord's Prayer recitation—but Murray filed a mandamus action for removal of the practice in its entirety, nonetheless. Unlike *School District of Abington Township v. Schempp*, however, an actual trial never ensued until oral arguments before the Supreme Court. A trial court dismissed the original *Murray* suit in 1961, stating that the Bible was not a sectarian document and that the school board's excusal amendment was sufficient to foster religious equality. The Maryland Court of Appeals upheld the lower court's dismissal the following year, citing Supreme Court silence as grounds. That silence became the backbone of *Murray's* federal appeal. After Madalyn Murray filed for certiorari in the Supreme Court, the FBI began monitoring the atheist petitioner, and Baltimore's Department of Public Welfare, Murray's longtime employer, fired her.[12]

During oral arguments, attorneys for the Baltimore school district argued that Bible reading and recitation of the Lord's Prayer were secular attempts to promote moral values. "Now, the practice, we maintain, has something in it other than religiousness itself," argued attorney Francis Burch for the school district, "it has a traditional teaching of moral and ethical values." "The literature of the Bible was historical," he continued, "the most widely read book of all books ever composed."[13] Obviously the Court could not accept such an argument after its *Engel* decision, which ruled that the sectarianism of a relatively innocuous Regent's prayer necessitated its public school removal. The Bible and Lord's Prayer, by comparison, unquestionably promoted a specific belief.

Generally, the overwhelmingly disgruntled public viewed the pending verdict as inevitable, as the Supreme Court had never upheld religious activities in the public schools. The Citizens for Educational Freedom characterized the verdict as "another step toward the elimination of God from all public American life." "Every time the Supreme Court restricts religious ceremony in the public schools," wrote commentator James Reston the day following the ruling, "this country suffers a twinge of conflict between its heart and mind." The conflict in Reston's heart and mind, however, could also be described as a conflict between two different versions of America's social identity. The cultural discourse's contradictory "Americanism" falsely offered religion as a replacement for equality, rather than an aid to it.[14]

Thus the affront when *Murray* reaffirmed the Court's former decisions while allowing the Bible a place in the secular realm of objective teaching on world religions. But the country's heart and mind lacked the Court's uniformity, and reaction was understandably diverse. Heritage and tradition arguments dominated early reaction to Supreme Court religion decisions, even prompting the normally reclusive former president Herbert Hoover to publicly warn of the 1962 *Engel* decision's "disintegration of a sacred American heritage." Dwight Eisenhower also called upon the national tradition to publicly disagree with the Court's ruling, and Justice Potter Stewart, in his *Engel* dissent, argued that denying children the opportunity to participate in the Regent's prayer denied them the "spiritual heritage of the nation." "I realize, of course, that the Declaration of Independence antedates the Constitution," said former President Eisenhower in response to the decision, "but the fact remains that the Declaration was our certificate of national birth."[15]

The most stringent post-*Murray* heritage arguments, however, came from the religious community. Billy Graham noted that religion had been a part of American heritage since the arrival of the pilgrims, adding, "Now a Supreme Court in 1963 says our fathers were wrong all these years." "We need more religion, not less," said Graham. "Why should the majority be so severely penalized by the protests of a handful?" The Catholic Archdiocese of New York, in a statement typical of Catholic reaction to *Murray*, noted that secularization of schools was a radical departure from American tradition. The Archbishop of Washington, Patrick A. O'Boyle, said of the

Court, "It is obvious that little by little it is discarding religious traditions hallowed by a century and a half of American practice." The decision was, in this scenario, the antithesis of American religiosity, creating a society of atheists and agnostics, and a decided U.S. policy shift. Others, including Jewish organizations such as the Synagogue Council of America, argued that America's legacy of religious freedom should take prominence over its legacy of religion and that a practice's duration does not necessarily ensure its constitutionality. "We fervently believe," declared the Council's president, Uri Miller, "that public institutions such as the public school should be free of such practices." Madalyn Murray herself responded to religious heritage arguments by positing that, "through history ... you find that nearly all who contributed anything ... were atheists or agnostics."[16]

Southern legislators disagreed, the most memorable exhortation pronounced by Representative George Andrews of Alabama who lamented, "They put the Negroes in the schools, and now they've driven God out." But local counterparts and constituents equally and ably matched the animus of their national politicians. Southern protest stemmed heavily from the segregationist community, which somewhat mitigated national ire and caused some citizens to alter their positions to avoid the appearance of racism. While mass disagreement with *Engel* and *Murray* emanated from every American region, the South proved far less acquiescent than the North and West.[17]

Representative L. Mendel Rivers of South Carolina, typically illustrating southern frustration with perceived judicial interference, declared in 1962 that the Supreme Court was "legislating—they never adjudicate—with one eye on the Kremlin and the other on the National Association for the Advancement of Colored People." A group of southern Senators offered a constitutional amendment after *Engel* that asserted, in part, "the right of each state to decide on the basis of its own public policy the question of decency and morality." Southerners, however, and conservatives in general, had no consistent defense against *Murray*, just as they did not have a unified defense against the Court's *Brown* decision in 1954, because in both instances, conservatives failed to anticipate judicial action based on legal precedent. Different agendas and different reasons for opposing judicial impositions made different positions inconsistent. One consistent similarity, however, involved the belief that the better judgment of each community should base decisions as to what a proper society should be. Alabama Governor George Wallace pronounced in 1964, in a manner strikingly similar to some of his more prominent integration denunciations, "We will not permit God and religion to be suppressed, outlawed, and banned from the institutions created by the people. Nor will we permit the State or any branch of our Government to order God out of our schools." While the Court's segregation decisions were implementable because the non-southern mind held a virtual consensus that the practice was morally wrong, no such consensus existed for the Court's *Murray* decision.[18]

Wallace and others were not arguing *for* religion, they were arguing *against* judicial interference. The arguments were prevalent, but did have detractors who favored a barrier between church and state. The prayer and Bible reading cases rallied the strict separation forces, whose varied religious and anti-religious makeups had previously kept the groups disparate. Prominent among the religious forces was Martin Luther King, Jr., who approved of the Court's *Murray* ruling and referred to it as "a sound and good decision reaffirming something that is basic in our Constitution, namely separation of church and state." Responses such as King's allied religious liberals with groups such as the American Ethical Union and the American Humanist Association, and while the response this coalescence created did not match the hard-line conservative zeal of a George Wallace or Strom Thurmond, it established a voice that had not previously existed. The American Ethical Union made a strikingly similar statement to King's after the previous year's *Engel* decision, declaring, "The principle of separation is a basic safeguard of freedom." "Even among the theistic religions," stated the Union's amicus brief for the petitioners in *Murray*, "the Bible readings heard by the children include doctrines not accepted by some sects or denominations." A similar brief filed on the petitioners' behalf by the American Humanist Association argued that public Bible reading and Lord's Prayer recitation aided "all religions against non-believers and aid those religions based on a belief in God."[19]

These separation arguments, along with southern railings against judicial interference, inevitably led to a debate over government neutrality, which featured two competing conceptions. An argument included on the opinion pages of the *New York Times*, as well as in the *Murray* opinion of Justice Tom Clark, stated that in order for government to remain neutral, religious exercises in the public schools must be removed. Clark quoted Cincinnati Judge Alphonso Taft, father of future Supreme Court Chief Justice William Howard Taft, in an 1870 opinion, "The government is neutral, and, while protecting all, it prefers none, and it disparages none." Justice Potter Stewart promulgated the counter-argument in his dissenting opinion and claimed that making the option of religious exercise obsolete promoted secularism and was fundamentally non-neutral. "For a compulsory state educational system so structures a child's life," wrote Stewart, "that if religious exercises are held to be an impermissible activity in schools, religion is placed at an artificial and state-created disadvantage."[20]

Proponents of removal-as-neutrality based their arguments on the work of James Madison, who insisted that governmental involvement in religious exercise degraded that exercise. A delineation of the public school religion cases featured in the *Columbia Law Review* echoed Madison in early 1963. It stated that government union with religion, even in the smallest forms, endorsed one faith as more appropriate than another, therefore encouraging the more "appropriate" faith and creating an indirectly "chosen" government religion. A 1963 article in the *Washington Law Review*, however, noted that *Murray* could be construed as promoting secularism over neutrality, because government denial of resources to a Christian community that had continually and historically received them effectively ruled against that Christian community. The critical flaw of neutrality theory was that in order to remain strictly neutral, the government must fund both secular and religiously affiliated organizations when the purpose of each was the same. Maryland's Attorney General, Thomas B. Finan, highlighted this flaw in his amicus brief to the Supreme Court on behalf of the respondents, arguing that to avoid funding any secular activity proposed by a religious organization, just because it was a religious organization, was not, by definition, neutral. Removal of the Lord's Prayer and Bible reading, argued Finan, would "by necessary implication impose upon the populace an atheistic or at least agnostic concept of our origin and end and will itself constitute the establishment of a religion." Adherents as diverse as Episcopal Bishop James Pike, Republican New York Senator Kenneth

Keating, and Harvard Law School's Erwin Griswold, echoed Maryland's reasoning and propagated these neutrality arguments as the basis for their disapproval of *Murray*.[21]

While Erwin Griswold portrayed the Court's prayer decisions as examples of judicial absolutism, his disagreement with the decision stopped short of accusing the Court of establishing a communistic secularism. Often, however, the overwhelming American fear of Soviet Communism saturated discussions of public school secularism. The juxtaposition of freedom and totalitarianism, after all, was an integral part of that overriding "Americanism." In 1962, for instance, West Virginia Senator Robert Byrd blamed the Court's public school religion decisions on a palpable Communist influence, and various school boards throughout the nation similarly assailed the decisions as "victor[ies] for communism," but the majority of this Communist rhetoric was simple hubris employed for argumentative emphasis. No evidence exists that links any of the eight concurring justices to Communist influence. Despite its fears, the nation was in no danger of a Red invasion of its public schools.[22]

While Communist charges, regardless of merit, remained relatively clear, evaluations of a proper definition of communism's counterpart and *Murray*'s inconsistency with the American status quo were far murkier. "In God We Trust" slogans on money, prayers in the legislature and other previously present official procedures basically, if not technically, established a national religion. While military chaplains, religious tax exemptions, and other public religious activities clouded the issue, Justice Brennan's concurring opinion in *Murray* argued that "the line we must draw between the permissible and the impermissible is one which accords with history and faithfully reflects the understanding of the Founding Fathers." While it did not untangle the governmental inconsistencies, Brennan's stance attempted to reassure doubters that the Supreme Court did not intend to secularize the nation. The Supreme Court had previously allowed public funding for buses and textbooks for parochial school children as well as off-campus religious instruction for public school students. Conservative commentator L. Brent Bozell ignored Brennan's reassurances, however, arguing in the month following the decision that *Murray* continued a logical governmental progression toward "every public action affecting religious interests constitut[ing] a *prima facie* case of unconstitutionality."[23]

Regardless of actual legitimacy, American ideology held concepts of "truth" and "consistency" as one and the same, describing positions held in contradiction to popular belief as wrong despite potential merit. The contradictory principles of neutrality and non-establishment, the changing definitions of "religious" and "secular," the varying conceptions of the wall of separation, and the common view of America as a Christian nation all left the Supreme Court searching for the proper application of principles to given situations, while the popular majority scrambled to maintain their religious hegemony. Justice Tom Clark, the Christian moderate who wrote the majority opinion in *Murray*, stated that the refusal of separation would only damage religious purity and confuse school children as to the divine or secular nature of religious exercise. "The place of religion in our society is an exalted one," declared Clark, "achieved through a long tradition of reliance on the home, the church and the inviolable citadel of the individual heart and mind."[24] Clark's value argument, endorsed by many makeshift pundits, acted as the primary countermeasure against popular coercion and consistency claims. President Kennedy, U.S. Commissioner of Education Sterling McMurrin, and New York Senator Jacob Javits each anticipated Clark after the Court's *Engel* decision, arguing that religion in the schools transferred spiritual responsibility from the church and home to public education, thereby weakening all three and disorienting children's conception of religious purpose. "We have in this case a very easy remedy," said Kennedy, responding to *Engel*, "and that is to pray ourselves." Following *Murray*, mainstream religious groups such as the National Council of Churches, the United Presbyterian Church, and the Synagogue Council of America—each with a vested interest in maintaining the unique sanctity of church life—made similar pleas as to the proper place of religion in American life. The National Council of Churches, in a representative statement, emphasized that, "neither true religion nor good education is dependent upon the devotional use of the Bible in the public school program."[25]

Devotional use, in fact, was the culprit. The sectarian nature of the Lord's Prayer and the Bible (and even the New York Regent's prayer) existed not only because the two promoted one belief system over another, but also because they distinguished between theism and atheism. This distinction became particularly relevant in light of the presence of a disbelieving petitioner and assumed a key role in the amicus briefs of the American Humanist Association and the American Ethical Union on the petitioner's behalf. The American Humanist Association's brief explained, "The reading of the Holy Bible in the King James, Douay or other version and the recitation of the Lord's Prayer presupposes a religious belief and a religion based on a belief in God," while the American Ethical Union described the practices as "necessarily offensive to children of followers of the Ethical religion, since they express official sanction of dogmas and practices to which these children cannot subscribe." Madalyn Murray argued that the purpose of public education was "to prepare children to face the problems on earth, not to prepare for heaven," and the petitioners' brief filed on her behalf prominently featured arguments against the sectarianism of the Baltimore practices. Religion in the public schools did not and could not in-and-of-itself create moral students. Clark's opinion and Murray's victory, however, did not fully convince a nation focused on conceptions of what type of students public schools should create.[26]

But that opinion and that victory remained, and Americans used their own understanding of constitutional history to justify a pro- or anti-*Murray* stance. The majority of the populace viewed the decision as a broad interpretation of the First Amendment after application of the Fourteenth but disagreed as to the correctness of that interpretation. The First Amendment itself stemmed from eighteenth-century Jeffersonian liberalism that, in turn, stemmed from the primarily Baptist and Presbyterian desire for more stringent protection of religion from state authority. The 1868 Fourteenth Amendment barred the states from passing laws that abridged the rights of any American citizen.[27] While these generalizations made original intent arguments appear obvious and standard judicial practice dictated application of the latter amendment to the former, opponents of the *Murray* decision asserted that the First Amendment's congressional mandate and the Fourteenth's preoccupation with the newly freed slaves mitigated the use of original purpose as valid argument. "*All* that is in question is what our 50 *states* (and their subordinate agencies) can or cannot do under the First Amendment," wrote Willmoore Kendall in 1964, "which is a matter about which the Framers of the First Amendment, directed as it is exclusively at Congress, certainly had no discernible intent." By emphasizing that the nation's Founding Fathers would have disapproved of total governmental absence from religion, *Murray's* detractors further portrayed religiosity as a national ideal and magnified the disbelieving minority's outsider status.[28]

The validity of that minority's position in a democratic society also understandably received much attention. Like "liberty" and "freedom," "democracy" served (and serves) as a vague term that supposedly set America apart, but its actual function and relationship with equality often fell victim to those prior assumptions. California Republican Don Clausen stated that the Court's *Murray* and *Engel* decisions punished the majority to accommodate a small minority, replacing the democratic theory of government with an American oligarchy. A 1962 editorial in the Catholic newspaper, *The Pilot*, railed against the "futility of following a course of public policy and public law which is based on the clamorous and constant protestation of a well-organized and litigious minority." "We must see to it that minority groups are protected," contributed a letter-writer to the *New York Times*, "but is their wish and whim to be the law of the land?" The concern from lawmakers and letter-writers, however, did not take hold in the pulpit. Many Protestant churches saw the need to safeguard religion, even if that religion happened to be a minority faith. In essence, theologians such as Arthur Lichtenberger, Presiding Bishop of the Protestant Episcopal Church, argued that assuming minorities only warranted toleration—even when that minority was, like the Murray family, atheistic—was inconsistent with the concept of religious pluralism. Such an assumption, pronounced a statement issued by the National Council of Churches prior to the Court's *Murray* decision, "endangers both true religion and civil liberties." Tolerance was not equality and, by definition, could never be equality. *Murray* and *Engel*, in Bishop Lichtenberger's conception, "reflect[ed] the Court's sense of responsibility to assure freedom and equality to all groups of believers and non-believers as expressed in the First Amendment to the Constitution." The subtle yet fundamental difference between tolerance and equality, however, remained elusive to the majority of Americans concerned about the minority's "wish and whim."[29]

When the "tyranny of the minority" arguments ran their course, opponents were left with the First Amendment. Violation of the Establishment Clause required one to demonstrate either "advancement" or "inhibition" of religion, while the Free Exercise Clause evaluated church and state separation from the bottom up, guaranteeing each citizen religious freedom. A decision hinged on Free Exercise therefore required a demonstration of coercion, whereas a decision based on the Establishment Clause did not. Essentially, establishment claims considered overt acts of governmental religious manipulation, while claims based on the Free Exercise Clause considered the protected population and the impact of any governmental policy on the equal participation or non-participation in the religion of one's choice. However, *McCollum*—itself based on a violation of the Establishment Clause—demonstrated a form of coercion, so a state could also establish religion by coercing or funding religious exercises. The Court's *Murray* decision also acknowledged an adequate demonstration of indirect coercion and used the establishment claims of *McCollum* and *Engel* as precedent.[30]

The Establishment and Free Exercise Clauses of the First Amendment, as presented in the *Murray* opinion, were inherently contradictory. Establishment encouraged government isolation while Free Exercise mandated government protection, a paradox of precedence in the petitioners' argument before the Supreme Court. Leonard Kerpelman argued for the petitioners that the Baltimore statute promoted a "free exercise" for the majority that "established" a dominant religion against minority claims. The establishment could be removed only after a reinterpretation of "free exercise" on the part of the school board. "I don't think that the free exercise of the majority can work that way," argued Kerpelman. "In exercising its right it is establishing a religion in the public school; by establishing the religion in the public school, they take away, of course, the right of the petitioners to be free of an establishment." With the variety of available interpretations, *Murray*'s eight concurring justices did not necessarily present a unanimous voice. Rather, each offered his own conception of how far the Establishment Clause reached, leaving the public to interpret the validity of those individual claims. Public opinion began at the water's edge of a shoreline created by these competing viewpoints.[31]

A brief swim from that edge, beyond the varied arguments surrounding the logic and legitimacy of *Murray*, lay the reality of action and implementation. The Court handed down its opinion on 17 June 1963, and before the close of the month, a barrage of Constitutional amendments appeared in both the House and Senate attempting to void the judicial decree. Delaware Republican Senator John Williams offered his amendment just two days following the ruling, the bill stating in part, "Nothing contained in this constitution shall be construed to prohibit the authority administering any school, school system, or educational institution supported in whole or in part from any public funds from providing for the participation by the students thereof in any periods of Bible reading or non-sectarian prayer if such participation is voluntary." Protesters picketed Justice Tom Clark, writer of the majority opinion, at a 28 June meeting of the National Council of Juvenile Court Judges in Knoxville, Tennessee. Representative Robert Ashmore of South Carolina even introduced a bill to place "In God We Trust" above the bench of the U.S. Supreme Court within days of the decision.[32]

Madalyn Murray, too, became a target of American resentment following her victory, suffering the murder of her cat and graffiti accusing her of Communism. "I've missed so, so much school this year," said Garth Murray, Madalyn Murray's youngest son, at the close of the 1963–1964 school year, "because of atheism and sinus and measles." Vandals inflicted severe property damage and threatened the family with death, but Christian ire fumed outside of Baltimore, as well. The atheist received threatening correspondence from across the nation. "You filthy atheist," wrote one disgruntled citizen, "Only a rat like you would go to court to stop prayer. All curses on you and your family. Bad luck and leprosy disease upon you and your damn family." "Lady," said another, "you are as deadly to our city as a snake. Return to Russia. (Signed) A True Believer in our God who gave you the air you breathe." Finally, direct death threats also emanated from Murray's mailbox: "You will repent, and damn soon a .30-30 (rifle bullet) will fix you nuts. You will have bad luck forever. You atheist, you mongrel, you rat, you good for nothing s__, you damn gutter rat. Jesus will fix you,

you filthy scum." Murray's war was not simply one of words, however. A physical confrontation with Baltimore police led to charges of assault and contempt of court, as well as the Murray family's flight from the city.[33]

Two days after the Court's opinion, the ACLU filed suit in California state court to remove "under God" from the Pledge of Allegiance in Los Angeles public schools. Murray continued her legal campaign the following year by unsuccessfully suing the city of Baltimore to halt the practice of exempting religious organizations from taxation. Judicial scholar Leo Pfeffer predicted in 1963 that governmental support and tax status of religious organizations would be the next major area of inquiry, and America's legal community, if not its Protestant populace, seemed firmly committed to the beneficial effects of church and state separation. The reality of public school implementation, however, proved differently.[34]

Ten years after the ordered removal of the Lord's Prayer and Bible reading from public schools, absolute compliance had yet to be achieved, though many school districts initially appeared relatively compliant. In Alabama, West Virginia, and other states, compliance actions stemmed from state court decisions that applied the Supreme Court standard judicially. In some states, such as Louisiana, Kentucky, and New York, attorneys general wrote official opinions declaring constitutional the general principle established by the Court, while many western states ratified state constitutional amendments firmly elaborating the Court's *Murray* position. While some southern state governments made overtures toward compliance, the only significant regional variation in successful implementation occurred in the South, which saw in *Murray* an opportunity to defy the Supreme Court without any tangible danger of Federal troops arriving to enforce decisions. As *Time* magazine noted in its coverage of *Murray*, "No federal authority is likely to call out the troops to take the Bible out of a teacher's hand or order children to unclasp theirs."[35]

In all, sociological compliance studies, intended to gauge local response to the Bible and Lord's Prayer removal in the years following the *Murray* decision, showed that school districts previously requiring some sort of devotional practice demonstrated a much stronger tendency to comply with the *Murray* decision than did those previously allowing a devotional practice without an actual physical requirement. The latter most likely assumed that sufficient compromise had already occurred, or that the Court's decision could not affect the less stringent devotional practices. Both groups, however, attempted to forward alternatives as religious supplements, the most popular of which was the moment of silence, adopted, in fact, by both Maryland and Pennsylvania, the home states of Murray and Schempp. Some school boards substituted a recitation of the fourth verse of the "Star Spangled Banner," which repeated the line, "In God is our Trust," and referred to the United States as a "heav'n rescued land." New York, home of *Engel's* Regent's prayer, found many of its school districts willing to recite the song as an opening ceremony. Another supplemental method, encouraging student-initiated prayer, assumed the lack of authority control would circumvent *Murray*, but proved unconstitutional during the Court's 1965 session in *Stein v. Olshinsky*. Many school districts offered released-time programs, allowing students to spend a portion of the school day receiving religious instruction off campus, but only Hawaii, Oregon, and Vermont created laws affirming the practice. Each supplement demonstrated religious America's reluctance to move toward a more secular and equal position.[36]

In these maneuvers, the adaptability of a system of thought positing religious patriotism as the only "Americanism" appears most evident. This American mind—this collective ideal held by a majority of religious Americans in the mid-1960s (and through the first years of the twenty-first century)—adjusted when forced to change. Interestingly, in an attack by America (the judiciary) on religion (school prayer and Bible reading), opinion sided *against* America in the name of Americanism. That was the strength of the religious-patriotic ideal, leaving atheist opponents with little room to maneuver. The religious patriotism of the majority American mind, however, never disappeared.

Texas and Kentucky both appeared before the Supreme Court in March 2005 to defend monuments to the Ten Commandments—Kentucky's inside the capitol, Texas's on the capitol grounds. In June, the Court demonstrated that uniformity was still impossible. A pair of split decisions ruled the Ten Commandments unconstitutional inside government buildings, but acceptable on their lawns. "The court has found no single mechanical formula," wrote Justice Stephen Breyer, "that can accurately draw the constitutional line in every case." Breyer quoted the *Schempp* and *Murray* decisions to demonstrate the historical frustration with inconsistency. Interestingly, Chief Justice Renquist, in his majority opinion endorsing the right of Texas to display a monument to the Ten Commandments on the capitol grounds, selectively quoted the *Schempp* and *Murray* opinion, repeating, "Religion has been closely identified with our history and government." His neglect of the final ruling in that opinion, however, stands as its own monument to the inconsistency so frustrating to Breyer.[37]

In April 2005, the Arkansas House of Representatives approved a bill disallowing school administrators from interfering in student-led public prayer on school grounds. Though it failed to receive a motion to appear on the Senate floor, the bill's overwhelming popularity in the House led representatives to promise its swift return.[38] Groups continue to fight America for America's sake—they fight the universal for the sake of the personal. And when outspoken atheist petitioners reappear, such as Michael Newdow and his unsuccessful attempt to remove "under God" from the Pledge of Allegiance, culminating in 2004, "mainstream" citizens follow the story in the popular media and damn their actions and characters as subversive at best, un-American at worst.[39]

The majority of the American populace receives Supreme Court rulings from news outlets rather than careful readings of opinions, as they did in 1963. The Court's *Murray* decision, then, created a controversy based more on its portrayal than the content of its written opinion. The pattern of responses upon responses only fomented public ire and exacerbated the negative reaction towards the opinion. In essence, the majority of the populace heard Alabama Representative George Andrews declare, "They put the Negroes in the schools, and now they've driven God out," before they heard Justice Tom Clark explain from his majority opinion, "The place of religion in our society is an exalted one." Exaggerated disapproval of every Supreme Court public school religion decision, *Murray* primary among them, stemmed from exaggerated initial coverage, while more thoughtful and accepting press evaluation and legal commentary prompted gradual acceptance.[40]

Acceptance, however, was reluctant. The *Murray* decision had a twenty-four percent approval rating in 1963. Twelve years later that figure rose to only thirty-five percent. In another survey, pollsters asked respondents whether someone who was ideologically opposed to all churches and forms of religion should be allowed to speak publicly. In 1954, thirty-seven percent of the population approved of the possibility, while in 1976 the number rose to sixty-four percent.[41] But hesitant compliance with the Supreme Court's *Murray* decision did not signal the American religious majority's willingness to grant full equality to non-believers. American citizens were products of their faith and nationalism, both of which assured them of a superiority based on beliefs and place of birth. That citizenry, however, was far less homogeneous than the anti-*Murray* majority assumed.

The growing ethnic and religious diversity in America aligned the 1963 Supreme Court with popular necessity, if not popular will. The broadest support for school prayer came from the section of the population with the lowest incomes and lowest education. African-Americans, for example, remained more devoted to school prayer than whites due primarily to lower socioeconomic status and heavier reliance on religion and church activities, especially in the area of civil rights. The Anti-Defamation League of B'Nai B'rith, representing another prominent American minority, referred to the Court's prayer decisions as "splendid reaffirmation[s] of a basic American principle."[42]

Decisions gain significance for a number of reasons. The *Murray* decision clearly acknowledged the virtual impossibility of absolute church and state separation. The continued acceptance of "under God" in the Pledge of Allegiance and similar customs made this impossibility clear, as did the fact that no Supreme Court decision had been an all-encompassing removal of religion from public schools. Even after *Murray*, the Bible could still be objectively and historically taught, but the religious majority consistently worried over the dismantling of structured religious activity in the public school system. They still do, though absolute separation remains impossible. The piecemeal-removal policy, however, regardless of the public outcry, stemmed (and still stems) from a pragmatic approach to the Establishment and Free Exercise clauses of the First Amendment.[43]

Whether John Dewey would recognize such judicial pragmatism as the Jamesian version of his youth is debatable. So too is the question of whether *Murray* logically elaborated on Horace Mann's original vision for

American public education. Regardless, the Court clearly demonstrated its willingness to view the church as an important social, if not national, institution, leaving the disbelieving minority to patiently wait for further elaborations. The religious patriotic majority clearly demonstrated *its* willingness to fight for its definition of "Americanism," proving, if nothing else, the resiliency of the American mind and the traditions it held dear. Each copy of the Ten Commandments on each piece of state property stands today as a monument to that resiliency. The retrenchment of majority sentiment following *Murray* ensured that judicial decisions would not immediately place atheists on the same equal playing field as the religious. The American God did not die, but neither did the minority challenge, and as the 1960s cycled toward their inevitable conclusion, Dewey and Mann were left spinning quietly, carefully in their graves.

Notes

1. *School District of Abington Township v. Schempp*, 374 US 203 (1963), http://laws.findlaw.com/us/374/203.html, accessed 31 January 2003 [hereinafter cited as *Abington Township v. Schempp*, 374 US 203.]; Horace Mann died on 2 August 1859. John Dewey died on 1 June 1952. "Educational Contributions of Horace Mann," http://www.cals.ncsu.edu/agexed/aee501/mann.html, accessed 24 February 2003; Louis Menand, *The Metaphysical Club* (New York: Farrar, Straus and Giroux, 2001), 438; Stephen Macedo, "Transformative Constitutionalism and the Case of Religion: Defending the Moderate Hegemony of Liberalism," *Political Theory* 26 (February 1998): 61, 72; and "Progressive Education," http://www.ilt.columbia.edu/publications/projects/ digitexts/notes/ilt_prog_education.html, accessed 24 February 2003.

2. "The Supreme Court, the First Amendment, and Religion in the Public Schools," *Columbia Law Review* 63 (January 1963): 84; and J.A. Leo Lemay, *Deism, Masonry, and the Enlightenment: Essays Honoring Alfred Owen Aldridge* (Newark: University of Delaware Press, 1987), 11–15, 158–160.

3. "On Writ of Certiorari to the Court of Appeals of the State of Maryland," No. 119, October Term 1962, Supreme Court of the United States; and "Appeal From the

United States District Court for the Eastern District of Pennsylvania," No. 142, October Term 1962, Supreme Court of the United States.

4. Frank Way, "Stability and Change in Constitutional Litigation: The Public Piety Cases," *The Journal of Politics* 47 (August 1985): 911; and Louis H. Pollak, "Public Prayers in Public Schools," *Harvard Law Review* 77 (November 1963): 63.

5. Macedo, "Transformative Constitutionalism and the Case of Religion," 63; Way, "Stability and Change in Constitutional Litigation," 913; Kirk W. Elifson and C. Kirk Hadaway, "Prayer in Public Schools: When Church and State Collide," *Public Opinion Quarterly* 49 (Autumn 1985): 318; D.L., "Constitutional Law— Establishment Clause of the First Amendment—Bible Reading and the Lord's Prayer in Public Schools," *New York Law Forum* 9 (December 1963): 544; *Cantwell v. Connecticut*, 310 US 296 (1940), http://laws.findlaw.com/us/310/296.html, accessed 2 October 2003.

6. *West Virginia State Board of Education v. Barnett*, 319 US 624 (1943), http://laws. findlaw. com/us/319/624.html, accessed 2 July 2003; D.L. "Constitutional Law," 545; *Minersville School District v. Gobits*, 310 US 586 (1940); and Robert L. Cord, *Separation of Church and State: Historical Fact and Current Fiction* (New York: Lambeth Press, 1982), 150–151.

7. *Everson v. Board of Education*, 330 US 1; *New York Times*, 21 June 1963, 28.

8. *McCollum v. Board of Education*, 333 US 203 (1948), http://laws.findlaw. com/us/333/203.html, accessed 10 September 2003; William C. McClure, "Constitutional Law—First Amendment—State Law Requiring the Reading of the Holy Bible in the Public Schools Violates the 'Establishment Clause' of the Federal Constitution," *University of Pittsburgh Law Review* 25 (October 1963): 89; "No Bible in the Schools?" *Life*, 12 April 1963, 63; *Zorach v. Clauson*, 343 US 306 (1952), http://laws.findlaw.com/us/343/306.html, accessed 7 July 2003; Paul G. Kauper, *Religion and the Constitution* (Baton Rouge: Louisiana State University Press, 1964), 59, 67; and *New York Times*, 26 June 1962, 17.

9. *Torcasso v. Watkins*, 367 US 488 (1961), http://laws.findlaw.com/us/367/488.html, accessed 2 October 2003; *New York Times*, 20 June 1963, 20; and D.L., "Constitutional Law," 549.

10. The Regent's prayer read, "Almighty God, we acknowledge our dependence upon Thee, and we beg Thy blessing upon us, our parents, our teachers and our country." *Engel v. Vitale*, 370 US 421 (1962), http://laws.findlaw.com/us/370/421.html, accessed 15 March 2003 [hereinafter cited as *Engel v. Vitale*, 370 US 421.]; *New*

York Times, 26 June 1962, 1, 16, 17; Dennis L. Thompson, "The Kennedy Court: Left and Right of Center," *Western Political Quarterly* 26 (June 1973): 263–264; and "Supreme Court: The Fourth 'R,'" *Newsweek*, 11 March 1963, 24.

11. "The Supreme Court: A Loss to Make Up For," *Time*, 28 June 1963, 13; *New York Times*, 18 June 1963, 1, 27; 26 June 1962, 17; Catharina Csaky Hirt, "The Efficacy of Amicus Curiae Briefs in the School Prayer Decisions" (Ph.D. diss., Vanderbilt University, 1995), 34; and Michal R. Belknap, "God and the Warren Court: The Quest for 'A Wholesome Neutrality,'" *Seton Hall Constitutional Law Journal* 9 (Spring 1999): 405. Further demonstrating the lack of religious uniformity, Abstracts of the United States for 1961 reported that thirty-seven percent of the American population was not religiously affiliated at the close of the 1950s. Larry H. Schwartz, "Separation of Church and State: Religious Exercises in the Schools," *University of Cincinnati Law Review* 31 (Fall 1962): 412.

12. *New York Times*, 18 June 1963, 27; G. Cohen, "Constitutional Law—Whether State Action Requiring Public Schools To Begin Each Day With Readings From the Bible Violates the First Amendment," *Chicago-Kent Law Review* 40 (Fall 1963): 168; Leo Pfeffer, "The Schempp-Murray Decision on School Prayers and Bible Reading," *Journal of Church and State* 5 (Spring 1963): 166; "Petition for a Writ of Certiorari to the Court of Appeals of Maryland," No. 119, October Term 1962, Supreme Court of the United States, 10–11; "Brief in Opposition to Petition for Writ of Certiorari," No. 119, October Term 1962, Supreme Court of the United States, 7.

13. "Oral Argument by Francis B. Burch, Esq., on Behalf of Respondents, Number 119—27 February 1963," in *Oral Arguments of the Supreme Court of the United States: The Warren Court, 1953 Term–1968 Term* (Paul M. Hebert Law Center, Baton Rouge; Frederick, MD: University Publications of America, Inc., 1984), text-fiche, p. 19, F17; and Pfeffer, "The Schempp-Murray Decision," 168. Leonard J. Kerpelman argued for the petitioners, Francis B. Burch and George W. Baker, Jr. for the respondents, and Thomas B. Finan for the State of Maryland *amicus curiae*. "Freedom of Religion … Bible Reading in Schools," *American Bar Association Journal* 50 (January 1964): 82; and *New York Times*, 18 June 1963, 27.

14. Cohen, "Constitutional Law," 172; McClure, "Constitutional Law," 89–90; Pfeffer, "The Schempp-Murray Decision," 172; and *New York Times*, 18 June 1963, 27, 36, 19 June 1963, 36.

15. *New York Times*, 27 June 1962, 20, 26 June 1962, 16, 29 June 1962, 26, 30 June 1962, 20, 19 June 1963, 36; Philip B. Kurland, "The School Prayer Cases," in *The Wall Between Church and State*, ed. Dallin H. Oaks (Chicago: The University of Chicago Press, 1963), 145; and *Engel v. Vitale*, 370 US 421.

16. *New York Times*, 18 June 1963, 27, 29, and 27 June 1963, 32; Daniel B. Ritter, "Constitutional Law: The Bible Reading Cases," *Washington Law Review* 38 (Autumn 1963): 657; "Brief of Synagogue Council of America and National Community Relations Advisory Council as Amici Curiae," No. 119 and No. 142, October Term 1962, Supreme Court of the United States, 7; "No Bible in the Schools?" 64; Jane Howard, "The Most Hated Woman in America," *Life*, 19 June 1964, 94; and Sanford Kessler, "Tocqueville on Civil Religion and Liberal Democracy," *The Journal of Politics* 39 (February 1977): 122, 142.

17. *New York Times*, 26 June 1962, 16, 27 June 1962, 1, 20, 30 June 1962, 20; and Belknap, "God and the Warren Court," 441–442.

18. *New York Times*, 27 June 1962, 20; Willmoore Kendall, "American Conservatism and the 'Prayer' Decisions," *Modern Age* 8 (Summer 1964): 250, 252, 258; Robert D. Smith, "Religion and the Schools: The Influence of State Attorneys General On the Implementation of *Engel* and *Schempp*," *Southern Quarterly* 8 (April 1970): 225; and Pollak, "Public Prayers in Public Schools," 62.

19. Martin Luther King, Jr., as quoted in Leo Pfeffer, "Prayer in Public Schools: The Court's Decisions," *National Forum* 68 (Winter 1988): 26; Bradley C. Canon, "The Supreme Court as a Cheerleader in Politico-Moral Disputes," *The Journal of Politics* 54 (August 1992): 650–651; "Brief of the American Ethical Union as Amicus Curiae," No. 119 and No. 142, October Term 1962, Supreme Court of the United States, 5 [hereinafter cited as "Brief of the American Ethical Union."]; "Brief of the American Humanist Association, As Amicus Curiae, and Motion for Leave to File Same," No. 119 and No. 142, October Term 1962, Supreme Court of the United States, 13, 19 [hereinafter cited as "Brief of the American Humanist Association."]; and *New York Times*, 29 June 1962, 26.

20. *New York Times*, 28 June 1963, 28; *Abington Township v. Schempp*, 374 US 203; and Stephen V. Monsma, "Justice Potter Stewart on Church and State," *Journal of Church and State* 36 (Summer 1994): 560.

21. Ritter, "Constitutional Law," 663, 665; William W. Van Alstyne, "Constitutional Separation of Church and State: The Quest for a Coherent Position," *American Political Science Review* 57 (December 1963): 865, 867; "The Supreme Court, the

First Amendment, and Religion in the Public Schools," 94; Wilber G. Katz and Harold P. Southerland, "Religious Pluralism and the Supreme Court," *Daedalus* 96 (Winter 1967): 181, 183; Bernard J. Coughlin, S.J., "Toward a Church-State Principle for Health and Welfare," *Journal of Church and State* 11 (Winter 1969): 38–39; "Brief and Appendix of Attorney General of Maryland, Amicus Curiae," No. 119, October Term 1962, Supreme Court of the United States, 3–4; "The Supreme Court: A Loss to Make Up For," 14; and *New York Times*, 28 June 1962, 17.

22. Pfeffer, "Prayer in Public Schools," 26; *New York Times*, 27 June 1962, 20; and Kendall, "American Conservatism," 246.

23. *New York Times*, 28 June 1962, 30; L. Brent Bozell, "Saving Our Children from God," *National Review*, 16 July 1963, 20.

24. Ellis M. West, "Justice Tom Clark and American Church-State Law," *Journal of Presbyterian History* 54 (Winter 1976): 387, 394–395; *Abington Township v. Schempp*, 374 US 203; and Bryan F. Le Beau, *The Atheist: Madalyn Murray O'Hair* (New York: New York University Press, 2003), 79–80.

25. *New York Times*, 17 June 1963 24, 29, 18 June 1963, 29, 22 June 1963, 23, 26 June 1962, 17, 28 June 1962, 1, and 30 June 1962, 20.

26. Schwartz, "Separation of Church and State," 409–410; "Brief of the American Humanist Association," 19–20; "Brief of American Jewish Committee and Anti-Defamation League of B'Nai B'Rith as Amici Curiae," No. 119 and No. 142, October Term 1962, Supreme Court of the United States, 10–11; "Brief of the American Ethical Union," 5; "No Bible in the Schools?" 64; and "Petitioners' Brief," No. 119, October Term 1962, Supreme Court of the United States, 11, 16.

27. D.L., "Constitutional Law," 542; *New York Times*, 26 June 1962, 17, 18 June 1963, 36; and U.S. Constitution, amend. 1, amend. 14, sec. 1.

28. The italics are Kendall's. Kendall, "American Conservatism," 252; Van Alstyne, "Constitutional Separation of Church and State," 866; "The Supreme Court, the First Amendment, and Religion in the Public Schools," 80–81; D.L., "Constitutional Law," 550; House, James Madison, June 1789, *Annals of Congress*, vol. 1, 1ˢᵗ Congress, 1789–1791 (Washington: Gales and Seaton, 1834), 434; and U.S. Constitution, amend. 1.

29. *New York Times*, 18 June 1963, 29, 29 June 1962, 26, 27 June 1962, 20; House, "The Supreme Court Decision on the Issue of Prayer in Our Public Schools," Extension of Remarks of Hon. Don H. Clausen of California in the House of Representatives, transcript of Living Waters Broadcast, 23 June 1963, 88ᵗʰ

Cong., 1ˢᵗ sess., *Congressional Record* 109, pt. 10 (24 July 1963): 13328; and Katz, "Religious Pluralism," 183.

30. Ritter, "Constitutional Law," 662; Van Alstyne, "Constitutional Separation of Church and State," 867; Cohen, "Constitutional Law," 171; D.L., "Constitutional Law," 548–549; and *Abington Township v. Schempp,* 374 US 203.

31. Coughlin, "Toward a Church-State Principle," 36; "Oral Argument by Leonard J. Kerpelman, Esq., on Behalf of Petitioners, No. 119—27 February 1963," in *Oral Arguments of the Supreme Court of the United States: The Warren Court, 1953 Term–1968 Term* (Paul M. Hebert Law Center, Baton Rouge; Frederick, MD: University Publications of America, Inc., 1984), text-fiche, p. 6, F17; Van Alstyne, "Constitutional Separation of Church and State," 865; and Barbara A. Perry, "Justice Hugo Black and the 'Wall of Separation Between Church and State,'" *Journal of Church and State* 31 (Winter 1989): 56.

32. Howard, "The Most Hated Woman in America," 92; *New York Times,* 20 June 1963, 20, 29 June 1963, 20, 26 June 1963, 43; Senate, "The Proposed Constitutional Amendment on Bible Reading and School Prayers," John J. Williams, 88ᵗʰ Cong., 1ˢᵗ sess., *Congressional Record,* 109, pt. 8 (19 June 1963): 11088; House, *A Bill to Provide for the Inscription in the Courtroom in the U.S. Supreme Court Building of the Phrase "In God We Trust,"* 88ᵗʰ Cong., 1ˢᵗ sess., H.R. 7252, *Congressional Record,* 109, pt. 9 (25 June 1963): 11529; Pfeffer, "The Schempp-Murray Decision," 174; and Bozell, "Saving Our Children from God," 34.

33. Howard, "The Most Hated Woman in America," 92; Robert Liston, "Mrs. Murray's War on God," *The Saturday Evening Post,* 11 July 1964, 86; and "Playboy Interview: Madalyn Murray," *Playboy,* October 1965, 65.

34. *New York Times,* 20 June 1963, 20; Howard, "The Most Hated Woman in America," 91–92; Richard E. Morgan, *The Supreme Court and Religion* (New York: The Free Press, 1972), 105; "Playboy Interview," 69; Katz, "Religious Pluralism," 183; Pfeffer, "The Schempp-Murray Decision," 175; and Theodore Sky, "The Establishment Clause, the Congress and the Schools: An Historical Perspective," *Virginia Law Review* 52 (December 1966): 1396.

35. Michael W. LaMorte and Fred N. Dorminy, "Compliance with the Schempp Decision: A Decade Later," *Journal of Law and Education* 3 (July 1974): 403–404; Schwartz, "Separation of Church and State," 399; and "The Supreme Court: A Loss to Make Up For," 14.

36. Smith, "Religion and the Schools," 227–228; Robert H. Birkby, "The Supreme Court and the Bible Belt: Tennessee Reaction to the 'Schempp' Decision," *Midwest*

Journal of Political Science 10 (August 1966): 309; *New York Times*, 29 June 1962, 17, 26, 19 June 1963, 1, 18, 29 June 1963, 25, 30 June 1962, 20, 22 June, 1963, 20; Pfeffer, "The Schempp-Murray Decision," 175; LaMorte, "Compliance with the Schempp Decision," 405–406; Oscar George Theodore Sonneck, *Report on "The Star-Spangled Banner," "Hail Columbia," "America," "Yankee Doodle"* (Washington, D.C.: Government Printing Office, 1909), 37; *Stein v. Olshinsky*, 248 F.2nd 999 (2ns Cir.), *cert. denied*, 382 US 957 (1965); Pfeffer, "Prayer in Public Schools," 27; Sky, "The Establishment Clause," 1396; and "Brief of Attorney General of Maryland, Amicus Curiae," No. 119, October Term 1962, Supreme Court of the United States, 5.

37. Quotations are from *Van Orden v. Perry*, the Texas decision. *Los Angeles Times*, 1 March 2005, A18; *New York Times*, 3 March 2005, A1; *Van Orden v. Perry*, 545 US 677 (2005), http://wid.ap.org/documents/scotus/050627vanorden.pdf, accessed 29 June 2005; and *McCreary County, Kentucky v. American Civil Liberties Union*, 545 US 844 (2005), http://wid.ap.org/documents/scotus/050627mccreary.pdf, accessed 29 June 2005.

38. Melissa Nelson, "Ark House Committee Approves School Prayer Bill," *The Associated Press State & Local Wire*, http://www.lexis-nexis.com, accessed 23 June 2005; and "Senate Panel Silent on School Prayer Bill," *The Associated Press State & Local Wire*, http://www.lexis-nexus.com, accessed 23 June 2005.

39. Newdow v. United States Congress, 292 F.3d 597 (9th Circuit 2002), http://caselaw.lp.findlaw.com/data2/circs/9th/0016423p.pdf, accessed 1 July 2003; *Elk Grove Unified School District v. Newdow*, 542 US 1 (2004), http://www.lexis-nexus.com, accessed 23 June 2005; *San Francisco Chronicle*, 27 June 2003, A1; and Howard Fineman, "One Nation, Under … Who?" *Newsweek*, 8 July 2002, 24.

40. *Abington Township v. Schempp*, 374 US 203; and Gregory Casey, "Popular Perceptions of Supreme Court Rulings," *American Politics Quarterly* 4 (January 1976): 4–5, 12.

41. Mariana Servin-Gonzalez and Oscar Torres-Reyna, "Trends: Religion and Politics," *Public Opinion Quarterly* 63 (Winter 1999): 620, 614.

42. Belknap, "God and the Warren Court," 402; and John C. Green and James L. Guth, "The Missing Link: Political Activists and Support for School Prayer," *Public Opinion Quarterly* 53 (Spring 1989): 42–43.

43. Coughlin, "Toward a Church-State Principle," 42–43.

Achilles, the Tortoise, and the Edmund Pettus Bridge

Language and Consistency in Historical Writing

A chilles surely balked when the tortoise challenged him to a footrace, standing flush as he probably was in the hot Greek sunshine. But his confidence, fatted from years of success, fell to the logic of the animal's pre-race jibes. After a suitable reptilian head start, Achilles would have to make up half the distance, then half of the remainder, then half of that, and half of that, ad infinitum. The hero was convinced he was beaten, and thus surrendered before even undertaking the race. (Millennia later, Muhammad Ali would employ a similar tortoisian scheme to great effect.)

And so Achilles was felled by Zeno's Paradox of motion, one of many such tales designed to prove the seeming fallacy of movement. Motion, Zeno seemed to be arguing, is simply the state of being in different places at different times. It is an illusion. At every instance of what appears to be motion, a still body is simply in a different position.

Two thousand years later, on Tuesday, 9 March 1965, Martin Luther King, Jr. walked across the Edmund Pettus Bridge, standing flush as he probably was in the hot Alabama sunshine. He sang songs along the way. As he reached the other side of the Alabama River, he spoke to police officers, arrayed to block the bridge's exit. He knelt in prayer, then stood up again. He turned around and walked back across the bridge to a nearby church.

His walk followed the infamous "Bloody Sunday" incident. Thousands of people trailed behind him, almost all expecting to continue walking to Montgomery and unaware that their leader struck a secret agreement to turn the marchers around. Historical interpretations of the stunted "middle passage" between Bloody Sunday and the Selma to Montgomery voting rights march have dissected political backroom dealings and police strategies to subdue the marchers and save face from public embarrassment. Each evaluation also includes a description of the event itself. Those descriptions, however, tell just as much as the intended historical accoutrements, make arguments with nothing more than their semantics and diction. The language employed in various historical descriptions creates another sort of Zeno's paradox: the description of someone's motion causes the recipient of the description to doubt its very possibility. It creates a false impression, or in the case of different histories, creates a variety of impressions presenting themselves as empirical fact.

But there is, in the end, very little empirical fact. There are few absolutes, even in the most routine descriptions. Each depiction of a historical event creates a new event. It is up to historians, then, to examine their words more carefully—to choose neither to run without thinking nor cower in the face of an ornery tortoise trying to psych them out. Instead, they should work to unravel the paradoxes presented and proceed from there.

Take these five accounts of the Edmund Pettus march, each stripped of the complex minutia before and after the event itself. The samples begin with the march and end at its conclusion. Nothing has been taken from the narratives in between those two points:

Sample 1

King proceeded with the march a day late as if, for the first time, he would defy a federal court order. He led about three thousand demonstrators across the Edmund Pettus Bridge and there encountered a federal marshal who advised him of the order and stepped aside. Also present in force were state troopers whose commander admonished King that the march could not continue. Then the troopers inexplicably moved out of the line of march. With the road to Montgomery open, King turned his followers back, in keeping with his agreement with federal negotiators.[1]

Sample 2

The two thousand singing and chanting marchers, ranks swelled by a Who's Who of religious notables and a large Unitarian contingent, recrossed the river. A forbidding line of troopers stopped them at the same point as on Sunday. King led the gathering in prayer, then ordered the long column to turn back. They retreated to Brown Chapel singing "Ain't Gonna Let Nobody Turn Me 'Round," the Selma theme song—an irony not lost on many. Back at the church he promised his followers that they would still get to Montgomery.[2]

Sample 3

Within a few minutes the column of two thousand marchers, many of whom were now whites, formed and began to move out. As it did so, with King at the head, Collins drove up, told him that "he felt everything would be all right," and handed him a small piece of paper.

Again turning from Sylvan to Water and then onto Broad, the column moved to the foot of the Pettus Bridge, where at shortly after 3:00 p.m. they paused while U.S. Marshall H. Stanley Fountain read to King Judge Johnson's order. Fountain then stepped aside as King indicated that he would proceed on across the bridge. As the column descended the other side of the bridge, several hundred yards ahead of them once again stood Major Cloud and the state troopers. Fifty feet from the officers King brought the column to a halt and requested permission to conduct several prayers. After the singing of "We Shall Overcome" and the leading of prayers by four different individuals, King turned so as to lead the column back across the bridge. As he did so, the troopers, in an unplanned move reportedly ordered over an open 'phone line from the governor's office in Montgomery, withdrew to the sides of the highway, leaving the road to Montgomery ostensibly open. Although each rank of the column wheeled in turn and followed King back into Selma, the surprise—and anger—at the meek retreat was widespread and strong among the SNCC workers and Selma teenagers, who had not received word of the late-morning negotiations.[3]

Sample 4

They moved on, five abreast down Sylvan Street, Martin arm in arm with Reverend Robert Spike and Bishop John Wesley Lord. In the forefront also was A.D. King, Fred Shuttlesworth, James Bevel, James Farmer, and James Forman, among others. "We Shall Overcome" alternated with stanzas of "Ain't Gonna Let Nobody Turn Me 'Round" as the huge interracial crowd turned into Broad Street. The weather was bright, clear, and cold, and the marchers saw, well ahead of them on the other side of Pettus Bridge, the phalanx of grim-faced troopers standing with legs apart and braced with clubs positioned at waist level. They trudged on through stanzas of freedom songs until the vanguard reached the bridge, where Federal Marshal H. Stanley Fountain intercepted it to read Judge Johnson's restraining order. Martin told Marshal Fountain that the march would continue, and the federal agent stepped aside. There was no singing now as the marchers crossed the bridge; the Alabama troopers were approximately one mile ahead. Fifty feet from the troopers, they halted on command of Major Cloud. "This march will not continue. It is not conducive to the safety of this group or the motoring public," the major barked. They wished to kneel in prayer, Martin said. His request was granted. When they had finished praying, the marchers rose to their feet. At that precise moment, Cloud ordered his men to break ranks and move to the shoulders of U.S. Highway 80, leaving the road to Montgomery open to the non-violent army. Mayor Smitherman had already charged that Martin was cautious to the point of cowardice, and the unexpected behavior of the troopers was intended to discredit him.

One can only tantalize over the question of what would have happened had the SCLC leader exploited the maneuver of the Alabama troopers. The marchers might still have been attacked. Worse, the snipers who were rumored to have been positioned by the Klan along the highway might have decimated their ranks before federal officers could act. Nor is it clear what penalty the federal court would have imposed for Martin's violation of its injunction. These hypotheses were not to be tested that day, however, for Martin turned to his followers and instructed them to retrace their steps. With an irony that must have graven itself into the minds of the SNCC students, the three thousand demonstrators headed back to the church, many of them singing "Ain't Gonna Let Nobody Turn Me 'Round."[4]

Sample 5

Once formed, the line took up all available space in front of the church and beyond it down the sidewalk and back into a large playground behind it. Few of the people could even hear Dr. King's final words, but his sentiments were unanimously shared: "We have the right to walk the highways, and we have the right to walk to Montgomery if our feet will get us there. I have no alternative but to lead a march from this spot to carry our grievances to the seat of government. I have made my choice. I have got to march. I do not know what lies ahead of us. There may be beatings, jailings, tear gas. But I would rather die on the highways of Alabama than make a butchery of my conscience."

Then the line set off, with the front ranks loaded down with religious celebrities. Hundreds of priests, rabbis and ministers followed, raising their voices in continuing choruses of "Ain't Gonna Let Nobody Turn Me Round." They passed groups of state troopers stationed in the center and at the corners of each block, up Sylvan Street to Water Avenue, then along the riverbank to Broad Street and the bridge.

At the foot of the bridge a U.S. marshal, H. Stanley Fountain, was waiting with a copy of Judge Johnson's order. King stopped the line when Fountain stepped in front of him, and listened gravely as he read it to them. Then Dr. King said "I am aware of the order," but insisted he was going ahead. "I am not going to interfere with this march," Fountain said. "Let them go." There were only a few city policemen on hand, and they stepped back to the curb with Fountain, while the long line began rolling past them.

The afternoon was cool but very clear, with bright sunlight making everything—the turgid river, the steel bridge girders, the people's faces—look especially vivid. The contrast in the atmosphere with that of the first march was marked; Sunday had been overcast, gray, gloomy and cold, befitting the occasion. Now as the front ranks reached the crest of the bridge, they could see the troopers' blue plastic helmets gleaming in the sun; the veterans noticed with relief that there were no gas masks dangling from their belts. Still the line fell silent again at the sight of well over a hundred men standing two deep under the heedless changing traffic signals, their clubs once more at the ready, all across the highway and along both sides for a hundred feet, forming a long, ominous cul-de-sac for the first dozen ranks. Major John Cloud was again in command, and he let King get within fifty feet before speaking through his bullhorn: "You are ordered to stop and stand where you are. This march will not continue."

"We have a right to march," Dr. King replied. "There is also a right to march to Montgomery."

Cloud repeated his order. King then asked if they could pray. "You can have your prayer," Cloud said, "and then you must return to your church."

Dr. King asked the marchers to kneel, and the line, stretching back up the ramp to the bridge for almost a mile, sank down. Prayers were offered, by Bishop Lord, Dr. George Docherty, and Rabbi Richard G. Hirsch of the Union of American Hebrew Congregations. The worship was quiet but fervent.

As the group finished and rose to its feet, Major Cloud abruptly turned and ordered the troopers to clear the road. If there was a secret script for the confrontation, the state then violated the agreement. The highway to Montgomery stood before the marchers, wide open.

What would have happened if Dr. King had tried to lead the march through this unanticipated breach? They had not been given permission to proceed, and who could tell what the troopers would have done if King had started forward? Apparently Wallace had either wanted to entice him into a clear violation of the federal court order or to make him look timid in the eyes of the more militant marchers. Or was there a more dangerous possibility—was it a trap? A federal official standing near the pavement was told by a high trooper officer a moment later that the withdrawal order came direct from the governor's office, where a second-by-second account was being monitored over an amplified telephone. In Washington, the attorney general sat in his office chain-smoking and listening to a similarly audible description from attorney John Doar, his representative at the scene.

Dr. King, if he hesitated at all, paused only a few seconds before direct-ing the line to turn and march back across the bridge to Brown Chapel. Those behind him moved forward to the place where the leaders had been stopped before making their turn, each rank wheeling around and trudg-ing up the ramp. Occasional verses of "Ain't Gonna Let Nobody Turn Me 'Round" could still be heard, although the song was now a little ironical.[5]

The traditional historical tendency would be to read the samples as a continuing aggregate of additions, a closed number set that rises with each comma-delineated value. Sample 1, for example, is relatively bare-bones, while Sample 3 fills in some of the narrative. Sample 2 takes the trinity from many in the marching party. Samples 4 and 5 progressively grow the story further. After reading the sample set as a series of rungs on a step-ladder, leading to a higher, fuller understanding of the march, the historian would then take elements from each, creating a conflation that would best represent the salient points and arguments from each sample.

Sample 1 tells us that the march was a day late. It reminds us that if the group did make it all the way across the bridge, it would be the first time that King defied a federal injunction. There were about three thousand marchers. The troopers' move from the protesters' path was inexplicable.

Sample 2 emphasizes the fame of the religious leaders amongst the marchers and gives special recognition to the Unitarians. This was the group's second time across the bridge. They had come from Selma's Brown Chapel and returned there, singing "Ain't Gonna Let Nobody Turn Me 'Round." It was intentionally ironic.

Sample 3 drops the number of marchers to two thousand and colors many of them white. LeRoy Collins, Community Service Relations Director, speaks. The narrative leads us through each street before arriving at the bridge. It was just after 3:00. A U.S. Marshal read Frank Johnson's order. King stopped the marchers fifty feet from the waiting officers. He asked permission to pray. Four of the leaders did. And they sang, "We Shall Overcome." The troopers moved as King was turning the crowd around. They were ordered to do so by the governor. Local Selma teenagers and

Student Nonviolent Coordinating Committee (SNCC) members were surprised and angry about the move, but they followed. Their shock stemmed from their ignorance of negotiations that set the turn in motion earlier that day.

Sample 4 describes the phalanx, now back up to three thousand, moving in lines of five. It names the leaders at the front, noting that King's arms were locked with Robert Spike and John Wesley Lord. "Ain't Gonna Let Nobody Turn Me 'Round" was on display en route, as well, presumably without its later irony. The sky was clear, the air cold. The troopers were armed with clubs, they were sullen. King told H. Stanley Fountain that the group would cross the bridge. As it did, the songs stopped. The troopers were a mile away. John Cloud spoke to the assembled. The troopers moved from the road when King stood from praying, intending to discredit him. Mayor Joseph Smitherman had already called him a coward.

Sample 5 tells us that the crowd filled the area around Brown Chapel. King spoke some final words, but most were so far back that they couldn't hear them. Religious officials numbered in the hundreds. Along the route, troopers were stationed at each block. Fountain was flanked by city policemen. King listened gravely as Fountain abdicated responsibility, then moved with the police away from the road. Sample 5 also gives us the dialogue. The afternoon was cool, not cold. Sunday had been cold and gloomy. The bridge was steel, the river turgid. The troopers wore blue helmets. They had no gas masks. There were more than one hundred, two deep. The traffic signals continued as if cars were waiting. The dialogue of King and Cloud. The prayer leaders' names. An amplified telephone provided the governor with immediate updates. Nicholas Katzenbach in Washington also received play-by-play from John Doar. He was chain smoking. King's pause was quick before turning.

It is part of the grand historical project to cull these individual statements of instance from each account, synthesize them, then create a new conflation, fuller and richer for the effort. But that is not the project of this paper, which reads such conflations as inherently problematic. It is a problem akin to that of Shakespeare scholars concerning the existence of three distinct versions of *Hamlet*. The *Hamlet* most of us have read and seen our entire lives is a conflation of two different versions, one from the First Folio of 1623, another from an earlier version published in quarto format. Or, it isn't really Shakespeare's *Hamlet*. In this example, three *Hamlet*s really means zero *Hamlet*s, because without documentary evidence and with a lifetime of conflations, the real, intended *Hamlet* is forever disguised.[6] If each of the sample set accounts is another folio of the Edmund Pettus drama, then the conflation becomes just as specious as each supposed quarto. King, in this interpretation, plays Hamlet: never crossing the bridge, never slaying Laertes, never actually existing.

The reason we do this, of course—conflate disparate elements of various secondary accounts—is that we assume each folio to be describing the same event, telling the same story. There is one King, one Pettus, one Fountain, one Cloud. Though each account is technically different, they are still functionally the same. This paper does not make such assumptions. The bridge between technical and functional, it argues, is not so easily crossed. It is, perhaps, an Edmund Pettus all its own. The void between continental idealism and British empiricism comes to mind here. Both sought to describe what was essentially the same world, but they did so in monumentally different ways, allowing them to draw monumentally different conclusions. In this metaphor, continental idealism stands in for an easy climb across the bridge between technical and functional. For faith. For assumption. British empiricism becomes disconnect by default.

But like all metaphors, that one eventually breaks down, too. The overriding commonality between thinkers on the continent and on the isles was the unerring belief that philosophical pursuits, however directed, would ultimately lead to valid truth claims that would eventually order the hitherto unknown. This paper doesn't do that, either. If we were to extend our metaphor as we drift lazily into truth claims, idealism and empiricism would play on the same team, standing in for the vast majority of historians. On the other side would be pragmatism, arguing that truth itself was contingent and ephemeral, randomly moving with the changing whims of historians, the linguistic choices of authors, and the state of existing conflations.

This paper argues that the five narratives of the Edmund Pettus march are both technically and functionally different. That they tell five distinct stories, each providing some measure of individual, provisional truth. They are unique. Conflating them would only create a sixth, unique story. Also different. Also provisional. Doing so would create six marches across the Edmund Pettus Bridge, six retreats back to Brown Chapel. And that being the case, like Hamlet's marches so many centuries prior, it would, in the effort, create zero.

The Role of Argument

At first glance, each of the five samples, though clearly different in many respects, make essentially the same argument. The effluvium surrounding the specific event of marching to and from the Edmund Pettus Bridge has been removed from the samples, leaving only the portion of the narrative that encompasses the actual event. So the arguments of each would seem to be consistent. But they are not. The first two samples provide an example of this phenomenon. If each sentence is listed as a set of propositions, arguments can be drawn from each.

Sample 1

1. King proceeded with the march a day late as if, for the first time, he would defy a federal court order.
2. He led about three thousand demonstrators across the Edmund Pettus Bridge and there encountered a federal marshal who advised him of the order and stepped aside.
3. Also present in force were state troopers whose commander admonished King that the march could not continue.
4. Then the troopers inexplicably moved out of the line of march.
5. With the road to Montgomery open, King turned his followers back, in keeping with his agreement with federal negotiators.

King led a march that complied with a federal agreement, though it appeared to those involved that he would not.

Sample 2

1. The two thousand singing and chanting marchers, ranks swelled by a Who's Who of religious notables and a large Unitarian contingent, recrossed the river.
2. A forbidding line of troopers stopped them at the same point as on Sunday.
3. King led the gathering in prayer, then ordered the long column to turn back.
4. They retreated to Brown Chapel singing "Ain't Gonna Let Nobody Turn Me 'Round," the Selma theme song—an irony not lost on many.
5. Back at the church he promised his followers that they would still get to Montgomery.

Religious protesters, many of them disgruntled, prematurely stopped a march they expected to continue.

If these two samples told the same story, if their collected set of propositions presented the same conglomeration of facts, then the arguments derived from each proposition set should be interchangeable. These accounts are part of broader narratives, providing accounts of a specific incident doing work to get their authors to their principal arguments about (in the case of Sample 1) symbolic representation in the press and (in the case of Sample 2) the religious mission of Martin Luther King. They are conduits taking their authors from one set of argumentative propositions to another. But in the simple telling of a simple event, the arguments of those conductive links take them in two different directions.

"Religious protesters, many of them disgruntled, prematurely stopped a march they expected to continue," could not be a viable inference from Sample 1. Nowhere in Sample 1's propositions is the religiosity of demonstrators mentioned. None of the five statements describes any state of frustration among them. Since Proposition 5 states that King was "keeping with his agreement with federal negotiators," the march cannot be said to have stopped prematurely. Furthermore, the marchers themselves are not the subject of Sample 1's argumentative scope.

Similarly, "King led a march that complied with a federal agreement, though it appeared to those involved that he would not," is not a legitimate argument deduction from Sample 2. The marchers, not King, are the subject of Sample 2's argumentative scope. There is no mention of a federal agreement. There is an element of deceptive appearances in Sample 2, but the feelings of the marchers are not directed towards compliance. Furthermore, while King leads the group in prayer, and speaks to them upon their return to the church, he does not, in Sample 2, lead the march.

The arguments of each are fundamentally different because the set of propositions that constitute each sample are fundamentally different. Further, inferences drawn from those arguments pull the reader further away from any reasonable proximity.

Sample 1 Argument

King led a march that complied with a federal agreement, though it appeared to those involved that he would not.

Inferences

1. King walked at the front of a group of people.
2. King was in league with the federal government.
3. King was a liar.
4. Those at the scene assumed King would do something different than what he did.

Sample 2 Argument

Religious protesters, many of them disgruntled, prematurely stopped a march they expected to continue.

Inferences

1. The protesters had a belief in the supernatural.
2. A selection of the protesters were frustrated by the cessation of the march.

3. All of the protesters participated in the cessation of the march.
4. Protesters at the scene assumed they would do something different than what they did.

The fourth inferences from both samples appear similar. The principal difference between them, of course, is that King is not present in the Sample 2 inference. It leads us to see the protesters as the authors of the action, whereas Sample 1 places King at the center of that action (see subject emphasis discussion below).

Though such a propositional argument analysis would be unwieldy for this type of paper, similar breakdowns would lead to similar results for all five of the samples. They give five distinct proposition sets, five different arguments, leading to five new groups of inferences to make about such arguments. Each are contingent, conditional, and ultimately temporary. Using Samples 1 and 2 as exemplary of the group, however, and leaving aside post-structural critiques of language as representative of other representations ultimately leading to nothingness, it is instructive to also seek out argumentative similarities—to see what, if any, absolutes can be derived from the sample set.

Common Inferences from Samples 1 and 2

1. King marched.
2. Protesters marched.
3. Troopers stopped the march.
4. Protesters turned from the troopers.
5. Protesters did not reach their goal.

All five of these common inferences can be drawn from samples 3, 4, and 5, as well. As the five elements of consistency among all five samples, they can be said to be the five true propositions of the sample set's depiction of King's march across the Edmund Pettus Bridge.

Truth Statements Concerning Edmund Pettus March

1. King marched.
2. Protesters marched.

3. Troopers stopped the march.
4. Protesters turned from the troopers.
5. Protesters did not reach their goal.

By default, propositions that deviate from the core truth statements are therefore false. There is no corroboration in the first two samples, for example, for the time of the march, the number of marchers, their religious persuasion, their attitude about turning around, the reason for the turn, or their destination upon retreating. Even prior to any discussion of adjective use or storytelling device, we can read all extraneous information deviating from the five truth statements as nonabsolute.

Prayer and Consistency

Even commonalities, however, prove problematic. Take, for example, the sentences relating to prayer, as parsing out their potential consistency will help to determine the congruity of the accounts. Sample 1 does not mention prayer, so sentences from Samples 2–5 will suffice:

Sample 2: King led the gathering in prayer, then ordered the long column to turn back.

Sample 3: After the singing of "We Shall Overcome" and the leading of prayers by four different individuals, King turned so as to lead the column back across the bridge.

Sample 4: When they had finished praying, the marchers rose to their feet.

Sample 5: Prayers were offered, by Bishop Lord, Dr. George Docherty, and Rabbi Richard G. Hirsch of the Union of American Hebrew Congregations.

It does not require a Bethian semantic tableaux to distinguish core differences in the accounts.[7] Both Samples 2 and 3 indicate leadership, but one designates King as the leader of prayer, the other "four different individuals." Those individuals lead "prayers," rather than "prayer." Putting aside that semantic difference, as "prayer," when referring to a group, can be functionally plural, the accounts still place two fundamentally different protagonists as subjects of leadership. In Samples 4 and 5, leadership disappears completely. In earlier sentences in Sample 4, King tells the troopers that the group wants to pray. The next sentence portrays this wish as a request. The lack of consistency within the sample itself is replaced in Sample 5 by a decided statement of request. King *asks* the troopers permission to pray. Then he *asks* the marchers to kneel. But nothing in either account indicates that he led prayers (or prayer). In fact, those who pray in Sample 5 are decidedly not King. Sample 5 lists three specific clergymen who "offer" prayers. In Sample 4, this specificity is substituted with the personal pronoun "they."

Even when allowing for assumption to penetrate interpretation of the account, the four samples cannot be rectified. Assuming that leading a prayer is nothing more than saying a prayer out loud, while others pray silently, Sample 3 gives us four vocal prayers. Sample 4's "they" is consistent with that number, and though it doesn't mention anything about vocalization of an act that can also be, and often is, undertaken silently, it doesn't have to. Its broad generalization keeps it consistent with the more specific Sample 3. Sample 5 deviates from Sample 3 in the opposite way, adding more specificity to the account. It lists three prayers, which makes it fundamentally incongruous with Sample 3. King is present in the paragraph, asking marchers to kneel, and it could also be assumed that if in fact there were four vocal prayer leaders, that the account in Sample 5 intends King to be the fourth. But this is not a safe or reasonable assumption. The presence of King in the paragraph and his place as the dominant subject of the sample itself indicate that the sample would most likely credit him with participation if in fact he did participate. Sample 5 includes the most detail of the sample set, utilizing a series of direct quotes and personal names to bring specificity to the account. If King had vocally prayed in Sample 5, Sample 5 would have mentioned it. But even if we leave that discrepancy aside, assuming for the sake of argument that King was the fourth vocal prayer giver, thus giving Samples 3, 4, and 5 consistency, Sample 2 cannot be rectified. The vocal prayer giver in Sample 2 is King. There are no plural pronouns in the sentence. The account is therefore inconsistent with the other three. Even with a Sample 5 concession to King, Samples 2 and 5 cannot be given any measure of equivalence, as the assumed King of Sample 5 is still one of four ministers to offer vocal prayer.

When that assumption is removed, generating consistency is even more difficult. "Four different individuals," "they," and "Bishop Lord, Dr. George Docherty, and Rabbi Richard G. Hirsch of the Union of American Hebrew Congregations" are not congruous. "They" is an indexical without a specific referent. "They" could mean anyone, without recourse to a specific telling of just who "they" designates. Similarly, "four different individuals" gives a specific body count but provides no indication of who those four different individuals might be. Their names, religions, status, etc., are absent from the account. And, of course, there are four of them. Sample 5 provides names, religions, and status, but the body count is a refutation of "four different individuals."

Ultimately, the generalization of Sample 4 makes it consistent with Sample 3 and Sample 5. But Sample 3 and Sample 5 are not consistent with one another. And none of the three is consistent with Sample 2 (to say nothing of Sample 1, which doesn't even mention prayer). If the prayer statements of the samples are inconsistent, then the samples themselves are inconsistent. And if that is the case, using those accounts to build upon one another is itself an inconsistent act. If you were one orange short of filling your juice container, for example, you would not squeeze an apple to complete the task, because apples and oranges are inconsistent, and the resulting product of the act would be something fundamentally different from orange juice. It would also be something fundamentally different from apple juice. So the process of amalgamating inconsistent entities would actually eliminate the possibility of either orange juice or apple juice. It would be, to wit, subtraction by addition. The same is true for reconciling historical accounts.

Three Kings

Existing alongside these more formal differences, accounts in the sample set also produce markedly different portraits of the major characters involved, principally those of King and the Alabama State Troopers. In Sample 4, King walks arm and arm with fellow ministers at the head of the marching pack. He is respectful but determined. He has, however, been accused by an elected official of cowardice. Though the option to continue the march is open to him, he chooses not to accept it, giving a measure of weight to the elected official's critique. Sample 3's King is forceful with his charges (bringing them to a halt) but submissive to those in his path (requesting permission to pray). With an open road in front of him, he turns the marchers back, angering those who do not want such a "meek retreat." In Sample 5, King opens the march with a rousing, defiant speech. "I would rather die on the highways of Alabama than make a butchery of my conscience." He is insistent with the U.S. marshal, "There is also a right to march to Montgomery." But when told to turn the march around, he does, just as insistently, ignoring the open road ahead. Samples 1 and 2 provide no substantial portrait of King (see emphasis discussion below), but the three that exist give decidedly different descriptions of the leader. Sample 5's King is an out-and-out liar, if not a traitor, provoking an expectant crowd before knowingly turning them away. In Sample 3, King leads his charges, but doesn't rouse them with false promises. His reaction to the confrontation with troopers is meek, but the description is variable. Many in the column find the meekness an improper reaction, but King's status as prayer leader (if not minister, which comes from the broader context surrounding the samples, though not the samples themselves) indicates that he ascribes to a theological system that values meekness as a virtue. His loyalty/morality/strategic scruples, then, remain a matter of interpretation. In Sample 4, the boisterous leader disappears, as does the traitor, and there is far less room for interpretation. The sample provides a contemporary accusation of King's cowardice, and follows that accusation with a demonstration of it.

King the traitor. King the meek. King the coward. In each sample, Martin Luther King is the protagonist of the account, the main character of the narrative. But he is a fundamentally *different* character in each. When the principal figure in ostensibly equivalent accounts takes on completely different personas, then the equivalency of each account cannot be maintained. And without that equivalency, the samples cannot be said to tell the same story. If all are telling different stories, then the lack of any better or worse description leaves us with no definitive description. As with the Hamlet discrepancy, three Kings leaves us with zero.

The character of King's opponents is similarly variably described. In Sample 1, troopers are "present in force," but serve at the behest of their commander. Their move from the street is inexplicable. Sample 2's troopers are "forbidding." They never move from the street at all. The troopers in Sample 3 move away from the street in "an unplanned move," but one that is ordered by the governor. They aren't forbidding. Instead, they are tools of higher officials not even present at the event. In Sample 4, troopers are an afterthought, as their commander is the forbidding presence. They recede in favor of a battle of wills between Cloud and King. The opposite is true of the troopers in Sample 5. The group wears blue plastic helmets, but they don't wear gas masks, lessening the threat they might pose to marchers. They have their clubs drawn, but it is less their presence than their numbers that prove intimidating, more than one hundred "standing two deep … forming a long, ominous cul-de-sac." So, again, there are five different sets of state troopers, each with different characteristics that create five fundamentally different groups: tools of a commander; tools of an unseen hand; complete afterthought; unyielding presence; intimidating force, weapons drawn, which yields strategically. Each set of troopers is different, unique, dealing with a group of Kings who are different and unique. Any discussion of functional reality in the sample set, considering the inherent differences of the principal actors, is impossible.

Hypotheticals

But the differences are more insidious than that. The crescendo of the action, the core of the controversy surrounding the event, is the troopers' move from the street, giving King and the marchers a clear path to

Montgomery, which King refuses. As mentioned above, the troopers in Sample 2 don't even move from the street. In Sample 1, the move is inexplicable. In Sample 3, the governor is responsible. In Samples 4 and 5, Cloud makes the decision (though Sample 5 notes the rumor that the governor's office was the reason for Cloud's order). The troopers' action cannot be both inexplicable and ordered by Cloud. They cannot move on account of the governor, then not move at all. Based on these five accounts, there is nothing definitive to say about the troopers' action. Their motion and the cause of it are both in question.

In the two samples that credit Cloud as the agent of action, the accounts take on the additional burden of hypotheticals. Sample 4 encourages readers to consider that despite the troopers' move, the marchers could still have been victims of attack. Snipers could have been waiting for them. The federal penalty for violation of an injunction could have been severe. Sample 5 poses its hypotheticals in the form of questions, wondering what would have happened had the marchers moved through the "unanticipated breach." Perhaps the troopers would have accosted them. Perhaps it was a trap.

The use of hypotheticals seems to be one of the most glaring differences between the various accounts. Sample 4 and Sample 5 add to the unreality of the event by posing scenarios that they acknowledge didn't happen. Though the hypotheticals appear to be the most obvious source of differentiation between the samples, however, their presence *does not* indicate inconsistency. The use of declarative and interrogative hypotheticals animates the narrative and serves as an authorial aside (in some cases) and a further elaborative aid for contextualizing the facts of the case. Declarative phrases such as "might still have been," "might have decimated," or "would have imposed" indicate to any reader that the embellishments are just that, thereby contributing to the author's interpretive framework, not the historical event itself. And since the interpretive framework is supposed to be different, since historical interpretation and argument are what should give uniqueness to historical accounts anyway, then the addition of hypotheticals, in whatever form, do not impinge on the factual root of the accounts. So among a cacophony of incongruity, the one element of the sample set that seems most incongruous is actually an innocuous distraction, which only serves to reinforce the incompatibility of the samples. Or, to wit, the exception proves the rule.

The Numbers of Words

If Sample 4's tantalization over potential outcomes is included, four of its twenty-one sentences (19%) are devoted to hypotheticals. The three interrogative hypotheticals in Sample 5 constitute only 7% of the selection's forty-three total sentences. Both numbers are statistically significant, devoting large sections of page space to wondering "what-if." (If the accounts were mapped out to the entire volumes from which they came, for example, and each of those volumes had 200 pages each, hypotheticals would take up 38 and 14 pages respectively.) Though Sample 4 includes only one more hypothetical than Sample 5, however—and that "one more" is an introductory sentence designed to entice the reader to participate—its fewer total sentences make the relative discrepancy between the two much larger. Thirty-eight pages of musings on possibilities for outcomes that never took place would prove inordinately distracting in a two hundred page book, for example. Sample 4's musings on potential take up more than two and a half times the total text than do Sample 5's. By viewing each sample as a repository of statistics, the constitution of each becomes clearer. Since all five are factual retellings of a historical event, it would be tempting to assume that those numbers, that constitution, would be similar. It is, however, the dissimilarity described in sections above that only becomes clearer by examining the structures of the narratives themselves.

At first glance, Sample 5 would seem to be the structural deviant of the bunch, considering its length. In fact, however, Sample 3's sentences diverge most clearly. Though Sample 5 uses 836 words to tell the Edmund Pettus story, its forty-three sentences average 19.4 words each, keeping it well within the average range. Sample 3's nine sentences, however, average 28.8 words, by far the longest of the group.

Sentence Length

	Sentences	Words	Words Per Sentence
Sample 1	5	94	18.8
Sample 2	5	90	18.0
Sample 3	9	259	28.8
Sample 4	21	408	19.4
Sample 5	43	836	19.4

When the subjects of those sentences are parsed out, determined by focus of action rather than necessarily emphasizing formal structure, the different emphases of each become clearer.

Subject Emphasis Sentence Count

	Sample 1	Sample 2	Sample 3	Sample 4	Sample 5
King	3 (60%)	2 (40%)	4 (44.4%)	6 (28.6%)	14 (32.6%)
Marchers		2 (40%)	4 (44.4%)	9 (42.9%)	12 (27.9%)
Troopers	2 (40%)	1 (20%)	1 (11.1%)	1 (4.8%)	2 (4.7%)
Cloud				3 (14.3%)	5 (11.6%)
Fountain					4 (9.3%)
Government				1 (4.8%)	5 (11.6%)
Weather					2 (4.7%)
Klan				1 (4.8%)	

Sample 1 makes King the clear focus of the account, while Samples 2 and 3 give equal time to King and the marchers. Sample 4 actually makes the marchers the dominant protagonists. When sentences listed for King that are actually his spoken words are removed from the total, only five of Sample 5's sentences keep King as a subject. Two of Fountain's and two of Cloud's are also direct quotations. When those are removed from the total, only five original sentences keep King as the locus of action, while seven emphasize Fountain, Cloud, and the troopers—to say nothing of the five sentences devoted to political entities in Montgomery and Washington. King's presence, then, rises as the accounts become shorter and less specific. As description of the event takes on more exactitude, and more judgment, King's presence diminishes. There are two possible reasons for this. First, it could be coincidence. As this paper has continued to argue, the variances in the accounts make them tantamount to descriptions of five unique events. Variation in protagonists' roles in five separate scenarios should not be inherently surprising. The problem with that explanation is that despite those differences, despite this paper's argument, authorial intent was to describe a known event, the same event featured in its fellow samples, which virtually eliminates the possibility of happenstance. The second reason is more pragmatic. King is a revered figure, a religious and secular hero alike, whose championing of civil rights led to a sea change in American social and cultural understanding. And this was not his finest hour. The more coverage the failed march across Edmund Pettus Bridge receives, the more paltry King appears. The tendency of historians—of authors—is to celebrate King when possible and limit, if not mute, criticism when criticism is called for. By exacerbating the role of the "bad guys" in the account, and thereby de-emphasizing King, authors can shape the narrative to recoup a measure of respect for the leader.

The character of the marchers also varies by account. Sample 1 counts three thousand demonstrators, but then removes them from the story entirely. Sample 2's count of two thousand is a major point of differentiation, but so too is its description. The marchers are "singing and chanting," the group is filled with famous religious leaders, and they are disenchanted by King's about-face. More importantly, they were comprised of a "large Unitarian contingent." On its face, this small phrase would seem relatively innocuous, but it comprises more than three percent of the ninety-word sample—more than six percent of the forty seven words of the two sentences featuring marchers as the dominant protagonists. The Unitarianism of the group dominates the description of the protesters in a way completely incongruous with the other samples, none of which even mention Unitarianism. Sample 3 notes that many in the crowd were white, but announces no religious denominations. Sample 4 mentions a bishop and reverend, but with the exception of noting the prayer before the group's turnaround, does not discuss the religious makeup of the crowd. Sample 5 adds a rabbi to the mix, and again discusses the prayers, but deals no more with the religiosity of the protesters. There are no Jews in Samples 1–4. The preponderance of Unitarianism in Sample 2, particularly in such a short selection, makes the character of the group decidedly different from its companions. The marchers take up different roles and different amounts of space in each sample, and when they are discussed, they look remarkably different. There are, in effect, five different groups of marchers, led by their five different Kings and opposed to five different sets of Alabama state troopers.

A Note on Sources

Though this paper is largely concerned with the scope of the narrative description of these accounts, a brief examination of the sources of those narratives can demonstrate further problems in conflating such texts as retellings of equivalent events. Were the samples to be arranged chronologically, their order would run 4, 5, 3, 1, 2. Sample 4, originally published in 1970, cites accounts of the march in the *New York Times* and *Time* magazine.[8] Sample 5, originally published in 1974, relies—despite their differences—on Sample 4, along with an unpublished description of the march by one of its participants.[9] Sample 3, originally published in 1978, is by far the most exhaustive in its notation. It cites a variety of sources for its reconstruction of events, including both Samples 4 and 5. The note also provides a long, extensive examination of King's motivation, parsing out the leader's own denial that any agreement with authorities existed and rebuttals to that claim by contemporary and historical sources.[10] In Sample 1, originally published in 1990, both Samples 5 and 3 provide the dominant source material for the account, along with an additional secondary retelling not cited by any of the others.[11] Sample 2, the shortest of the group, originally published in 2004, cites a separate work by the author of Sample 3, remarkably similar in content to its sister publication.[12]

In other words, the samples are participants in the conflation process. Though they are fundamentally different in description, emphasis, and argument, each sample builds off the other, using its fellows to create its own version of events. The source consistency, and its incongruity with the narrative inconsistency, demonstrates the fallacy of such attempts. What exactly is being conflated? As is demonstrated above, there are five translatable facts appearing in each sample, five constants that readers can take to be unquestionably true.

1. King marched.
2. Protesters marched.
3. Troopers stopped the march.
4. Protesters turned from the troopers.
5. Protesters did not reach their goal.

If such is the core of the conflation process, then why are so many additional sources cited? The five accounts of the episode differ on questions of fact (the number of marchers), emphasis (the Unitarianism of the crowd, the intent of the troopers), and interpretation (King the liar, King the dupe). And yet they rely on the presence of one another in footnoted text to ground their accounts and give them a historiographical lineage—one that will prove both a lack of ignorance of those who have come before them and a stunning breadth of historical legwork. But all things considered, this doesn't seem like historical legwork at all. And citing the work of giants in the field appears relatively unhelpful when new accounts veer from the old.

In other words, it may very well be that assuming historians are familiar with the seminal texts in their field is a far safer gamble than assuming their work is proceeding logically and consistently from those texts.

The authors of the samples are justifiably lauded, as are their books, for sound research and fresh analysis. But the sources and the narratives don't match.

Conclusion

Other differences abound. Sample 4 creates a sense of ambiance by noting that "the weather was bright, clear, and cold." Sample 5 further establishes setting by describing the river, the bridge girders, the sunlight reflecting off each. The girders can be assumed from Samples 1, 2, and 3, the nature of bridges leading to any reasonable assumption that they exist. The existence of a river is at least possible in the first three samples, as bridges are often built over rivers, but it doesn't necessarily exist, as bridges can be built over many things other than rivers, as well. The sun doesn't shine in the first three samples. The sky isn't clear. The air isn't cold. The stories exist in a comparative vacuum.

The settings are different. The protagonists, the antagonists, and the choruses are different. Here presented are five distinct accounts of Martin Luther King's aborted march across the Edmund Pettus Bridge, each functionally unique in all of its descriptive facets. Of course, the arguments of each author will differ, their interpretation will differ, but such fall beyond the scope of this analysis. This paper argues that their descriptions of the events themselves also differ, are functionally inequivalent and incongruous, and thus cannot be considered to describe the same event. Though they seek to move toward the same goal, they are—in their fundamental narrative differences—ever moving halfway, then half of the remainder, then half of the remainder, ad infinitum.

Of course, in the end, Achilles could have won the race had he accepted the challenge. And Zeno's Paradox can be solved. By adding the half distance (1/2) to the next half distance (1/4) and so on, the sum will ultimately be one, the actual distance of the race. It is what mathematicians refer to as a summable infinite series. Grading the race by time rather than distance also gets the job done.

More to the point, Lewis Carroll created an additional version of Zeno's Paradox. So too did Douglas Hofstadter. It would be just as easy to measure and evaluate their versions of the paradox in the same manner as King's walk across the Edmund Pettus Bridge.

There is no great answer to what I will call here the Edmund Pettus Paradox. If historians only wrote in agreed upon absolutes, the language would suffer, arguments would diminish, and the evolution of historical debate would recede into the ether. The purpose of this paper isn't to fix historical writing, because, for the most part, it doesn't need fixing. Instead, it is a call for we as historians to think more clearly about our sentences, and the propositions that stem from each. Even in those descriptive moments between the flight and fancy of our argumentative flourish, we create something fundamentally new. By being better readers—or, perhaps, more conscientious readers—we will ultimately become better writers, better stewards of the information entrusted to us by common assumption. We do not need to give up. And we do not need to race without proper introspection. We need to solve our paradoxes, remove our ambiguities, then run.

Notes

1. Richard Lentz, *Symbols, the News Magazines, and Martin Luther King* (Baton Rouge: Louisiana State University Press, 1990), 151.

2. Stewart Burns, *To the Mountaintop: Martin Luther King, Jr.'s Sacred Mission to Save America, 1955–1968* (New York: Harper Collins, 2004), 275–6.

3. David J. Garrow, *Protest at Selma: Martin Luther King, Jr., and the Voting Rights Act of 1965* (New Haven: Yale University Press, 1978), 86–7.

4. David Levering Lewis, *King: A Critical Biography* (New York: Praeger, 1970), 279–80.

5. Charles E. Fager, *Selma, 1965* (New York: Charles Scribner's Sons, 1974), 102–5.

6. For more on the controversy amongst Shakespearean scholars, actors, and directors, see Ron Rosenbaum, *The Shakespeare Wars: Clashing Scholars, Public Fiascoes, and Palace Coups* (New York: Random House, 2006).

7. Beth's proof method for formal systems intends to parse out truth statements in formal logic, which falls beyond the scope of this paper. See Evert Willem Beth, "Semantic Entailment and Formal Derivability," in *The Philosophy of Mathematics*, ed. J. Hintikka, 9–14 (London: Oxford University Press, 1969; originally published 1955).

8. The articles cited by Sample 4 are Roy Reed, "Dr. King Leads March," *New York Times*, 10 March 1965, 22; and "Civil Rights, the Central Point," *Time*, 19 March 1965, 23–30. Lewis, *King*, 411.

9. Along with the Lewis account, Sample 5 cites an account by Richard Leonard, housed in the Harvard College Library. Fager, *Selma, 1965*, 229.

10. Though Sample 3 notes that "many accounts have been referred to in constructing this narrative of the events of March 8 and 9," the two given the most credit in its reconstruction of the march are Lewis's *King* and Jim Bishop's *The Days of Martin Luther King, Jr.* (New York: G.P. Putnam's Sons, 1971), 386–8. Additional source material includes the Fager account, along with James Forman, *Sammy Younge, Jr.* (New York: Grove Press, 1968), 76–8; Alan F. Westin and Barry Mahoney, *The Trial of Martin Luther King* (New York: Thomas Y. Crowell, 1974), 172–4; Andrew Kopkind, "Selma: 'Ain't Gonna Let Nobody Turn Me 'Round,'" *New Republic* 152 (20 March 1965): 7–9; John Herbers, *New York Times*, 10 March 1965, 22 (an account of the event on the same page as Roy Reed's, cited in Sample 4; Reed's version of the story is not cited, though Lewis's construction of events based on Reed's article is one of the two principal sources for Sample 3's narrative); Dean Peerman and Martin E. Marty, "Selma: Sustaining the Momentum," *Christian Century* 82 (24 March 1965): 358–60; Max L. Stackhouse, "The Ethics of Selma," *Commonweal* 82 (9 April 1965): 75–7; and Warren Hinckle and David Welsh, "Five Battles of Selma," *Ramparts* 4 (June 1965): 32. Garrow, *Protest at Selma*, 273–4.

11. Lewis and Garrow precede a citation for Clayborne Carson, *In Struggle: SNCC and the Black Awakening of the 1960s* (Cambridge: Harvard University Press, 1981), 159–60, which had yet to be published when samples 4, 5, and 3 first appeared in print. Lentz, *Symbols, the News Magazines, and Martin Luther King*, 151.

12. Sample 2 cites David J. Garrow, *Bearing the Cross* (New York: Vintage, 1988), 400–405. Burns, *To the Mountaintop*, 471.

Hurry Sundown

Otto Preminger, Baton Rouge, and Race, 1966–1967

On 31 March 1966, more than 5,000 screaming Baton Rouge fans watched as Elvis Presley's gold limousine made its way down Third Street, moving slowly so that everyone could have a glimpse. There were another thousand in front of the Gordon Theater as the parade ended, the limo arrived, and the stars of Presley's *Frankie and Johnny* (1966) disembarked. Over a crowd that was so loud that it could barely hear what was transpiring on the platform above, Donna Douglas, a Baton Rouge native, thanked the crowd for its warm hospitality. It was so good to be back in Louisiana. She was so glad that her new movie was premiering in her hometown. Douglas was named an honorary mayor. Her co-stars Sue Ann Langdon and Nancy Kovak were named honorary citizens. It was a crowd and a city hungry for the bright lights of Hollywood, an economy ready to please.[1]

In two months, however, Baton Rouge would have a new movie coming to town. Otto Preminger's *Hurry Sundown* (1967) revolves around a speculator's attempt to buy up as much land as possible in a small Georgia farm town in the months following World War II. Two families won't sell—one white, one black. While the story centers on the travails of the black family's resistance to sales pressure, bigotry, and violence, the story's

Thomas Aiello, "Hurry Sundown: Otto Preminger, Baton Rouge, and Race, 1966–1967," *Film History: An International Journal*, vol. 21, no. 4, pp. 394–410. Copyright © 2010 by Indiana University Press. Reprinted with permission.

denouement comes when the poor white family joins forces with its black neighbors against the adamant speculator. The film itself was a critical flop, and its production serves as one in a long line of examples of white Hollywood's clumsy, ham-handed, stereotypical treatment of race before the final fall of the Production Code. But it also demonstrates the South's continued racial intransigence, even as the sixties moved into their twilight and there was real money to be made from location filming. The Louisiana capital seemed to corroborate most of Preminger's heavy-handed racial messages. Though the director's clumsy attempt at race activism and Baton Rouge's clumsy handling of the location shoot had different intents, the consequences of both looked strikingly similar.

But as the Hollywood beauties waved from a gold limousine, everything was optimism. And as summer approached, that optimism seemed inordinately justified. A Louisiana State University comparative study of May's fiscal numbers in 1965 and 1966 demonstrated marked progress. Building permits were up almost 30 percent. Department store sales up more than 7 percent. Grocery store sales, electric power use, bank deposits, registered telephone users. Everything was up. Baton Rouge and its surrounds were showing progress in every economic category.[2]

Baton Rouge wasn't alone. "As warm to the heart of Dixie as the old browned Confederate daguerreotype in the parlor is its defiant battle cry: 'The South will rise again,'" wrote the Associated Press. "Now, at long last, it is." Industry had finally, slowly, moved south. New businesses and their accompanying new jobs flooded the region in the 1960s, lured by states desperate for industry and eager to provide incentives to willing companies. Most began offering significant tax breaks. Some states (Louisiana not among them) allowed municipalities to buy land and build plants for corporations using the sale of bonds. Many southern states sponsored vocational training schools to prepare workers for new jobs. In the summer of 1966 alone, Baton Rouge opened eight 'neighborhood service centers' to help facilitate employment and education opportunities for area residents at or below the poverty level. "Dixie today is a land of boosters, and the voice of the Chamber of Commerce is heard throughout the land," the report continued. "By any standards the growth has been remarkable."

But race was still a problem, ever threatening to counteract the more attractive aspects of the South. "The social revolution which has occurred here in recent years," said Roger Blough, president of US Steel, "has tended, perhaps, to counteract the attractiveness of other advantages which the South affords to new capital investment." Baton Rouge, its civic leaders, and its press knew the benefit of keeping racial threats and attacks against visiting industry (no matter how temporary those visits might be) off the front pages.[3]

To address some of those problems, Governor John McKeithen created the Louisiana Commission on Human Relations in January, intending that the advisory board would work to salve the region's racial tension. In late June, the legislature passed a bill to replace the slogan "Sportsman's Paradise" on Louisiana license plates with "Right-to-Profit State," in hopes of bringing new business to the region. McKeithen designated July "Tourist Appreciation Month" to draw in more visitors.[4] By July, however, a group of visitors had arrived who didn't feel quite so appreciated.

It was 17 November 1964 when director Otto Preminger announced the purchase of Bert and Katya Gilden's novel, *Hurry Sundown*, a sprawling account of race in postwar Georgia that took the couple (writing as K.B. Gilden) more than a decade to complete. "It was very long," Preminger later said of the original draft of the novel, "longer even than the published version, which is also very long, and I was fascinated by the people, and by the whole implication of the South in 1946 after World War II which, in my opinion, was the starting point of the Civil Rights Movement." By early 1965, the book had found its way onto most bestseller lists.[5]

Horton Foote began the screenplay soon after the purchase, creating a draft that ultimately set the plot of the film. Foote had written *To Kill a Mockingbird* (1962) and had experience with southern subjects. But after a disagreement about the script (a disagreement that Preminger's manic biography made almost inevitable), Thomas C. Ryan arrived to finish the project. Foote never liked the Gildens' novel, and saw their story as overwrought and "far-fetched." Still, it was style, not racial substance that ultimately led to his dismissal. Preminger "wanted more melodrama and ultratheatricality than I gave him," said Foote. Ryan had worked with the director before, and would share a writing credit with Foote, but "I ask now," noted Foote, "not to have it on my résumé."[6]

Foote, however, would not be the production's only casualty. Ryan himself was released after talking to Rex Reed, in conjunction with a *New York Times* piece the critic was writing about the filming. Preminger would also fire a secretary, a script girl, and Gene Callahan, the Baton Rouge native who found and negotiated the movie's locations. "Learning that Preminger is a champion of civil rights may surprise some," wrote Thomas Meehan, "for he has frequently been called a Nazi, especially by actors who have worked under him."[7]

But Preminger had proved before that he could be both. In 1954, the director completed *Carmen Jones*, Oscar Hammerstein's adaptation of the 1875 Bizet opera *Carmen*, with a World War II setting and an all-black cast. He rode the actors as he always did, but horror stories of his tyranny never emanated from the production, probably because an affair with Dorothy Dandridge, the film's star, somewhat mellowed him. When he directed *Porgy and Bess* four years later, he again proved fearless in making movies with a black cast. But this time his relationship with Dandridge had soured. Preminger engaged in screaming matches with Sammy Davis, Jr. Sidney Poitier walked off the set, refusing to return until the director apologized and agreed to take a softer tone. By 1967, Preminger's reputation for both black advocacy and oppressive filmmaking were well established.[8]

The story is set in Georgia, and originally the plan was to film there, all the better for authenticity. But there was trouble. Biographer Willi Frischauer framed this struggle—like so many of the *Hurry Sundown* struggles—as a racial one. "Georgia would have nothing, nothing at all to do with a movie showing 'niggers gettin' the better of whites' or 'noble blacks scoring off white trash.' He next tried Atlanta but the answer was as dusty: 'Not here!'" But Frischauer's staging of events is problematic. It assumes first that no other factors but race were included in Georgia's decision, and it thereby makes Louisiana look gracious by default. But Georgia's role in the potential staging of *Hurry Sundown* was far more sympathetic, and Louisiana's far less so. New studies of the film by Chris Fujiwara and Foster Hirsch argue that it was, above anything else, a union dispute that led Preminger to Louisiana. In the incestuous world of film crew unions, Georgia was considered territory controlled by New York. The union there refused to renegotiate the shooting schedule to accommodate the heat, and made salary demands beyond what Preminger was able to pay. Louisiana, on the other hand, was in the grip of the Chicago union, which proved far more accommodating. So the Georgia story moved west, facilitated by production manager Gene Callahan, a Baton Rouge native with connections in the region. Callahan wasn't chosen for his Louisiana roots, but used them to help sway Preminger west. "Otto trusted Gene on this," said production manager Eva Monley, "because Gene was from the Deep South." Callahan and Monley scouted the locations in and around Baton Rouge, all to the approval of Preminger.[9]

In late April, Preminger prepped for the production by pressing the flesh in Louisiana and meeting with local and state leaders to ensure their support. "I am especially grateful to Governor McKeithen and Mayor-President [Woody] Dumas for their complete cooperation and helpful attitude," Preminger told reporters. He met with the governor, with the Baton Rouge mayor. He met with a group of civic leaders from nearby St. Francisville, where much of the shoot would take place. He met with the West Feliciana Parish police jury to negotiate the use of the parish courthouse in St. Francisville. He met with the Louisiana Division of Employment Security about the casting of extras. "We found only one other employment service in the nation that keeps any kind of file we may use," said the director, "and it was not as thorough as the Baton Rouge one."[10]

The state employment office began accumulating files of locals with acting experience in 1960, when William F. Claxton's Desire in the Dust (1960) filmed in the region, and the office went out of its way to prove its preparedness to Preminger's crew. Louisiana, it seemed, was desperate to please.[11]

Baton Rouge and its surrounds had a long history as a film location, and actively courted the motion picture industry. In 1917, Tarzan of the Apes (1918) filmed in nearby Morgan City. In 1929, the silent cinema returned with Dolores Del Rio for Evangeline (1929). More recently, director Robert Aldrich filmed the horror film Hush, Hush, Sweet Charlotte

(1964) in St. Francisville and Ascension Parish. Bette Davis's portrayal of a rapidly deteriorating spinster, however, had little in the way of political polemic. The following year, the cast of *Alvarez Kelly* (1966), starring William Holden and Richard Widmark, arrived near the Amite River to film a Civil War western in which a Confederate and Unionist join forces to steal a Union cattle herd to feed a group of desperate, hungry Rebels. *Hurry Sundown* came with the same kinds of stars, the same large budget, but it was fundamentally different from its predecessors.[12]

When Preminger arrived in late May, the Baton Rouge *Morning Advocate* announced the integrated cast, but assured its readers that Preminger promised that the film would not be "political propaganda." The company would "be here to make a movie and not to be active in politics."[13]

The *Morning Advocate* was clearly a southern paper. In early July, when the House Judiciary Committee voted to exempt homeowners from an open-housing provision of proposed civil rights legislation, the paper applauded the move as "a significant revolt against political opportunism in the administration and aggressive extremism in the civil rights movement." Editorials called for "common sense and fair play in civil rights legislation." It wasn't a fire-eating paper in 1966, but it still kept a guarded defense of the white South.[14]

Its readers did, too.

The 125-member crew stayed in the massive Bellemont, a hotel and convention center built in 1946 as a sprawling mock-antebellum plantation. Amongst the banners paraded over the entrance was the Confederate battle flag. It would, perhaps inevitably, become the theater for one of the cast's most notorious incidents. "It was evident from the first day of shooting that many of the local people didn't want us there because we had a mixed cast," said Eva Monley, in an interview with Foster Hirsch. The campus had three pools, "and I'll never forget the first day one of the Negro actors jumped into [one]," remembered Jane Fonda. "People just stood and stared like they expected the water to turn black!" But they did more than that. After a bomb exploded in the pool, hotel management informed Preminger that integrated swimming would not be permitted. The Bellemont was already taking a calculated publicity risk by allowing the mixed cast to stay in the hotel. Though John Philip Law claimed that

Preminger solved the problem by renting the motel, other accounts argue that his solution was far more calculating and far less expensive. The director threatened to remove the cast and crew and default on the bill if the pool did not remain open to all its guests. The Bellemont's reputation was already suffering. It couldn't afford now to lose payment for the endeavor. The pool remained open and the production stayed, but the continued threats to the cast and its hotel meant that armed state troopers had to guard the *Hurry Sundown* wing of the complex.[15]

Preminger responded to the threats and violence by contacting the governor's office. When he discovered that an aide was an aspiring playwright, the director suggested that he might be interested in producing a play on Broadway. He used a charm not often seen on the set to woo the governor's help. McKeithen made Preminger an honorary colonel on his staff. The legislature invited him to speak, then gave him a standing ovation upon the conclusion of his talk. McKeithen assigned a patrol of Louisiana state troopers to guard the cast and crew.[16]

The armed protection, however, not only made the cast feel as though they were on lockdown, it also failed to ease the fear that beset them. "The place was guarded by soldiers as though it were an armed camp," wrote Gerald Pratley, a journalist on location with the production. One police officer expressed his displeasure to Michael Caine, informing the actor that he "bettah get his nigga-lovin' ass the hell outah heah."[17]

Still, the negotiation demonstrates the disconnect between the state and its people. Louisiana, and Baton Rouge in particular, understood the money it stood to make from such endeavors, and therefore willingly placed its law enforcement resources at the production's disposal. At the same time, the understanding that such protection would be necessary indicated that all would not be well. Average civilians, Ku Kluxers, and even racist police officers expressed their displeasure at the intrusion, even as their tax dollars funded its protection. Significantly, none of the anger engendered by those in and around Baton Rouge focused on the government's willing cooperation. The complicity of the police, the legislature, or the governor never became a prominent part of the dialogue. The unpowerful were raging while the powerful were protecting, covering up, and profiting, but it was only the outsiders that became targets.

The Baton Rouge *Morning Advocate* acknowledged the presence of state police, but argued that they were there to make sure "no passersby or visitors inadvertently wandered into camera range during outdoor filming at the site." It assured its readers that shooting was progressing according to schedule. There were no disturbing incidents to report.[18]

The incidents, however, were just beginning.

Cast member Madeleine Sherwood received a variety of death threats, she suspected, because she had been actively involved in the Civil Rights Movement. Frightened—and seemingly isolated from the rest because of her activism—Sherwood called Preminger, who met her outside at the pool after a particularly harrowing round of threatening phone calls. He raised their hands into the air and screamed, "Shoot!" into the dark night beyond the fence. Nothing happened. Her fear abated. The death threats slowed to an eventual stop.[19]

The cast received dozens of threatening letters from garden-variety racists and more violent Ku Klux Klan members. Locals shot cast trailers, leaving bullet holes strewn along their sides. At one point, someone chased a crew member from a local washeteria because he was washing the bedsheets of a black cast member. Even when there weren't any overt acts or threats of violence, cars would slowly drive around cast locations. It was a reminder to all involved that they were unwelcome guests, that the locals were watching, ever watching. "You can cut the hostility with a knife," said Diahann Carroll. "Down here, the terror has killed my taste for going anywhere."[20]

But going anywhere was part of the job. And the incidents only escalated when the cast moved from the city to its rural location shoots in outlying areas.

"Located in Feliciana Parish," said critic Rex Reed of the St. Francisville location, "it is the kind of place where ladies still wear gardenia corsages in the drugstore, where men in ice-cream suits still sip bourbon toddies on their porches at sundown, and where you are nobody unless your family has lived there at least 100 years." It was "a fading remnant of old-world decadence, it is white Protestant, old-guard and crumbling. It is also the center of Ku Klux Klan activity in Louisiana." That it was. In St. Francisville, the Klan warned the crew to be gone by eight o'clock p.m.

They were. "It's like going to the Vatican to make a movie about Martin Luther," said one resident, "or going to a synagogue to make a film about putting down the Jews."[21]

The Klan's presence was palpable in the summer of 1966. The House Un-American Activities Committee was investigating the group. In addition, the federal government began the second of two trials against a group of Georgia Klansmen accused of killing Lemuel Penn, a public school teacher and Army Reservist returning from Fort Benning to his home in Washington, DC. Penn was a decorated World War II veteran, and the murder happened just days after the Civil Rights Act of 1964, ensuring that the case would receive national attention. After an all-white jury acquitted his murderers, the federal government stepped in. The trial continued throughout the *Hurry Sundown* production.

But public Klan problems were far closer to home than that. A July meeting of the seventeen chapters of the New Orleans area Ku Klux Klan was broken up by police, leading the ACLU to come to the Klan's aid. "In this instance," said an ACLU spokesman, "the Klan was fully within its rights." In April, two disgruntled Klansmen bombed the truck of Lynn Rivere, the exalted cyclops of Baton Rouge's Klavern of the United Klans of America. Motions in the trial continued throughout the summer. In August, as the movie shoot was coming to a close, a local congressional race became heated when incumbent Jimmy Morrison accused his challenger John Rarick of being associated with the KKK. Rarick never denied that the Klan supported his candidacy, but continued his refrain that he had been slandered. Still, statements such as, "If the congressman will repudiate his CORE votes and NAACP bloc votes, yes, I'll repudiate what he calls extremists," certainly didn't do much to warn off such charges. In fact, they made Rarick more popular than ever—the race candidate in a population still divided by race, even if the official line was something else.[22]

Returning from a location shoot one evening, the group's caravan of vehicles suffered a hail of gunfire from the thick trees lining the street. No one was hurt, but as Robert Hooks noted to Foster Hirsch, "The shooters had made their point. All of us were convinced that we were surrounded by some of the dumbest and meanest people on the face of the earth, to say nothing of being the most cowardly."[23]

Film critic Gerald Pratley was on location with the cast and crew at St. Gabriel. He noted the heat and Preminger's notorious temper. He noted the Gildens, also on location to watch their book brought to life. Pratley flew in to New Orleans, where a policeman picked him up and drove him to the set. "Hollywood's so-called stereotypes," he reported, "are disturbingly true to life." The officer blamed 'niggers' for the poor traffic, and did his best to explain to Pratley the way of life in which he found himself. The signs designating 'white' and 'colored' were long gone, victims of an extensive freedom movement and the Civil Rights Act of 1964, but "don't worry about that. Nothing's changed," he said. "Do you think we are going to let the niggers use our toilets? Would you want to sit on a toilet used by a black? We've got ways of taking care of this. We ain't got nothing against the niggers. They know their place down here, we keep them in it and there ain't no trouble. To them, I'm king. I patrol around the town and I take care of them." But then there were those rare disturbances to the order of things. It was those, not the virtual apartheid system, that caused so many problems. "When these outside folks come here to make trash like this movie, then there's always trouble. The fine people of Louisiana are real upset by this film." The policeman noted that Jane Fonda was seen kissing Robert Hooks. "The townspeople won't stand for such things."[24]

In another instance, Jane Fonda was posing for photographs from French journalists. While standing with a young black child in the cast, Fonda leaned down and kissed him. A photographer snapped a picture. "You can't do that," Preminger reported a local policeman as saying. "You can't kiss that nigger!" Only a subterfuge between the director and photographer—switching the film before he turned the roll over to the officer—saved the picture. It was later published in *Paris-Match*.[25]

The racial tension surrounding both the set and story also infiltrated the production. During a particularly tense scene, staging the death of Beah Richards's character, Preminger continued calling for take after take after take. Richards, satisfied with her work and wanting to stop, questioned her director's motives. "How do you know what a black woman in this situation would feel and act? What do you know about it, white man?" There are two distinct accounts of what happened next, but both demonstrate Preminger's desire to keep such tensions from the set. The director was notorious for multiple, seemingly unnecessary takes. According to Richards's co-star Robert Hooks, the outburst prompted a prolonged uncomfortable silence before Preminger ordered another take. After that final performance, he was satisfied. According to another version recounted by Chris Fujiwara, Preminger responded by asking, "How do you know I've never been black?" The shoot then continued successfully. Either way, the temporary racial crisis abated, felled by nothing more than the pace and demand of work.[26]

Such pressures ultimately translated into at least some measure of missionary zeal amongst the cast, which translated into more typical instances of southern racial intransigence. When an integrated collection of stars tried to dine at Brennan's restaurant in New Orleans, for example, they were refused entrance, the establishment noting that it did not serve blacks. The actors only compounded the problem by trading on their star power, asking the manager if he knew who they were. He did, and it didn't matter.[27] This incident, however, must be considered fundamentally different from the violent reaction to the company's presence in Baton Rouge. While it was reasonable to expect that the infusion of cash into the local economy was a fair trade for allowing an integrated cast and crew to film in the area—even to film a story that condemned southern race standards—trying to force a new standard by entering a segregated restaurant was fundamentally unreasonable. Such rules may have been unstated, but they weren't unknown. If the racial status quo allowed for public integrated dining, then the political thrust of the movie would have been largely unnecessary.

Of course, confrontations with the locals were one thing. Negotiating with the state's power structure was another. A starstruck John McKeithen continually sought the company of Preminger and the movie's white stars for a dinner at the governor's mansion. The director refused, reasoning that if the full, integrated cast wasn't welcome, none would attend. Instead, he invited the governor to a dinner for a coterie of French journalists covering the filming. McKeithen eagerly attended, only to find that none of the movie's actors were present. This was soft rebellion on Preminger's part, but it was rebellion nonetheless. "Otto behaved beautifully through it all," said Eva Monley. "He refused to negotiate and continued to demand equal treatment for everyone in his cast and crew."[28]

Preminger noted similarly in his autobiography that Lester Maddox, who would later become the virulent segregationist governor of Georgia, owned a restaurant in the area and invited members of the production to dinner. But when he discovered that among the guests would be Diahann Carroll and Robert Hooks, he cancelled.[29]

Still, Baton Rouge did make an official effort at welcome hospitality. In late June, the Baton Rouge Community Chorus and Playhouse staged Lorraine Hansberry's *A Raisin in the Sun*. An integrated group of actors from *Hurry Sundown* attended the 25 June performance. The locals received permission to premiere music for the movie at the event. (There was no incident.) The Baton Rouge Community Chorus sang three songs from the production to an approving audience. Additionally, John Phillip Law's *The Russians Are Coming* was in Baton Rouge theaters during the shoot, and the actor made a personal appearance at Baton Rouge's Broadmoor Theatre in early July to promote the film and salve relations between the *Hurry Sundown* production and the locals.[30]

Then, on 22 June, Preminger addressed the Louisiana legislature—a guest of East Baton Rouge Parish representative Luther Cole—sharing the stage with Alabama governor George Wallace. George Weltner, head of Paramount, flew to the capital city for the event, watching as Preminger and Wallace stood behind the dais. The director went first. "I am a naturalized American citizen, and only in America could such two diametrically opposed speakers share the same podium." He lauded the American tradition of peaceful disagreement. Of course, "we don't say all of our films are good any more than you say all of your speeches are good." Preminger nodded to the state's push to bring new business to Louisiana, claiming to be proud to "join other great industries which have come here and made this state a very prosperous place … Wherever I go I see prosperity and hope we contribute a little." Significantly, while Preminger expressed a hope that his films demonstrated all the best of the democratic spirit and freedom of expression, he tempered his call by assuring his audience of "the restraint of responsibility." We are different, he seemed to be telling the legislature, but even though I'm making a race movie, I will not betray you. He closed with a peon to the state itself. "We hope you in Louisiana will like us as much as we like you." The assembled politicians gave him a standing ovation. Preminger acknowledged the applause, moved slowly back to his seat.[31]

George Wallace followed the director, part of a wide-ranging press junket in the region, and he gave the assembled legislature a version of the speech he was giving elsewhere. "Since 1954," he told them, in a not-so-veiled reference to *Brown v. Board of Education*, "the precedent and the law have been repeatedly broken." At an honorary dinner that night, he reassured the more than 2,000 in attendance that "there are millions of people throughout the country who possess the spirit and hold the philosophy of the South." He railed against the Supreme Court and Communism. It was the opening salvo in what would become a 1968 presidential bid. "This is not a sectional fight in which we are engaged," he announced, somewhat paradoxically, "it is a national fight."[32]

That national fight seemed palpably close to home as the shoot continued. In June, as filming was well underway, James Meredith, who had integrated Ole Miss in 1962, began a protest march from Memphis, Tennessee to Jackson, Mississippi. His "March Against Fear," however, came to an abrupt end when he was shot by a white Mississippi segregationist and hospitalized. In response, the SCLC, CORE, and SNCC all volunteered to continue the march for him. It was a hot night in the replacement marchers' camp when young Stokely Carmichael, leader of SNCC, gave a powerful speech with a new message: "Black Power," he screamed. "Black Power!" The crowd called back to him, echoing a new mantra that would fundamentally change the dominant strategy of Civil Rights activism. But just as that activism was becoming more militant, progressing to a new stage in its evolution, Preminger's film seemed a study in regress, harkening back to the days of patronizing white liberalism.[33]

In early July, as filming continued, the NAACP publicly decried what it interpreted as a deliberate attempt by Hollywood to exclude black actors and crew members from movies and television shows. The studios defended themselves on the 'deliberate' count, but really had no defense for the exclusion. The NAACP was right, but it certainly wasn't the first time such criticisms appeared.[34]

Hollywood was historically slow in its response to race progress. In 1961, Los Angeles NAACP president Edward Warren publicly asked "that movies show the truthful American image. Any time they have a crap game they show plenty of Negroes. But when do you see a Negro doctor or lawyer?" he asked. "They will show you a scene with a baseball crowd and you don't see a single Negro. You will see city street scenes and not a single Negro. This is ridiculous." After the NAACP campaign, Hollywood began taking notice. In 1963, Wendell Franklin was hired as an assistant director on *The Greatest Story Ever Told* (1965), the first black man to hold such a position for a studio film.[35]

Then, in April 1964, seven months before Preminger's announcement, Anne Bancroft presented the Academy Award for Best Actor to Sidney Poitier, the first black man to receive such an honor. His movie, *Lilies of the Field* (1963), told the story of a journeyman who works with a group of German nuns to build a new chapel, everyone finding a baseline mutual respect along the way. It wasn't a political movie, but politics pulsed through the hall as the award was being announced. A violent summer in Birmingham had passed. A violent Freedom Summer in Mississippi was still to come. But though Poitier was visibly moved by the honor, he had no illusions. "Did I say to myself, 'This country is waking up and beginning to recognize that certain changes are inevitable?' No, I did not. I knew that we hadn't 'overcome,' because I was still the only one."[36]

Nor was this the first time that the industry made such an attempt down South. In 1961, Roger Corman filmed *The Intruder* (1962)—the story of a white supremacist who travels throughout the South organizing resistance to *Brown v. Board of Education* in the mid-1950s. Corman brought his cast and crew to Charleston, Missouri, in the southeast corner of the state. Police warned the group to develop an escape plan, arguing that if the town became angry enough, there would be nothing they could do to stop them from attacking. Paranoia gripped the set. Death threats arrived frequently. The police and National Guard had to guard the group's motel. The movie, however, finished on schedule, and everyone escaped without harm.[37]

Everyone would escape from Baton Rouge without harm, as well. But the film that shoot produced seemed to miss the point of Louisiana's intransigence, to miss the point of all the race progress swirling around it. Donald Bogle has argued that the movie is a repository of every filmed racial stereotype: "the Southern Belle, the Simon-Legree massa, the white idiot child, the faithful mammy, the white Liberal, the New Educated Black Woman ..., the New Good Sensitive Negro, the Corrupt Old White bigot, the Po' White Trash."[38]

Time acknowledged Preminger's intent, but the director "chooses strange ways to display his big brotherhood. One sequence shows Negro sharecroppers singing a white-eyed hallelujah number reminiscent of those '40s films that pretended to liberalize but patently patronized. Two hours of such cinematic clichés make the viewer intolerant of everyone in the film, regardless of race, creed or color." For Bosley Crowther, the film was "a massive mishmash of stereotyped Southern characters and hackneyed melodramatic incidents."[39]

Stephen Farber also criticized the film's stereotypes, frustrated by the use of tropes to make its point. But then the point itself was part of the problem. "Though it takes an apparently unequivocal stand on the race question, it does not have a new or interesting point to make on the plight of the Southern Negro, and its offensively sweet, industrious Negroes have nothing in common with today's Black Panthers, who might challenge a complacent audience. Art forces us to consider things we'd rather squirm away from, but *Hurry Sundown* congratulates us on the liberalism we picked up in the sixth grade, and never forces us to test that liberalism in any unsettling, radical ways."[40]

The film's frustrated reviewers were right. The movie didn't fit the time. The tropes used in the film existed in the South. There were lots of mean, ignorant white people. There were lots of poor blacks who were either compliant or rebellious. And there were even associations between poor whites and blacks. But in the age of Black Power, such stories entered a climate that had seen such characters all too many times before. Those who would respond to such messages had already reached a new stage in their thinking about race relations. Meanwhile, southern whites would only find that teaching pedantic.

But in other ways, contemporary reviews exaggerated Preminger's misfire. There was no "white-eyed hallelujah number." The brief group song by the black sharecroppers only lasted seconds, a plot device allowing the sheriff and his makeshift deputies to sneak onto the property to arrest Reeve Scott, the rebellious black farmer played by Robert Hooks. And while Beah Richards's mammy character is certainly stereotypical, Michael Caine's character, the villain Henry Warren, mentions at the beginning of the film that the land belongs to his wife's old mammy. So, to be fair to Preminger, he wasn't using that stereotype as a stand-in for something more complex. He wasn't trying to hide anything. He admits it at the front of the movie, trying to provide an understandable code to the nation for the only plausible relationship between a rich white southern man and a poor black woman. In addition, the lawyer who represents Reeve at trial admits to having a black half-brother, demonstrating the incestuous nature of some of these relationships. He is problematic for the court because he is a white man representing a black defendant, because he denigrates the proceedings as illegal, and because he is from nearby Bay City. Bay City is where the judge had to move his daughter's wedding, where Rad McDowell, John Philip Law's character, threatened to purchase dynamite when the local store wouldn't sell, and then where the new slick lawyer came from. Bay City represents the town's competition. It's better just down the road. The attempts at subtlety are there, they simply remain overshadowed by the clumsy racial messages and the film's broader problems.

And the film had broader problems. While the critics harped on the film's racial content, they didn't fail to note that the movie was bad without it. The film drags on for two hours and twenty minutes as the stories of the lives of three families slowly unfold. The meandering progression also leaves Preminger less room for time with the film's central plot. There is no great crisis moment, for example, to bring Law's character to decide to unify with his neighbor. A decision that unfolds agonizingly over several pages in the Gilden novel is made with a few stern looks away from the camera in the film. The story spends its time developing side stories that don't further the plot, but leave massive plot points aside. It is, along with its race problems, a bad movie.

Later commentators Anne and Hart Nelsen cite the movie as subtly prejudicial. The reversed hierarchy of black heroes, poor white aides, and rich white villains, according to the Nelsens, establishes a state of cognitive dissonance, forcing the viewer to either reject the formulation for a more common understanding of order—and thus ridiculing the actions of the stereotyped black characters—or disconnecting from the plot progression entirely. The false choice is aided by the fact that the black characters never move outside the white power structure to achieve their ends. They "completely lack the emotions of fear, anger, and lust, while the whites, if overdone, do display numerous human frailties."[41]

Even as actress Beah Richards was suffering at the hands of her notoriously cruel director, and at the hands of a racist community that didn't want her in Louisiana, she remained, in a sense, part of the problem. Richards was from Vicksburg, educated at Dillard University in New Orleans. This was an area and a people she knew well. Donald Bogle sees Richards's role as a late permutation of a film stereotype present since the medium's inception. The "desexed, overweight, dowdy *dark* black woman" began as a formal type in 1914 with the short feature *Coon Town Suffragettes* (1914) and dominated available roles for black female actresses through the 1930s and 1940s.[42]

Her co-star Robert Hooks plays a returning World War II veteran and is intended to be a representation of the new black militancy. Instead, argues Bogle, Hooks is "pliable and decent," a "tom's tom." Diahann Carroll was a black woman cast to fit a white ideal, "one more dehydrated and lifeless accruement of a decadent capitalist society." Playing the role of a black schoolteacher in *Hurry Sundown*, Carroll was supposed to demonstrate the horror and indignance perhaps typical of a racist, segregated situation. But to Bogle, Carroll "seemed more bored by the racism in the picture—or amused—than irritated." Ultimately, for Bogle, the movie "presented archetypal scenes and characters that audiences associated with the South, with bigots, with liberals, and with touchy racial situations. Although it was cluttered with clichés and misrepresentations, *Hurry Sundown* was directed as one big glorious comic strip with pop scene after pop scene, and thus it succeeded on a primal level as a popularization of current events."[43]

But for southerners—for those Louisianans so upset about the location shoot—archetypal scenes were the farthest thing from their minds. Critics of the film emphasized its offenses to white liberalism and contemporary black equality claims. But there was plenty in *Hurry Sundown* for southern whites to abhor. Of course, what white liberals saw as stereotypical was still frustratingly reactionary to those who would think to terrorize the movie's filming. But there was more than just the story to offend.

"You know I was ten years old before I learned that 'damn' and 'Yankee' were two separate words?" said Julie Ann Warren, played by Jane Fonda, in one of the opening scenes. The white stereotypes, too, could make Louisianans just as mad as friendly talk about blacks. There was also stunted dialogue and forced, inaccurate accents that always drove southerners crazy. Burgess Meredith's character, an educated judge, uses phrases like "me and my womenfolk." The educated are racist, which is understandable, but they are also stupid. They don't just speak with accents, they speak improperly. Vivian's great subtle insult to the judge, once she strokes his ego and outwits him into allowing her to look in the city records is, "You're such a perfect example of everything southern." Whites are easily duped. The sheriff is placated with food and kind gestures in similar ways as the judge. When he goes to arrest Reeve, his black guests mollify the sheriff with food and drink. He doesn't make the arrest.[44]

Michael Caine's character, Henry Warren, was even more problematic to the white southern mind. Warren is, at base, the character most 1960s southern white men wanted to be. He is the rich family man with the nice house and beautiful wife who was important to the town and its development. But he is melodramatically evil. He bilks people out of their land, leaves his small child tethered to a crib, then locks him in a room defenseless against dynamiting in the area. He tricks his wife into selling out those she cares about, carries on an extramarital affair, and rapes his wife. Then, after two hours of Preminger's pillaging the postwar South, Warren launches into a considered disquisition on the saving power of California. "There ain't a dream been dreamed, can't come true out there." The message was clear. The South needed saving, and California—Hollywood—could do it.

The Nelsens see these caricatures as fundamental usurpations of the Gildens' original novel. The complexities of the black characters have been eliminated. The plight of the poor whites has been distorted, the group celebrated as the moral superiors of everyone else. When the black and white poor unite in the movie, they do so in a personal, superficial way, whereas the novel describes a broader organizational movement. This is true, of course, but in this regard Preminger is doing what almost every Hollywood adaptation does. The Gildens' novel is over one thousand pages long. Even with an overly long production like *Hurry Sundown*, shorthand for such relationships is, if not justified, at least forgivable. It isn't a blatantly racist movie, but in its use of stereotypes, both white and black, it depicts a false reality of the southern condition.[45]

Such is in contradistinction to the one positive historical treatment of the film. Historian Foster Hirsch is far more sympathetic. The movie was overly long and far from his best artistic work, but "it is another example of Preminger tackling previously off-limits subject matter." He disagrees with Fujiwara's assessment that 1960s values have been imposed on the narrative. For Hirsch, the characters "transcend stereotype"; they are neither simplistic nor contrived. The black characters aren't filled with retributive rage, haven't yet developed a Civil Rights mind. While the older white characters are racially intransigent, the younger characters slowly develop a race consciousness through the plodding story.[46]

The Gildens, for their part, were upset with the changes the movie made to their manuscript, too, but made little noise about their displeasure, as the Paramount Pictures payment more than salved their wounds. The movie is relatively faithful to the book's plot. And though the film version of *Hurry Sundown* was a critical failure, it did make money. With a budget of $3.8 million, the film topped $4 million in rentals. It was certainly no economic watershed, but it did finish its run in the black.[47]

The film was condemned by the National Catholic Office for Motion Pictures, but that event was far from rare. The group had condemned four other major studio productions during the year, as well. It condemned seventeen in total in 1967, more than any other year in its history. Still, it was the first film condemned that was approved by the industry's new Production Code. The group saw the movie as "superficial and patronizing in its treatment of racial attitudes and tensions." Preminger gave the response little thought. "This powerful group is not powerful," said the director. "It is like other pressure groups, only as powerful as the power we give them." He was right. The flurry of 1967 condemnations was one of the last gasps of a dying beast. The director actually screened the film at Creighton University, a Catholic school in Omaha, Nebraska, which completely ignored the condemnation. In the culturally permissive climate of the 1960s, such a rebuke could only have helped the film's box office cause.[48]

For Baton Rouge, however, such condemnations were angels dancing on the heads of so many pins. It would be tempting to characterize local anger as a reaction to militants in the cast like Richards, Hooks, and Jane Fonda. That seemed to be the case with Madeline Sherwood. But Richards and Hooks were problematic for white Baton Rouge not because of their political affiliations, but rather for the perceived reason behind those affiliations: they were black, and that was reason enough. Furthermore, Jane Fonda had yet to become the radical activist she would later become. Louisiana's anger wasn't over any specific political baggage Fonda brought to the set.[49]

In fact, Fonda credited her move toward militancy, at least in part, to her experience in Baton Rouge, where she suffered at the hands of an angry racist populace and first learned from her co-stars about "black militants." Fonda was struck by a cross burning on the lawn of the Bellemont. By the anger over a picture of her kissing a young black extra. By the gunshots and the repeated refrains of "nigger lover" coming from the natives. She heard Robert Hooks and Beah Richards talk about black nationalism and black power. It would not be long before she became active in civil rights and other protest movements.[50]

Regardless, it was integration that gave locals their cause, both in the cast and on the screen, even as Louisiana was trying to downplay its race problems and gild its corporate image. When Diahann Carroll went on the Tonight Show in 1967, part of the normal press junket for the film, she told Johnny Carson about the cast's experience. Locals felt betrayed. For all of the clandestine threats and violence, it was a minority of area residents who threatened the cast and crew. The police and the press worked to keep such violence out of the newspapers. Now their secret was out. For a city hoping to develop a thriving film industry, this was the nightmare scenario.[51]

Even during the shoot, such cover-ups were in evidence. It is significant in-and-of itself that the Baton Rouge *News Leader*, a local black weekly edited by Doris Gale and particularly dedicated to exposing such abuses, did not provide any kind of exposé on the violence. Neither did the *Louisiana Weekly*, the state's largest and most influential black weekly. The paper reported in early April on Diahann Carroll's appearance on NBC's *Sammy Davis, Jr. Show*. Late in the month, it profiled Wendell Franklin, the first black assistant director for major studio movies. But nothing on the filming in Baton Rouge. It was in the best interest of everyone involved, it seemed, to keep such incidents quiet.[52]

The St. Francisville paper was far more willing to voice complaints about the production than was the *Morning Advocate* or the black weeklies, but it, too, steered completely clear of race. An old café was converted to a hardware store, the courthouse was temporarily overrun. Traffic was interrupted. Parking spaces were unavailable. These were the typical headaches of a Hollywood location shoot. The integrated cast was never mentioned. Neither were the threats, the violence, the intimidation.[53]

When the crew returned for a second shoot weeks later, officials were ready. The new filming permit required the production to allow cars through. It specified certain hours for filming. Violation would lead to cancellation of the permit. By this point, St. Francisville residents had seen the integrated cast; had fumed for weeks about the fundamental indecency of the event. Traffic problems provided just the excuse they needed. Still, Preminger was ready. The cast and crew kept to the strict guidelines, ensuring that the town couldn't revoke their privileges.[54]

Still, the headaches had yet to end. In late July, a meeting of the Board of Aldermen devolved into a heated back-and-forth, as a contractor hired to do work on a block being used by the production was unable to complete the job until the movie was complete. The Teamsters, however, sided with Preminger, and the production's strict adherence to the town's traffic provisions gave it no reason to revoke the movie's permit. With the resolution unresolved, the Teamsters announced that they had struck a separate project by the same contractor. When the contractor attempted to work, pickets forced him to compromise. The production continued.[55] Significantly, however, though race permeated the shoot and clearly angered the St. Francisville population—was, in fact, the reason behind this minutia of conflict—it was never the focus of any official complaint. Such were saved for the cover of anonymity.

Hammond, another of the film's locations, belied no such trouble. Crowds gawked at movie stars Burgess Meredith and Michael Caine. The college men ogled Jane Fonda. As the tedious drone of shooting and reshooting continued, the crowd dissipated, bored with the tedium of the reality of such work. The most dramatic moment of the day, according to Hammond journalism, came when Preminger's wife fainted, a victim of the 100-degree heat.[56]

"Hammond will it ever be the same? In reality it probably will be, but for those playing roles in segments of scenes from the movie production," reported the *Hammond Daily Leader*'s Edna Campbell, "it will stand out for many years to come as a red-letter day in their lives. This was a very 'first' for Hammond, and a thrill for the local participants and spectators." The paper included features on Burgess Meredith and Jane Fonda, fawning at every turn, and pictures of the white cast, the locations, and the spectators watching their every move. Never was race mentioned. Never was anger.[57]

As the *Hurry Sundown* crew was packing up and leaving town, John Martzell, the Louisiana Commission on Human Relations' executive director, trumpeted its success. "The fact is that Louisiana stands out in the nation," he said. "There has been no serious racial strife in Louisiana since the commission was established." The production had proven that not to be the case, but the press conference demonstrated Louisiana's determination to control the message about its own racial sensitivity.[58]

When filming closed on 13 August, the cast and crew fled hurriedly back to Hollywood, leaving Baton Rouge to handle spin control. "Having a major movie produced entirely in the Baton Rouge area has been quite an experience for the community," reported the *Advocate*'s Anne Price, "and a financial boon in the bargain." Locals were employed, money was spent. "Preminger and the rest of the company have been generally highly pleased with the results of their Baton Rouge stay." Generally. Price reported that the production had "been well received." It "had good community cooperation … So the whole operation has been quite satisfactory for everybody involved." While Price's report was patently untrue, there was plenty of reason for she and others to believe it. Baton Rouge was a boom town, Hollywood had come and gone, and the racial threats that permeated the set were quieted from the beginning. "Baton Rouge hasn't seen the last of

Hurry Sundown," concluded Price, "for Preminger has promised to stage the world premiere of the production here."[59]

But that was not to be. Though Preminger and his employees said all the right things to all the right people, no one had any intention of coming back to Louisiana. When the movie premiered in February 1967, it didn't do so in Baton Rouge. It didn't appear there the next week. Or the next. The movie that caused so much of a stir throughout the hot Louisiana summer of 1966 never played in the place where it shot. The Paramount, the Dalton, the Regina, the Broadmoor, the Robert E. Lee—none chose to show *Hurry Sundown*.[60]

True, the movie was a critical flop. That, however, wasn't why it never appeared. Preminger's film was a local product, using locals as cast and crew. But to those who fumed over the integrated cast, berated the blasphemy of "nigger-lovers" in their midst, it was as foreign as foreign could be.

Notes

1. Ann Price, "Home Town Girl Gets Top Billing at Premiere: Fans Give Stars Rousing Welcome," Baton Rouge *Morning Advocate*, 1 April 1966, 1A, 16A.

2. "Baton Rouge Area Participates In Economic Growth, Study Says," Baton Rouge *Morning Advocate*, 8 July 1966, 7B.

3. Sid Moody, "'The South Will Rise Again' Takes On New Truth as Industry Moves In," Baton Rouge *Morning Advocate*, 24 July 1966, 3F; and Ann Pierce, "Community Advancement Opens Neighborhood Centers," 29 July 1966, 16A.

4. "House Passes Tag Slogan Change," Baton Rouge *Morning Advocate*, 24 June 1966, 12A; "July Designated Tourist Month In Louisiana," 29 June 1966, 9A; and "Governor Names Month of July As Tourist Month," *St. Francisville Democrat*, 30 June 1966, 1.

5. The amount of the purchase was undisclosed, but the payment reportedly exceeded $200,000. The novel itself eventually sold around 300,000 copies. Chris Fujiwara, *The World and Its Double: The Life and Work of Otto Preminger* (New York: Faber and Faber, 2008), 343; Foster Hirsch, *Otto Preminger: The Man Who Would Be King* (New York: Alfred A. Knopf, 2007), 410; and Thomas Meehan, "Otto the

Terrible," *Saturday Evening Post*, 8 April 1967, 27. Preminger quote reproduced from Gerald Pratley, *The Cinema of Otto Preminger* (New York: Barnes, 1971), 154.

6. Foote quote reproduced from Hirsch, *Otto Preminger*, 411–412.

7. "Reed," said the director, "is a frustrated little man who wanted to become an actor but couldn't make it." Preminger welcomed the young critic, only to feel betrayed by Reed's portrayal of a tyrannical director. Preminger quote reproduced from Otto Preminger, *Preminger: An Autobiography* (Garden City, NJ: Doubleday & Company, 1977), 174; Fujiwara, *The World and Its Double*, 343–344; Hirsch, *Otto Preminger*, 423; and Meehan, "Otto the Terrible," 28.

8. Hirsch, *Otto Preminger*, 219–224, 292–294.

9. The movie was filmed in Baton Rouge, St. Francisville, Liverpool, Bains, and Hammond, as well as on land owned by St. Gabriel prison. Willi Frischauer, *Behind the Scenes of Otto Preminger: An Unauthorized Biography* (New York: William Morrow & Co., 1974), 223; Fujiwara, *The World and Its Double*, 345; Hirsch, *Otto Preminger*, 414; and "Preminger Picks Area Film Locale," Baton Rouge *Morning Advocate*, 16 April 1966, 14A.

10. Anne Price, "Filming of Preminger Movie In BR Area Starts June 8," Baton Rouge *Morning Advocate*, 22 April 1966, 1A, 9A; and "Part of Movie To Be Shot Here," *St. Francisville Democrat*, 28 April 1966, 1. Preminger quote reproduced from "State Employment Service Simplifies Movie Casting Job Here," Baton Rouge *Morning Advocate*, 12 June 1966, 1E.

11. Created by Jerry Leggio, the file was maintained by Charles Denstorff, director of field services for the employment office. Both worked closely with Preminger and casting director Bill Barnes to choose the extras. "State Employment Service Simplifies Movie Casting Job Here," Baton Rouge *Morning Advocate*, 12 June 1966, 1E.

12. Chere Coen, "On Location: Movie Makers Have Given the Baton Rouge Area Its Fair Share of Screen Time," Baton Rouge *Morning Advocate*, 1 May 1998, A20; Louisiana Film Commission, "Motion Pictures Filmed in Louisiana," *Southern Quarterly* 23 (Fall 1984): 85–86. For more on film and the representation of Louisiana, see H. Wayne Schuth, "The Images of Louisiana in Film and Television," *Southern Quarterly* 23 (Fall 1984): 5–17.

13. "Otto Preminger Ready to Begin Work on Movie," Baton Rouge *Morning Advocate*, 31 May 1966, 10A.

14. "Common Sense (Just a Little) in Civil Rights," Baton Rouge *Morning Advocate*, 5 July 1966, 8A.

15. Fonda and Law claims in Fujiwara, *The World and Its Double*, 346; Eva Monley quote reproduced from Hirsch, *Otto Preminger*, 415; Meehan, "Otto the Terrible," 27; Colleen Kane, "The Bellemont," *Abandoned Baton Rouge*, http://abandonedbatonrouge.typepad.com/abandoned_baton_rouge/2008/05/the-bellemont.html, accessed 8 February 2009; and Preminger, *Preminger*, 183–184.

16. Eva Monley was made an honorary sheriff to protect her. She changed cars every day to be safe. Preminger, too, was made honorary sheriff. Meehan, "Otto the Terrible," 29; Hirsch, *Otto Preminger*, 415; and Frischauer, *Behind the Scenes of Otto Preminger*, 228.

17. Fujiwara, *The World and Its Double*, 415; and Gerald Pratley, *The Cinema of Otto Preminger* (New York: Castle Books, 1971), 14.

18. "Filming Crew Now Working In Baton Rouge," Baton Rouge *Morning Advocate*, 1 July 1966, 12C.

19. Hirsch, *Otto Preminger*, 417.

20. Fujiwara, *The World and Its Double*, 225, 346; Carroll quote reprinted from Mark Harris, *Pictures at a Revolution: Five Movies and the Birth of the New Hollywood* (New York: Penguin, 2008), 180; Pratley, *The Cinema of Otto Preminger*, 14; Meehan, "Otto the Terrible," 29; and Preminger, *Preminger*, 184–185.

21. Rex Reed, "Like They Could Cut Your Heart Out," *New York Times*, 21 August 1966, 105; and Frischauer, *Behind the Scenes of Otto Preminger*, 226.

22. "Jury Being Picked for Trial of Klansmen," Baton Rouge *Morning Advocate*, 3 July 1966, 12A, "Ex-Klansman Testifies at Trial in G[eorgi]a.," 7 July 1966, 4B, "Motions Are Filed in BR Klansman Case," 9 July 1966, 13A, "Klan Leaflet Claims 17 Units In New Orleans," 9 July 1966, 6B, "ACLU Comes To Aid of KKK In Controversy," 12 July 1966, 7C, "Separate Trial Is Granted In Klan Bombing Case Here," 14 July 1966, 14E, "KKK Membership Down During Probe, But Climbing Again," 22 July 1966, 3D, "Rarick Says He'll Sue Morrison For Slander-Libel in KKK Link," 9 August 1966, 8B, "Klansman Gets 20-Year Term In Shooting," 14 August 1966, 2A.

23. As the tension built on the set, the cast moved to nearby Plaquemine, but on their first and only day there, the heat from the lights set off the local hospital's sprinkler system, flooding the building and causing $1,200 in damages. The cast moved back

to St. Francisville. Hirsch, *Otto Preminger*, 416–417; and Reed, "Like They Could Cut Your Heart Out," 105.

24. Pratley, *The Cinema of Otto Preminger*, 9, 12–14.

25. Preminger, *Preminger*, 184.

26. Hooks kept a diary of the production. The quote comes from Hirsch, *Otto Preminger*, 422–423; and Fujiwara, *The World and Its Double*, 348.

27. Hirsch, *Otto Preminger*, 416.

28. Quote reproduced from Hirsch, *Otto Preminger*, 417; and Frischauer, *Behind the Scenes of Otto Preminger*, 226.

29. Preminger, *Preminger*, 185.

30. The chorus sang Hugo Montenegro's "Hurry Sundown" and "I Got the Spirit," and Fred Caruso's "Don' Bother Me." "Movie Actors To Attend Play By Local Group," Baton Rouge *Morning Advocate*, 24 June 1966, 11D, "Hurry Sundown," 2 July 1966, 8E, "John Phillip Law Sets Appearance At Broadmoor," 10 July 1966, 8E; and "BR Community Chorus and Playhouse Stages Lorraine Hansberry's *A Raisin In the Sun*," Baton Rouge *News Leader*, 5 June 1966, 1, 6.

31. Hirsch, *Otto Preminger*, 424; Preminger quotes reproduced from "Preminger Gives Solons Short, Unprepared Talk," Baton Rouge *Morning Advocate*, 23 June 1966, 6B, "People and Events," 26 June 1966, 8E.

32. Edgar Perez, "Wallace Addresses Testimonial Dinner," Baton Rouge *Morning Advocate*, 23 June 1966, 1A, 10A; and "Wallace Tells Solons Law Is Disappearing: Citizens Urged To Join Fight," *Hammond Daily Leader*, 22 June 1966, 1, "Wallace," 23 June 1966, 1.

33. "Ambushed Meredith Vows 'I Shall Return': Civil Rights Groups Plan To Continue March Against Fear," *Louisiana Weekly*, 11 June 1966, 1; and James K. Cazalas, "Shotgun Blasts Wound Meredith," Baton Rouge *Morning Advocate*, 7 June 1966, 1A, 8A.

34. "Hollywood Hiring Practices Hit by NAACP," Baton Rouge *Morning Advocate*, 8 July 1966, 15A.

35. Jack Temple Kirby, *Media-Made Dixie: The South in the American Imagination* (Athens: The University of Georgia Press, 1986), 112–116; and Harris, *Pictures at a Revolution*, 56–57.

36. Harris, *Pictures at a Revolution*, 53.

37. William Shatner, *Up Till Now: The Autobiography of William Shatner* (New York: St. Martin's Press, 2008), 68–74.

38. In a similar vein, Chris Fujiwara has highlighted the incongruity of the film's music. Though the film is set in the 1940s, the score maintains a 1960s sound, subtly making the point that such racial problems had yet to dissipate. The message, therefore, and its contemporary relevance, were central to the narrative, even if it meant sacrificing authenticity. It is simple and bold by design. Its lack of subtlety is intentional. But not only do such sacrifices harm the function of the narrative, they misinterpret the southern racial situation in both the 1940s and 1960s. The plodding evolutionary cycle that ultimately eroded Jim Crow was not simple, and while its arc was plotted at monumental bold points, it was defined far more by its subtle motion than its expository denouements. Fujiwara, *The World and Its Double*, 350; and Donald Bogle, *Toms, Coons, Mulattoes, Mammies, & Bucks: An Interpretive History of Blacks in American Films* (New York: Continuum, 1992), 208–209.

39. For the *New Yorker's* Brendan Gill, *Hurry Sundown* was "a terrible movie, and it is terrible in a way that Mr. Preminger has made his very own." It was "meretricious nonsense from start to finish." *Esquire's* Wilfred Sheed felt much the same. Brendan Gill, "The Current Cinema," *New Yorker*, 8 April 1967, 145; *Time*, 31 March 1967, 95; *New York Times*, 24 March 1967, 22; and Hirsch, *Otto Preminger*, 425.

40. Or, as Judith Crist wrote, far less subtly, "Gather roun', chillun, while dem banjos is strummin' out 'Hurry Sundown' an' ole Marse Preminger gwine tell us all about de South." Historian Mark Harris, in a common reaction to the film, deemed it "a disaster; no trace of comprehension of the very real contemporary racism that the cast and crew had experienced in making the film under the shadow of the Klan in Louisiana had rubbed off on the movie itself." Crist quote reprinted from Harris, *Pictures at a Revolution*, 288; and Stephen Farber, review of *Hurry Sundown*, in *Film Quarterly* 20 (Summer 1967): 78–79.

41. Anne K. Nelsen and Hart M. Nelsen, "The Prejudicial Film: Progress and Stalemate, 1915–1967," *Phylon* 31 (2nd Qtr. 1970): 145–147.

42. The italics are Bogle's. Thomas Cripps, review of *Beah: A Black Woman Speaks*, in *Journal of American History* 91 (December 2004): 1141–1142; Bogle, *Toms, Coons, Mulattoes, Mammies, & Bucks*, 9, 15; and Stephanine Greco Larson, *Media and Minorities: The Politics of Race in News and Entertainment* (Lanham, MD: Rowman & Littlefield, 2006), 26–27.

43. Bogle, *Toms, Coons, Mulattoes, Mammies, & Bucks*, 210–212, 213.

44. Of course, those who heard the messages of Black Power and the new arguments of second wave Civil Rights knew that whites weren't so easily persuaded.

45. Nelsen, "The Prejudicial Film," 145–147.

46. Hirsch, *Otto Preminger*, 425.

47. For Gildens' reaction, Helen Yglesias, "Chronicle of the Class Wars," *The Women's Review of Books* 7 (July 1990), 16–17; for film finances, Hirsch, *Otto Preminger*, 427.

48. Furthermore, Preminger had been in trouble with the Office before, earning condemnations for *Forever Amber* and *The Moon Is Blue*. The group's bevy of condemnations in 1967 was a testament to its newfound irrelevance, ultimately proven when it condemned *Rosemary's Baby* the following year, to no avail. *New York Times*, 8 March 1967, 52; Harris, *Pictures at a Revolution*, 361; Catholic Office quote reproduced from Nelsen, "The Prejudicial Film," 143; James M. Skinner, *The Cross and the Cinema: The Legion of Decency and the National Catholic Office for Motion Pictures, 1933–1970* (Westport, CT: Praeger, 1993), 82–86, 165–166; Gregory D. Black, *The Catholic Crusade Against the Movies, 1940–1975* (New York: Cambridge University Press, 1998), 56–65, 119–128; Vincent Camby, "Filmmakers Show Less Fear of Catholic Office," *New York Times*, 13 October 1967, 35; and Preminger quote reproduced from Preminger, *Preminger*, 180–181.

49. In mid-June, Fonda's brother Henry was charged with marijuana possession in California, but the controversy never touched his sister. Preminger, *Preminger*, 162; Bill Davidson, *Jane Fonda: An Intimate Biography* (New York: Dutton, 1990), 118–119; and "Peter Fonda Is Charged in Marijuana Case," Baton Rouge *Morning Advocate*, 22 June 1966, 6C.

50. Jane Fonda, *My Life So Far* (New York: Random House, 2005), 170–172, 211–213.

51. Chere Coen, "On Location: Movie Makers Have Given the Baton Rouge Area Its Fair Share of Screen Time," Baton Rouge *Advocate*, 1 May 1998, A20.

52. See Baton Rouge *News Leader*, John B. Cade Library Archives, Southern University at Baton Rouge; and "Diahann Carroll On Sammy Davis Show Friday Night," *Louisiana Weekly*, 2 April 1966, 2–11, "W. Franklin, Hollywood's First Negro Ass't Director," 30 April 1966, 2–11.

53. "Movie Crew Begins Filming Here This Week," *St. Francisville Democrat*, 9 June 1966, 1.

54. "Movie Shooting Continues In St. Francisville," *St. Francisville Democrat*, 14 July 1966, 1.

55. "Town Council Hears Movie Problem At Meeting Tue.," *St. Francisville Democrat*, 28 July 1966, 1, "Movie Crew Now Shooting Scenes At Parish Courthouse," 4 August 1966, 1.

56. Marg Eastman, "'Hurry Sundown' Film 2 Scenes at Grace Church," *Hammond Daily Leader*, 11 July 1966, 1, 8; and "Movie Shoots Scenes in Hammond," Baton Rouge *Morning Advocate*, 12 July 1966, 6C.

57. Edna Campbell, "'Sundown' Causes Sensation In Church Neighborhood," *Hammond Daily Leader*, 11 July 1966, 2, Marg Eastman, "Burgess Meredith: From 'Hamlet' to 'Batman'—Then 'Hurry Sundown' Here," 12 July 1966, 8.

58. Bill Neikirk, "Louisiana Racial Climate Changed, Martzell Believes," Baton Rouge *Morning Advocate*, 11 August 1966, 7A.

59. Ann Price, "Success All Round," Baton Rouge *Morning Advocate*, 14 August 1966, 10E.

60. "Movie Listings," Baton Rouge *Morning Advocate*, 5 February 1967, 9E, "Movie Listings," 12 February 1967, 9E, "Movie Listings," 19 February 1967, 9E, "Movie Listings," 26 February 1967, 9E, "Movie Listings," 5 March 1967, 9E, "Movie Listings," 12 March 1967, 9E, "Movie Listings," 19 March 1967, 9E, "Movie Listings," 26 March 1967, 9E.

Scrabble Tiles Can Help Decipher the Devil's Messages

From Baby-Killing Nuns to Baby-Wanting Witches in American Fiction and Culture

R osemary Woodhouse sat on the floor of her apartment in 1966, frantically trying to make Scrabble tile anagrams from the title of the book *All Of Them Witches*. She then attempted the same thing with "Steven Marcato." She finally found the name of her neighbor in the arrangements, cluing her in to the grand diabolical experiment of her pregnancy. Maria Monk stood on hard convent ground in 1834, receiving orders from her Mother Superior to fetch coal from the cellar. Upon her journey through the cavernous basement, she came across a deep hole, perhaps fifteen feet in diameter. There was lime strewn all around it, cluing her in to the grand diabolical practice of murdering the offspring of priest-nun rape. Both characters stood as representatives of the American Protestant desire to protect themselves against perceived threats.

Maria Monk's *Awful Disclosures of the Hotel Dieu Nunnery of Montreal*, the revised edition published in 1836, sold over 300,000 copies by 1860, only outsold by *Uncle Tom's Cabin*. Ira Levin's *Rosemary's Baby*, published in 1967, was also a bestseller—seventh on the fiction list for that year—and became a film that was a box office success. Though published 131 years apart, the books carried many similarities that contributed to their popularity. They both featured a heroine who entered a dark, mysterious, labyrinthine house (Monk the nunnery, Rosemary the Bramford apartment building), both heroines were subject to the horror of the "evil" taking place in each building (Monk the rape and torture of herself and the other nuns, as well as the murder of any baby born of those rapes; Rosemary the rape by the devil, brought about by the trickery of the building's residents trying to bring about the spawn of Satan). There were also notable differences. Rosemary was generally unaware of the evil goings-on around her, while Monk was all too aware. Rosemary grew, in the end, to begrudgingly accept her fate (at least, if nothing else, her role as mother), while Monk escaped the convent all together. Monk's tale was presented as fact, Rosemary's as fiction.

The most significant difference, however, is that the early nineteenth-century secret evildoers were Catholics, while the late twentieth-century secret evildoers were Satanists. Were the two antagonists switched, neither book could probably have been published, much less purchased by hundreds of thousands. Though the formulas were similar, the enemies were very different. The anti-immigrant nativist sentiment of the early 1800s made people far more disposed to fear/hate Catholics. The Protestant Puritan roots of the country and the growing uneasiness at the onset of the industrial revolution (and its attendant immigration) made Catholics a far greater threat to the God-fearing populace of the 1830s. Satanists, certainly, were not filling the available jobs in new American industrial centers. In the 1960s, by contrast, the ultra-religious Cold War climate that had been burgeoning for two decades since the close of the Second World War was far more concerned with the prospect of "evil." Those American values of the 1830s were now threatened by Soviet Russia, and communism and its attendant atheism were portrayed as the apotheosis of evil. In the 1960s, Christians were easy to understand, non-Christians, because of the Soviet threat, were suspect. So there was a different sort of Christian/American distrust permeating the populace in the two eras—the first, afraid that Catholic immigrants would infiltrate the country and erode the bedrock Protestant foundations of the nation; the second, afraid that Communists would infiltrate the country and destroy the Christian democracy they so cherished.

Monk's *Awful Disclosures* outraged the American populace. Investigators flocked to Montreal to examine the Hotel Dieu Nunnery, but when they arrived, they found no corroborating evidence to back Monk's claims of debauchery. Monk's mother claimed her daughter's head had been run through with a slate pencil as a child, thus triggering a mental imbalance. William L. Stone produced his own narrative, *Maria Monk and the Nunnery of the Hotel Dieu, Being an Account of a Visit to the Convents of Montreal and Refutation of the "Awful Disclosures."*[1] The Catholic response and the refutation of the most outlandish of Monk's claims attempted in small measure to counter the quick sales of her account, as well as other similar accounts of the era. A group of nativist, anti-Catholic ministers helped ghostwrite Monk's account and profited from the healthy sales. Monk's feelings of betrayal and the swirling controversy surrounding her caused the author to flee New York for Philadelphia in 1837. Though the events of the last twelve years of her life remain relatively unknown, Monk died in poverty in 1849.[2]

After *Rosemary's Baby* became a bestseller in 1967, it became a successful film the following year. The novel was Ira Levin's first in fourteen years, following his 1953 thriller, *A Kiss Before Dying.* Its success, along with the success of Roman Polanski's film version, prompted a far more rapid publication schedule, with Levin producing three novels in the 1970s. The story also highlighted new theological and feminist turns, directly mentioning *Time* magazine's coverage of Thomas J.J. Altizer's Christian Atheism and clearly portraying the pitfalls of pregnancy in modern times.[3] *Rosemary's Baby's* 1836 predecessor finds neither atheism nor Satanism as problematic hurdles, but *Awful Disclosures* does find a significant pitfall in pregnancy. The resemblance of the two works, however, moves far beyond the birth narrative.

Maria Monk's *Awful Disclosures* begins in Victorian gentility, assuring readers that though the acts of the portrayed Catholics are vile, "the virtuous reader need not fear."[4] Monk promises to be discreet. She first describes her early childhood and the varieties of nunnery in Montreal. The group with which she would eventually be involved was the Black Nunnery.

Though the name serves to conjure illusions of evil, "black" was simply the color of the nuns' robes. Monk came from a nominally Protestant, relatively irreligious family, though she attended religious schools. Unlike Rosemary, when Maria entered the convent, she was fully acquainted with the exhausting ritual of the building's religion.

"At length," wrote Monk, "I determined to become a Black nun." After inquiries were made, Maria was accepted into the convent as a novice. With no individual rooms, she was afforded no privacy. She spent her days learning the rituals required of her, but soon she grew tired of the nun's life and left her novitiate behind. After a disappointing life outside the cope of the church, including a hasty marriage, Maria paid her way back into the nunnery with money stolen from her mother and loaned from her friends. She was surprised upon her return to find that "great dislike to the Bible was shown by those who conversed with me about it." She persevered, however, and took the veil in a ceremony that required her to lie in a coffin on the altar of the church. After the haunting ceremony, her Mother Superior informed her, "One of my great duties was to obey the priests in all things; and this I soon learnt, to my utter astonishment and horror, was to live in the practice of criminal intercourse with them."[5]

The priests reassured her that doubts were the enemies of all properly devout Catholics. And yes, they also told her, sometimes infants are born. "But they were always baptized and immediately strangled! This secured their everlasting happiness."[6] Monk estimated that hundreds of babies died during the time of her brief tenure in the Hotel Dieu.

Father Dufrésne was the first priest to rape Maria, but rape, she soon discovered, was a regular—near daily—event at the Hotel Dieu. The emphasis on regimentation as a purifying element spread to even the less pure of the nunnery's activities. Lying to the relatives of novices also became commonplace, and Maria's doubt was met with a priest's approbation: "What, a nun of your age, and not know the difference between a wicked and religious lie!" What was good for the Catholic church was good for God. The priests, in fact, wielded unbridled power: "They often told me they had the power to strike me dead at any moment."[7] Priests even used confessions as staging grounds for rape, once raping a fourteen-year-old girl to death.

The supposed Catholic hatred of Protestants remains a refrain throughout Monk's narrative. At one point in the narrative, Maria is even told not to pray for Protestants. She notes that the Protestant Bible was considered throughout the convent as a dangerous book. The story even circulated among the nuns that a priest refused to help quell a city fire until it threatened Catholic neighborhoods. Similar stories constantly filled the nunnery. Murders and rumors of murders hid behind every corner, but Maria soon gave empirical evidence, describing her forced participation in the suffocation of a fellow nun as punishment for disobedience. Along with murder, infanticide, and rape, Monk also accused the convent of keeping a makeshift prison in a dark, near-deserted basement below the Hotel Dieu.

As if this were not enough, penances for mundane offenses were particularly exaggerated. Kissing the floor was common, as was consuming meals with a rope tied round the neck of the penitent. Nuns drank the water used to wash the feet of the Mother Superior. They branded themselves with hot irons, they whipped themselves, they stood in a crucifixion pose for extended periods of time.[8]

Monk also emphasizes the building itself and its dark corridors as a principal character in the horrific drama. After learning the Hotel Dieu's floorplan as best she could, Maria decided to escape, maneuvering her way through the labyrinthine corridors into a world free of the evils of Catholicism, on to New York, where freedom-loving Americans guarded against the papist menace.

More than a century later, in the same town, the fictional Rosemary Woodhouse hoped that she and her husband Guy would be approved for residency in the exclusive Bramford apartment building. After inquiries were made, Rosemary and Guy were accepted into the building as residents. Her friend and surrogate father, Edward Hutchins, disapproved. He told the couple stories of bizarre deaths, ritual murder, cannibalism, witchcraft, and satanic ceremony. Hutchins, known to Rosemary as "Hutch," described the life of Adrian Marcato, an 1890s witch who claimed to have conjured Satan. The Bramford was "a kind of rallying place for people who are more prone than others to certain types of behavior," Hutch argued. "Or perhaps there are things we don't know yet—about magnetic fields or electrons or whatever—ways in which a place can quite literally be malign."[9] Like the

Hotel Dieu, the Bramford apartment building is itself a central character in Levin's narrative. Its dark hallways, mysterious residents, and secret passages loom over Rosemary's long pregnancy. Though the author never explores the connection further, Hutch tells the couple that the church next door owns the old Victorian building, inherently implying that church apathy contributes to the dark doings inside.

Rosemary's alienation in the old building is relieved initially in a way Maria's never is—she does her laundry with Terry Gionoffrio, a drug addict and prostitute taken in by Roman and Minnie Castavet, the couple living in the apartment adjacent to the Woodhouse's on the seventh floor. Terry wears a charm around her neck filled with foul-smelling "tannis root," given to her as a gift by her new surrogate family. The relationship is brief, however, as Terry commits suicide later that week—a tragedy that leads to Rosemary and Guy's own acquaintance with the Castavets. Consolation leads to gratitude, which leads to a dinner and a secret conversation between Roman and Guy. Though Rosemary and her readers do not discover the scope of the conversation until the novel's conclusion, Roman lures Guy into a Satanic quid pro quo—Rosemary's womb for Guy's professional acting success.

Ritual is paramount in the Bramford as it is in the Hotel Dieu, and the Woodhouses wryly comment on the bizarre chanting coming from the Castavet's next-door apartment. Although rituals constitute Maria's torment in *Awful Disclosures*, it is the secrecy surrounding them that constitutes Rosemary's. And whereas Maria is raped by priest after priest, Rosemary is raped by the devil himself. Even this traumatic event is shrouded in secrecy, as a drugged chocolate mousse kept Rosemary drifting tenuously in and out of consciousness through the entire ordeal. Meanwhile, Guy's acting career begins to flourish as his chief rival for a major part inexplicably goes blind.

While *Awful Disclosures* catalogues the various atrocities in the Hotel Dieu, *Rosemary's Baby* allows Rosemary and the reader to construct the possible scenarios of evil hidden behind the compulsions of her husband and neighbors. When Hutch finds even more evidence for treachery amongst the Bramford, he immediately falls into the clutches of an unexplained coma. And, Hutch excepted, no one outside the hotel sees the evil hidden inside the corridors of the dark building. Monk emphasizes the same secrecy—the cloister of the imposing structure adding magnitude to the dark deeds perpetrated within its walls.

Chosen outsiders, however, are "in" on the plot. The Castevets urge Rosemary to replace her obstetrician with their own, Abraham Saperstein. "He delivers all the Society babies and he would deliver yours too if we asked him," Guy concurred, "[w]asn't he on *Open End* a couple of years ago?"[10] Saperstein, however, is party to the larger Satanic plan. Like the priests who come from all over Montreal to secretly partake in the rape of nuns, Saperstein continues a regular practice of helping others in his daily life, but spends his spare time at the Bramford, participating in the ritual and ensuring that Rosemary's pregnancy continues according to the Castevets' plan.

The smell of the "tannis root" gives him away. Eventually—using the tannis root and a methodical piecing together of available clues—Rosemary uncovers the entire plot, including Saperstein's participation, and decides to escape. Her attempt, however, is not as successful as Maria's. Though her range of motion extends beyond the confines of her building, Rosemary is still unable to escape. She makes contact with her former obstetrician, who feigns sympathy before turning her over to her husband and Saperstein. Like Maria's Dr. Nelson, who volunteers at the charity hospital, Rosemary's doctor does not believe in the evil-doings surrounding her because he has no reason. "We're going to go home and rest," Saperstein told his fellow doctor. Rosemary's unwitting betrayer smiled. "That's all it takes, nine times out of ten."[11]

Soon after Rosemary returns to the Bramford, she goes into labor. When she awakes from sedation, the Bramford residents give her the sad news that her baby, a boy, died soon after birth. The group takes Rosemary's milk daily and claims to throw it away. She soon discovers the plot, however, and makes her way through a secret passage (again the treachery of the building itself) into the Castevets' apartment, where her baby—the son of Satan—is resting in a black bassinet. Satanist tourists from all over the world are present, fawning over her son and taking pictures. Though Rosemary never acknowledges the hold of the Satanists over her child, she finds joy in her son, regardless of whether his eyes are the yellow eyes of the devil or not.

The stories are very similar, and the heroines of each narrative experience surprisingly similar circumstances. But Maria Monk could never have been supplicant in the hands of Satanists. Her feigned Victorian gentility could not even allow her to describe her sexual encounters with priests. In presenting herself as a victim because she was a proper lady—it was, after all, her dignity as a female that made these crimes so heinous—Monk's narrative takes a romantic tone to emphasize that her heroine (herself) was, in fact, a lady. Further, Satanists were virtually unheard of in nineteenth-century America, and certainly posed less of a threat to the average reader of popular literature than did Catholics. Similarly, Rosemary Woodhouse could never have been supplicant in the hands of infanticidal, rapist Catholics. American culture's political correctness would never have allowed such a book to become a bestseller. During the Cold War, Catholics were fellow Christians and Christians were the last line of defense against the atheistic communist menace. Americans were encouraged to hate and fear communism, but economic theories are often obtuse and do not properly permeate the popular mind. The Soviet rejection of religion as counterproductive to a communist society, however, was an act that every Christian American could understand and fear, thus uniting them in their status as believers.

The Protestantism following the American Revolution was a liberal, tolerant Protestantism, flush with the ideals of the new nation, but its welcoming spirit did not last. Immigration did its part, particularly Irish Catholic immigration, as Europeans sought jobs created by the growth of cities in the New World. In the 1820s, America's fastest-growing city was Rochester, New York, a product of the Erie Canal, completed in 1825. A transportation revolution brought roads and railroads along with the canal, and upstate New York became a vital center in the new United States. Paul Johnson argued in *A Shopkeeper's Millennium* that the religious revivals that followed this growth were the result of the tumult brought by economic change.[12] More likely, however, the economic growth of the region and the religious revivalism that swept through the area fed off one another in a reciprocal relationship that sustained both.

Either way, the resulting religious fervor set the region "on fire" for God, creating what historians now understand as the "burned over district" of upstate New York. The leader of this Second Great Awakening was Charles Grandison Finney, a former lawyer who modernized the revival experience by creating a formula for the salvation of souls. Finney argued that certain tactics could be employed to convince someone of his own iniquity and need for God's grace. He prayed for people in his audience by name, he created an "anxious seat" whereby people who needed a salvation experience could sit, with the audience looking on, and find saving grace. His tactics worked. Finney's success and the broader American acceptance of the evangelical principles of the Second Great Awakening made fundamentalist Protestantism the standard by which all other faiths were judged. And Catholicism was far from fundamentalist Protestantism.[13]

The emphasis on fundamentalist Protestantism grew into strong anti-Catholicism, and the first anti-Catholic newspaper, *The Protestant*, appeared in 1830. Four years later, prompted by an escaped novice who told of unspeakable acts of Catholic treachery, much as Monk would do, a Boston mob stormed the Ursuline Convent and burned it down.[14] Not surprisingly, anti-Catholic secret societies and religious groups became commonplace. In the early 1850s, two of those secret societies, The Order of the Star-Spangled Banner and the Order of United Americans, joined together to form a larger political body. Members, sworn to secrecy, were told to reply "I know nothing" to queries. Thus, the Know-Nothing Party began, and grew to more than one million members by 1854. This anti-Catholic sentiment was rampant throughout the antebellum period, and Monk's tale is one of many similar, though less popular, stories of Catholic debauchery. Susan Griffin argues that American nativism gave authors a "cultural shorthand" for depicting Catholic characters, allowing these popular melodramas—all presented as exposés rather than fictions—to flourish.[15]

As the nineteenth century became the twentieth, however, religious belief became more important than the specific church in which it appeared. From 1926 to 1950, church membership increased at over twice the rate of the national population growth. In 1953, ninety-five percent of Americans claimed to be Protestant, Catholic, or Jewish. The following year, ninety-six percent of Americans claimed to believe in God, and in 1957, ninety percent of the population believed that Jesus was divine. Sunday School enrollment increased markedly in the 1950s, as did new church construction, and a majority of citizens clearly identified an increasingly important role for religion in their lives. In 1958, almost 110 million Americans held religious affiliations, compared to eighty-five million in 1950. In such a climate, those who do not believe at all are far more dangerous than people who simply believe differently.[16]

In 1954, the US Congress added the phrase "under God" to the Pledge of Allegiance. The bill passed unopposed. In 1955, the body added the slogan "In God We Trust" to American currency. The following year, "In God We Trust" became the official national motto. Throughout the decade, the House Un-American Activities Committee investigated potential communists. One of the tell-tale signs of a communist was a lack of religion. The Soviet Union was the new great enemy after the fall of Nazi Germany, and though most average Americans could not specifically identify the specific "evil" in Russian economics, they could find fault in a nation professing atheism.[17] As a counterbalance, evangelists and politicians publicized American religion as the first line of defense against communism. Christianity was Christianity, whether Catholic or Protestant. At least it was not atheism (read: communism).

In 1960, seven years prior to the publication of *Rosemary's Baby*, Americans elected a Catholic president, John F. Kennedy. Though the evidence must necessarily remain circumstantial, it is unlikely they would have elected an atheist, much less a Satanist. They never have. Just as a Catholic president would be unthinkable in an era when the anti-Catholic Know-Nothing party garnered over one million members, an atheist or agnostic candidate could never proclaim himself (or herself) to be representative of the US constituency. Though Rosemary Woodhouse was born a Catholic, she had renounced her faith for the agnosticism of her husband, and both ridicule religious faith throughout the first chapters of *Rosemary's Baby*. Thus, Congress asserted from the halls of government that atheism leads to communism, and Levin elaborated on the proposition by portraying atheism as leading directly to the devil himself.

In 1963, Lee Harvey Oswald assassinated America's only Catholic president. Significantly, however, it was communism, not Catholicism, that prompted the murder. That same year, the Supreme Court removed public prayer and Bible reading from public schools, a decision that prompted outrage throughout the nation.[18] Madalyn Murray, the petitioner in the case, became a target of American resentment following her victory, suffering the murder of her cat and graffiti accusing her of communism. Vandals inflicted severe property damage and threatened her family with death. She received threatening correspondence from across the nation. "You filthy atheist," wrote one disgruntled citizen, "[o]nly a rat like you would go to court to stop prayer. All curses on you and your family. Bad luck and leprosy disease upon you and your damn family." "Lady," said another, "you are as deadly to our city as a snake. Return to Russia. (Signed) A True Believer in our God who gave you the air you breathe." Finally, direct death threats also emanated from Murray's mailbox: "You will repent, and damn soon a .30-30 (rifle bullet) will fix you nuts. You will have bad luck forever. You atheist, you mongrel, you rat, you good for nothing s__, you damn gutter rat. Jesus will fix you, you filthy scum."[19]

Still, what this reaction should demonstrate is the general consensus that Catholicism was no longer the problem. While Rosemary Woodhouse sat in Abe Saperstein's obstetrical office, she read a *Time* magazine, the cover of which asked "Is God Dead?" Though Rosemary's story was fiction, the issue of *Time* was real. The cover story offered a relatively elementary summation of Christian atheism and wondered about the existential crisis of American faith. "Belief," it quoted University of Chicago theologian Langdon Gilkey as saying, "is the area in the modern Protestant church where one finds blankness, silence, people not knowing what to say or merely repeating what their preachers say."[20] Though Gilkey describes Protestants, the article quotes Protestants and Catholics throughout under the broader description of "Christian." Jo Agnew McManis noted soon after the novel's publication, "Levin has made us believe, at least for the moment, in witches."[21] If all else fails, she seems to be saying, remember that it is a novel. Unlike Monk's tale, readers need not be afraid when the book is finally concluded.

Literary scholar Robert Lima noted that the period was one "of ecumenical realignment." He describes the Castavets as Satanists spurred to action by debates such as that in *Time* magazine. Just as Rosemary's religious uncertainty led her down a path of unrighteousness, society's uncertainty about its true religious state leads to works like Levin's.[22] That uncertainty, however, was a function of social progress. The hardened certainty of the 1830s led to the hatred and demonization of Catholics, and thus to the exponential sales of works such as Maria Monk's *Awful Disclosures*. By the 1960s, the hardened certainty against American believers, whatever their belief, had dissipated. As a result, Levin's *Rosemary's Baby* saved its demonization for demons themselves, a far less destructive target for the maintenance of stable society.

A stable society was just what the United States felt it needed in the face of the communist threat. The strong anticommunist stance of the Catholic Church ensured that it would not be categorically included with the possible "enemy within." Thus, a faux-nonfiction account of the murderous, perverted tendencies of Catholics would never have been welcomed by a Christian community united against the communist monolith, but it became the second bestselling book of the nineteenth century. A fictitious account of the birth of Satan's son, which would never have eluded the Victorian gentile sensibilities of an antebellum editor, became a 1967 bestseller. Both found success because they responded to the contemporary American religious culture that surrounded them.

As Rosemary fiddled with her Scrabble tiles, trying desperately to make *All of Them Witches* into clues, her baby began kicking inside her. "You're going to be a born Scrabble-player, she thought."[23] Some of her frustrated attempts at anagrams were "comes with the fall," "who shall meet it," and "we that chose ill"—three phrases that Maria Monk, 131 years prior, would have understood all too well.

Notes

1. Jenny Franchot, *Roads to Rome: Antebellum Protestant Encounter with Catholicism* (Berkeley: University of California Press, 1994), 160–161.

2. Ray Allen Billington, "Maria Monk and Her Influences," *Catholic Historical Review* 22 (October 1936): 286, 296.

3. Lucy Fischer, "Birth Traumas: Parturition and Horror in *Rosemary's Baby*," *Cinema Journal* 31 (Spring 1992): 4.

4. Maria Monk, *Awful Disclosures of Maria Monk, or, The Hidden Secrets of a Nun's Life in a Convent Exposed* (London: The Camden Publishing Co., Ltd., 1836), 4.

5. Ibid, 23, 39, 47.

6. Ibid, 49.

7. Ibid, 71, 78.

8. Ibid, 175–179.

9. Ira Levin, *Rosemary's Baby* (New York: Signet, 1997; originally published 1967), 27.

10. Ibid, 139.

11. Ibid, 266–267.

12. Paul E. Johnson, *A Shopkeeper's Millennium: Society and Revivals in Rochester, New York, 1815–1837* (New York: Hill and Wang, 1979), 15–18.

13. Charles E. Hambrick-Stowe, *Charles G. Finney and the Spirit of American Evangelicalism* (Grand Rapids, MI: Eerdmans Publishing, 1996), 103–104; and Ray Allen Billington, *The Protestant Crusade: 1800–1860* (Chicago: Quadrangle Books, 1964; originally published 1938), 41–42.

14. Reuben Maury, *Wars of the Godly* (New York: Robert M. McBride and Co., 1928), 53–54.

15. Susan M. Griffin, *Anti-Catholicism in Nineteenth-Century Fiction* (Cambridge: Cambridge University Press, 2004), 17.

16. George H. Gallup, ed., *The Gallup Poll: Public Opinion, 1935–1971*, vol. 2, *1949–1958* (New York: Random House, 1972), 1293, 1481, 1482.

17. Richard M. Fried, *Nightmare In Red: The McCarthy Era in Perspective* (New York: Oxford University Press, 1990), 9.

18. *School District of Abington Township v. Schempp*. 374 US 203 (1963).

19. Jane Howard, "The Most Hated Woman in America," *Life*, 19 June 1964: 92.

20. "Toward a Hidden God," *Time* 8 April 1966: 83.

21. Jo Agnew McManis, "*Rosemary's Baby*: A Unique Combination of Faust, Leda, and 'The Second Coming,'" *McNeese Review* 20 (1971–1972): 36.

22. Robert Lima, "The Satanic Rape of Catholicism in *Rosemary's Baby*," *Studies in American Fiction* 2 (Autumn 1974): 215.

23. Levin, *Rosemary's Baby*, 221.

The Man Plague
Disco, the Lucifer Myth, and the Theology of "It's Raining Men"

To determine the nature and function of the Devil, is no contemptible province of the European Mythology. Who, or what he is, his origin, his habitation, his destiny, and his power, are subjects which puzzle the most acute Theologians, and on which no orthodox person can be induced to give a decisive opinion. He is the weak place of the popular religion—the vulnerable belly of the crocodile.[1]

—Percy Bysshe Shelley, 1819

Tonight for the first time, at just about half past ten—for the first time in history—it's gonna start raining men.

—The Weather Girls, 1982

I n the 1970s and early 1980s, American disco clubs proved to be the vulnerable belly of the crocodile. New York City was in turmoil at the onset of the 1970s. From 1966 to 1973, the city's murder rate rose 173 percent. There was a growing bureaucracy and steadily decreasing social services. The city had a three-billion dollar budget deficit by 1975. Gang violence and race agitation threatened middle class whites who often

Thomas Aiello, "The Man Plague: Disco, the Lucifer Myth, and the Theology of 'It's Raining Men,'" *The Journal of Popular Culture*, vol. 43, issue 5, pp. 926–941. Copyright © 2010 by John Wiley & Sons, Inc. Reprinted with permission.

expressed their fear by absconding to the suburbs. But others found a more esoteric form of escape. Disco was a function of "baroque indulgence" in the face of this overwhelming social and economic breakdown.[2] Indiscriminate sex, heavy drug use, dancing, and drinking all served as a form of motivated escapism—a sort of protest through studied nonchalance that girded its acolytes against the decay that grew around them. They responded to the moral degeneracy of Babylon not by knocking down the tower, but instead by building it higher, higher, higher.

And so disco began in the dance clubs of New York City as the 1960s slowly became the 1970s (though historian Peter Shapiro traces its cultural roots back to Nazi-occupied Paris during World War II, where a thriving jazz and dance culture would give way in the postwar period to clubs such as the Whiskey à Go-Go. This celebratory spirit would cross the Atlantic, where it would combine with the rock-and-roll dance and drug culture, setting the stage for the development of what would become disco).[3] As the 1970s progressed, it spread throughout the country, finding corresponding West Coast homes in the nightclubs of Los Angeles and San Francisco. By 1982, disco was at its low ebb, but the style and energy of the music had made its way into the broader popular music scene. That year, an unlikely hit made the transition from San Francisco dance clubs to the American mainstream:

Hi, we're your weather girls.
And have we got news for you.
You'd better listen.
Get ready, all you lonely girls,
And leave those umbrellas at home.

The humidity's rising,
The barometer's getting low.
According to all sources,
The street's the place to go.

'Cause tonight for the first time,
Just about half past ten,

For the first time in history,
It's gonna start raining men.

It's raining men.
Hallelujah! It's raining men.
Amen!
I'm gonna go out,
I'm gonna let myself get
Absolutely soaking wet.

It's raining men.
Hallelujah! It's raining men,
Every specimen:
Tall, blond, dark and lean,
Rough and tough and strong and mean.

God bless Mother Nature,
She's a single woman, too.
She took from the heaven,
And she did what she had to do.
She bought ev'ry angel.
She rearranged the sky
So that each and ev'ry woman
Could find the perfect guy.[4]

"It's Raining Men" was fun. It was popular. But it provided its listeners, whether wittingly or unwittingly, with stark and disturbing religious imagery rooted in the historical tradition of Christian theology. It was, through the hustles and shakes, the lights and mirrors, a radical reinterpretation of the Lucifer myth.

§

Izora Rhodes was considered a musical prodigy from an early age, and her young talent led from a religious childhood in Texas to the San Francisco Conservatory. It was there, in the mid-1970s, that Rhodes met San Francisco native Martha Wash while both were singing in the gospel group News of the World (NOW).[5]

After their stint with NOW, the women took a very different musical direction, turning to San Francisco's popular disco scene and the flamboyant performer Sylvester. As accompanists for the singer, Rhodes and Wash lent backing vocals to Sylvester's gold album *Step II* and garnered critical acclaim for their sound and ability.[6]

Sylvester James had, like Rhodes and Wash, also come from a religious family (his from Los Angeles) and began his career by singing in a traveling gospel choir as a child. But he gave it up in his teens, following the compulsions of his rebellion to San Francisco, where he developed careers as a drag queen and disco performer. After playing with various Bay Area bands, Sylvester (as he had taken to calling himself, dropping his last name in a common display of androgynous popular bravado) was "discovered" by Motown producer Harvey Fuqua, who helped the singer cull a professional band and signed him to the Fantasy Records label.[7]

Fuqua had worked with Marvin Gaye in Detroit before coming west, and when he arrived, Sylvester was not the only talent he discovered. The producer moved Rhodes and Wash from NOW to the disco singer's house band, where they found immediate success—success that seemed immanently translatable to a starring role. So Fuqua moved them again, recording Rhodes and Wash, both excessively obese, as Two Tons of Fun in 1979. After two relatively marginal albums, the duo then moved to Columbia records and renamed themselves the Weather Girls. It was there at Columbia where the two teamed with producer Paul Jabara.[8]

Jabara began his career as an actor, performing in the original Broadway cast of *Hair* before moving on to movies and television. He also wrote and performed music, earning Grammy and Academy Awards in 1978 for his song "Last Dance." When Jabara met with the Weather Girls, he pitched them a new song he co-wrote with Paul Shaffer.[9]

From the small, isolated town of Thunder Bay, Ontario, Shaffer had come to New York in 1974. The following year, he began playing piano and keyboards for Saturday Night Live, leading to guest spots on the show and side projects with members of the cast—most notably serving as musical director for Dan Aykroyd's and John Belushi's Blues Brothers tour.[10] But he was also a songwriter, and together with Jabara, Shaffer crafted a seemingly lighthearted dance number using rain as a trope for the virtually limitless availability of perfect, single men. Barbara Streisand had turned down the opportunity to perform the song. So too had Donna Summer. But the Weather Girls were in no position to reject songs composed by a Grammy-winning songwriter. They accepted Jabara's offer, and in September 1982, Columbia released "It's Raining Men."[11] The song was nominated for a Grammy Award. It topped the United States disco charts and reached number forty-six on Billboard's Hot 100. But the Weather Girls were never able to capitalize on the song's success, producing a string of relatively lackluster follow-ups throughout the 1980s.[12]

Such do not seem the conditions to foster the authorial impetus for a fictional takeover of heaven. But that they were. "God bless Mother Nature," the Weather Girls sang. "She's a single woman, too. She took from the heaven, and she did what she had to do. She bought ev'ry angel. She rearranged the sky so that each and ev'ry woman could find the perfect guy." The song describes the takeover of heaven by Mother Nature, who bribes angels in a revolt against the ordained regularity of God's creation, all in an attempt to change water into eligible men. The radicalism of the story certainly veers from the canned, mundane lyrics of most American popular music, but the subtlety of the message and the celebratory attitude surrounding the celestial coup have generally kept that radicalism hidden. Of course, they have also made the message all the more radical.

Both Izora Rhodes and Martha Wash came from religious backgrounds. Neither Paul Jabara nor Paul Shaffer have demonstrated religious axes to grind in their other songs. There is little evidence that either the authors or singers intended sacrilege. But popular culture is created by the public reception of authorial messages, not the intent of individual authors. Listeners, readers, and watchers create the meaning, validation, and emotional impact of artistic work. When authorial content enters the public domain, authorial intent becomes meaningless. "It's Raining Men" is no different. Though Jabara and Shaffer's lyrics tell the story as listed above, listeners—driving in their cars, dancing in a nightclub, cloistered away through personal headphones—don't have access to formal, written lyrics. They interpret lyrics through the mediation of the singers. And their interpretations reveal a far darker portrayal of this battle. Internet lyrics sites depict the song in two different manners, each fundamentally changing the message of the original.

> God bless Mother Nature, she's a single woman too
> She took on the heavens, and she did what she had to do
> She fought every angel, she rearranged the sky
> So that each and every woman, could find the perfect guy[13]

This version presents an even more radical story of the holy war. Mother Nature, in sympathy with her gender to the detriment of her affiliation as a supreme being, doesn't "take off from the heaven." In this instance, she is far more active, "taking on" heaven, attacking the full panoply of heaven's defenders. There is no conniving here. No bribery. This version is far more visceral, as violence becomes the principal mode of achieving her ends. Still another reinterpretation of the lyrics changes the story yet again.

> God bless Mother Nature, she's a single woman too
> She took off to heaven and she did what she had to do
> She taught every angel to rearrange the sky
> So that each and every woman could find her perfect guy[14]

Here again Mother Nature is far more active, more atavistic than she is in the original story. She "takes off" to heaven, demonstrating a sense of urgency that doesn't necessarily belie violence. She neither fights nor bribes the angels. In this instance, she teaches the angels to do her bidding, which at the very least leaves open the possibility that she has God's support in the endeavor. This doesn't seem likely, considering the full panoply of examples demonstrating God's unwillingness to have his divine plan questioned or challenged. Still, the relatively mild connotations of "teaching," along with the prefix of "God bless Mother Nature," at least extend the possibility. But "God bless Mother Nature" begins each of the quatrains, and seems to serve in this role as a colloquial phrase of approval, a dodge against the more sinister actions that follow. He makes no other appearances, either before or after the heavenly war passage. Despite the quatrain's opening, this is still an act of seemingly unprovoked aggression.

The next point of significance surrounding the passage—in all of its forms—is its celebratory tone. The Weather Girls announce the event as historic, using religious language—Hallelujah!—to express their approval. The passage does not have a first-person narrator, but the third-person narrator clearly sees Mother Nature as the protagonist of the story, sees the coup as beneficial. And the narrator does find the possibility of the takeover personally gratifying. "I'm going to go out," she sings. "I'm going to let myself get absolutely soaking wet." Inherent in this triumphalism of two women singing about the success of Mother Nature against the traditional role of heavenly hosts is a critique of the historical sexism of the Bible, its theological interpretations, and practical consequences. A woman is taking over the understood role of men, in aid of offering God's female creations something he has not adequately provided them. And so the song is not simply revolutionary in its use of violence. It demonstrates an inherent critique of Judeo-Christian dogma as it applies to gender relations—a functional denunciation of the Bible's treatment of women. "Every vow," proclaims the book of Numbers, "and every binding oath to afflict the soul, her husband may establish it, or her husband may make it void."[15] Here that decree has been reversed. "It's Raining Men" presents a vision of women being independent, using their power to create a virtual upper hand in negotiations with men. Men are being created for the pleasure of women, created by a woman to serve as functional dependents for those who have traditionally been seen as subservient.

This is a complete reversal of the portrayal of women as pulled from Adam's rib—a reversal that can only come through revolution. And that revolution can only come through implicit or explicit violence. Mother Nature, then, in her role as antagonist of God (whatever her motive), becomes a stand-in for Lucifer in biblical and literary reinventions of the war for heaven and the Satanic fall from grace.

But before the Devil appeared at the disco, the attempted takeover of heaven—by Lucifer or Satan or both—had a much longer, much less successful history. Lucifer and Satan, in fact, are not represented as the same entity in the Christian Bible.[16] In the Old Testament book of Isaiah, the prophet compares the glutinous, overindulgent king of Babylon to Lucifer, translated in different texts as "morning star," "day star," or "light-bearer." In the Isaiah chronicle, Lucifer is cast from heaven for feigning to exalt his throne above that of God and is punished by being cast into hell.[17] The story of God's holy war with Satan comes in the New Testament, when Jesus notes his witness to Satan's fall from heaven (Luke 10:18) and when John gives a more explicit account of the heavenly war that resulted in such a fall. John's version provides no analysis of the motives behind the battle, but portrays the contest as a fight between two sets of angels, led on the virtuous side by the Archangel Michael and on the evil side by Satan.[18] It would be Saint Anselm, archbishop of Canterbury (1034–1093) who initiated the popular conflation of the two entities as one and the same.[19]

In every version of the heavenly war story—conflation, fiction, or otherwise—the Devil marshals a force of angels and battles another group of angels, defending the throne and honor of God. He loses and is cast down from heaven. In almost all accounts, whether the Devil is the aggressor or defending himself against a vengeful God, the impetus for the split is pride, noted in Proverbs to bring destruction.[20] Some early interpretations place the event before the creation of man, with Lucifer's refusal to bow before God's throne sparking Michael's vengeance, and thus war. But the Talmud moved the story forward, arguing that the Devil's rivalry wasn't with God, but with man. After Adam, God had a new favorite, and the angels were required to bow to God's most favored creation. Satan refused (his vanity now pointed in a new direction) and God threw him out of heaven. The Qur'an, too, places man at the heart of the contest, when Iblis refused to worship Allah's new creation and thus was thrust from the sky.[21]

The concept of heavenly war, whatever its genesis, highlights one of the principal theological paradoxes of every monotheistic religion: a holy, omniscient, all-powerful creator God presides over a creation in which evil is present. But if God is holy, omniscient, and all-powerful, then evil cannot exist. Its presence is a functional nullification of the monotheistic God concept.

The paradox could be solved by eliminating God's pure holiness, his omniscience, or both, but most theologians under the cope of the popular monotheistic religions (Christianity, Judaism, Islam) tend to accept holiness and omniscience as *a priori* and instead attempt a maneuver around the evil paradox. Evil, in this formulation, could be a means toward the greater good. It could be the state of non-being (which is, in the final analysis, a semantic cop out following the assumption that being itself, when experienced under the watchful eye of a holy, omniscient creator, must be good; anything not good, therefore, does not functionally exist). Evil, since it creates suffering, could be a method of punishing humans for their sins, perhaps for teaching them lessons. But the most common maneuver around the evil paradox comes from Augustine.[22]

Augustine argued that goodness cannot exist without choice, so God created sentient beings with the ability to choose properly. Value statements about states of being such as "good" or "evil" are meaningless—impossible, in fact—without intentionality. (That said, intentionality can only go so far. It doesn't, for example, solve the problem of an omnipotent God, as omnipotence carries within it the ability to know the outcome of each intentional moral choice by every created being.) So God created angels. And Augustine's angels were just as fallible as humans. Many fell to solipsism. And though Augustine's angels didn't attack, didn't storm the gates of heaven, they did love themselves more than they loved God, causing their fall from grace. Humans, then, were God's second attempt (again leaving omnipotence to twist in the wind).[23]

The historical Devil has taken a number of different narrative forms. He has been the fallen angel—the Frankenstein's monster—the creation of God that turned on his master. But he has also been portrayed as an entity completely independent of God (an effort to eliminate the holy omnipotent creator paradox; God can't be blamed for creating evil if He didn't create it, can't be blamed for allowing evil if there is an element of the cosmos over which He doesn't have dominion). Similarly, the Devil has also been described not as a physical entity, but rather as a symbol of human evil or fallibility. This conception is, more than anything else, a new point of entry for the Augustinian free will argument. Humans failed a test, and God gave that failure a name.[24]

But in the legend of the fall, the Devil is always the one who fails. And that failure has been interpreted by hundreds of writers through tens of centuries.[25] The first significant non-biblical account of the fall came from the Carthaginian Blossius Aemilius Dracontius in his fifth century *De laudibus Dei*, followed by the early English poet Caedmon in the seventh century. Dutch playwright Hugo Grotius published *Adamus exul* in 1601 and Joost van den Vondel published his own version, *Lucifer*, in 1654. Poets Jacob Cats, Andrew Ramsay, Alvares de Azevedo, Luis de Camoens, Guillaume de Salluste Du Bartas, and Phineas Fletcher all covered the story in verse from the sixteenth to the nineteenth centuries. Lord Byron, Percy Shelley, James Thomson, Charles Swinburne, and George Du Maurier did, as well. From Freidrich Leopold Stolberg's *Jamben* (1783) to Giosue Carducci's *Inno a Satana* (1863), from August Strindberg's *Lucifer or God* (1877) to Richard Dehmel's *Lucifer* (1899), authors have struggled to make sense of the fight, to blur the lines in the sand between good and evil in an effort to see the Devil's point of view. In the twentieth century, novelist Anatole France published his satirical novel *Revolt of the Angels* (1914), using the Lucifer myth as an allegory of French politics, reviving interest in the fall as a topic of popular debate.[26] For all of these accounts, however, the most influential treatment of heavenly war came from John Milton's *Paradise Lost* (1667–1674).

In Milton's hands, the image of the Devil functionally changes. No longer is he purely evil, purely vile. Milton's Devil has the vanity of the biblical story, but he is a fully-drawn character with a sharp intellect and a reasoned mind about his station in the heavenly hierarchy. He knows from the beginning of his quest that the project is doomed, but he fights anyway, led by—however misguided it might be—principle. In Milton's hands, the Devil becomes a sympathetic character, distraught at his fall not solely for his own selfish ends, but sincerely empathetic towards those angels who fall with him and compassionate towards man, whom he has doomed in the endeavor:

To mortal men, he with his horrid crew
Lay vanquisht, rolling in the fiery Gulf
Confounded though immortal: But his doom
Reserv'd him to more wrath; for now the thought
Both of lost happiness and lasting pain
Torments him; round he throws his baleful eyes
That witness'd huge affliction and dismay
Mixt with obdúrate pride and steadfast hate.[27]

But though there is in Milton the most effective presentation of sympathy for the Devil, his is ultimately a Christian-inspired text. The Devil is, for all of his narrative wholeness, the bad guy, and Milton is careful to remind his reader that the war was ill-conceived and destructive. *Paradise Lost* is not a celebration of heavenly war. Through the luster of baroque prose, a firm denunciation of the Satanic act remains paramount. When Jesus dies on the cross, for example, He "shall bruise the head of Satan, crush his strength/Defeating Sin and Death, his two main arms."[28]

"It's Raining Men" seems an unlikely descendent of this literary evolutionary line, and it differs from its forebears in two principal regards: authorial and demonic intent. Isaiah, John, and Milton all sought to further the Judeo-Christian project with the legend of the fall. It was, ultimately, a morality play demonstrating the insidiousness of pride and the eventual triumph of good over evil. Therefore, they seem to be saying, it would behoove any reader to choose the side of good, if for no other reason than its eventual, inevitable victory. The Weather Girls, however, don't leave listeners with the onus to choose sides. Mother Nature is no one to be feared, and God is caricatured through a common colloquialism. And if a listener does choose to side with one force or another, the song's celebratory tone really only leads her in one direction. Like Milton, the Weather Girls demonstrate a sympathy for the Devil (Mother Nature), but don't offer any of the Christian qualifications of their seventeenth-century counterpart. Their sympathy is grandiose, boisterous—and it comes as a culmination, a third act denouement rather than prefatory first act character development. While *Paradise Lost* leaves the reader ultimately lamenting the Devil's plight, "It's Raining Men" makes its listener openly root for God's opponent. It makes the argument that God was wrong in designating water as the core constituent of vapor condensation, that making eligible bachelors the rightful material to gather in clouds and fight against pressurized convection is the proper way of things.[29] Mother Nature is fixing God's error.

And so "It's Raining Men" is an argument against God's perfection and omnipotence. The Weather Girls do not base the imperfection of the world on human choice, however preordained. Good here is not defined through the necessary counter-presence of evil. Women do not make a conscious choice to turn away eligible men already available to them. They find the men God provides for them unsatisfactory, and thus celebrate Mother Nature's attempt to stand on their behalf. Here is the song's other principal difference with its forbears. Demonic intent is unselfish. Whereas pride always plays a role in previous recitations of heavenly war, "It's Raining Men" portrays a Lucifer-substitute acting out of concern for a group treated unfairly. The flaw in the combatants lies with God, not with the Devil, who makes a baroque, unselfish effort to buy, teach, or fight the host of angels, to stand as a representative of womankind on Earth. In *Paradise Lost*, angels stand with the Devil. In "It's Raining Men," the Devil stands with all of female humanity.

But it isn't the Devil. It's Mother Nature. And in the use of a demonic surrogate to precipitate (no pun intended) this heavenly conflict, the Weather Girls take their place among the authors seeking a way out of the aforementioned evil paradox. (Even though, as mentioned above, the song invalidates any omniscience claims with its condemnation of God as an unsatisfactory facilitator of women's needs. The importance of understanding the song's situation in relation to the evil paradox is not to find consistency in its overarching message. It is instead to gauge its relationship to those attempts that have come before it.) The presence of evil is a functional nullification of the monotheistic God concept of a holy, omniscient, and all-powerful creator. The Weather Girls work around the problem through a presentation of the Devil as a unique reinterpretation of one of those early historical narrative forms: they create a being completely independent of God. Mother Nature is an entity (or conglomeration of a series of entities) stemming from a variety of different polytheistic faiths.

There has never been room for a Mother Nature figure in the dominant monotheistic religions.[30] By using a counter-deity such as Mother Nature as a Devil-surrogate, "It's Raining Men" places God in contest with a section of the universe that isn't His. And God can't be blamed for creating evil if He didn't create it, can't be blamed for allowing evil if there is an element of the cosmos over which He doesn't have dominion.

§

And so, "It's Raining Men" participates in the long evolutionary line of religious and literary interpretations of the Lucifer myth. But it also remains at the tail end of another, less austere evolutionary line—disco. But rather than demonstrate a lyrical commonality with its musical counterparts, the song veers sharply, providing significant religious imagery in a genre that almost categorically shunned political, social, or theological messages. This was a culture of narcissism. Disco reveled in artifice, pomp, and superficiality as a salve against the broader, depressing culture outside the club doors.[31] It celebrated drugs, sex, and dancing as viable goals in-and-of themselves. Americans were "seeking escapism," noted a record executive in the late 1970s, "a respite, however fleetingly, from the seemingly insurmountable hassles of gasoline lines, high food bills, uncertainty about whether they will have enough heating oil to keep warm during the winter and the growing dilemma of trying to find and keep a roof over their heads."[32] In this escapism-as-politics culture, there was little room for meaningful, message-oriented lyrical content. Such content was, in fact, shunned as overbearing and ultimately beside the point.

In November 1975, for example, Silver Convention reached number one on the Billboard Hot 100 with their song, "Fly, Robin, Fly."

Fly, robin, fly
Fly, robin, fly
Fly, robin, fly
Up, up to the sky.[33]

The music was the message. The lyrical content was tertiary. In June of that year, the Bee Gees' "Jive Talkin'" reached Billboard's number one. In July, it was "The Hustle," by Van McCoy and the Soul City Symphony. From KC and the Sunshine Band's "Get Down Tonight," (1975) to Johnnie Taylor's "Disco Lady," (1976) from Gloria Gaynor to Donna Summer and beyond, disco artists purposely created a medium largely devoid of lyrical content. Of course, lack of content was the point.

And so the Weather Girls' "It's Raining Men" deviates from the established disco pattern. It is not part of a larger religious project among disco artists. It has no corollary among its contemporary peers. It managed instead to cordon off its own unique space in the twilight of a dying genre, depicting—however subtly—a revolutionary retelling of the Lucifer myth in the face of a discipline that encouraged apathy as an abiding mantra. The message, at least in this instance, was more than just the music. The Weather Girls gave a decisive opinion on the nature and function of the Devil. In so doing, they managed to find what Percy Shelley noted as "the weak place of the popular religion—the vulnerable belly of the crocodile."

Notes

1. Percy Bysshe Shelley, "Essay On the Devil and Devils," in *Shelley's Prose, or The Trumpet of a Prophecy*, ed. David Lee Clark (Albuquerque: The University of New Mexico Press, 1954), 264–265.

2. Peter Shapiro, *Turn the Beat Around: The Secret History of Disco* (New York: Faber and Faber, 2005), 4–13.

3. Shapiro, *Turn the Beat Around*, 15–30. Radcliffe Joe, an earlier chronicler, agrees with Shapiro's narrative, but gives far more weight to the development of the specific American dance evolution from the big bands of the 1920s through the birth of rock and roll. Both, however, see disco and dance music as a vital protest, albeit a narcissistic one—dance as a form of revolt against war, depression, or other crises. Radcliffe A. Joe, *This Business of Disco* (New York: Billboard, 1980), 12–21.

4. Paul Jabara and Paul Shaffer, "It's Raining Men," in *The Disco Collection*, published under license from Alfred Publishing Co., Inc., http://www.musicnotes.com, accessed 10 May 2008.

5. Pierre Perrone, "Obituary: Izora Rhodes-Armstead, Singer with the Weather Girls," *The Independent*, 27 September 2004, 35; and "Weather Girls," in *The New Encyclopedia of Rock and Roll*, eds. Patricia Romanowski and Holly George-Warren (New York: Rolling Stone Press, 1995), 1062.

6. Roberta Morgan, *Disco* (New York: Bell Publishing, 1979) 43; and "Fantasy Records," in *The Guinness Encyclopedia of Popular Music*, 2nd edition, vol. 2, *Clarke, Kenny-Gleason, Jackie*, ed. Colin Larkin (New York: Stockton Press, 1995), 1408.

7. Fantasy Records, founded by Max and Sol Weiss in 1949, had undergone many reinventions over the years. The label recorded jazz, poetry, comedy, and rock and roll. By the mid-1970s, Fantasy was also publishing popular music and disco. "Fantasy Records," 1408–1409.

8. Perrone, "Obituary," 35.

9. Claudette Jabara Hadad and Henry Hadad, "Biography," Olga Music, Inc. http://www.pauljabara.com/home.html, accessed 8 April 2008.

10. Eirik Knutzen, "Un-Hip, Un-Hip, Hurrah!" *The Toronto Star*, 27 June 1987, S16.

11. Bob Esty and Paul Jabara, producers, Colombia Records, catalog number 44 03181, 1982.

12. Perrone, "Obituary," 35.

13. "It's Raining Men," http://www.lyricsdownload.com/weather-girls-its-raining-men-lyrics.html, accessed 8 April 2008. This version is also used by http://www.lyrics4all.net/t/the-weather-girls/u/its-raining-men.php, accessed 8 April 2008.

14. "It's Raining Men," http://www.lyricscrawler.com/song/45692.html, accessed 8 April 2008.

15. Numbers 31:13.

16. The name "Satan" itself indicates its functional difference. The Hebrew *stn* and the Greek *diabolos* both translate as forces of opposition. So Satan himself can have no other function than that of an adversary. His existence is purely contingent upon the presence of an opponent, in this case God. Neil Forsyth, *The Old Enemy: Satan and the Combat Myth* (Princeton: Princeton University Press, 1987), 4.

17. "How art thou fallen from heaven, O Lucifer, son of the morning! How art thou cut down to the ground, which didst weaken the nations! For thou hast said in thine heart, I will ascend into heaven, I will exalt my throne above the stars of God: I will sit also upon the mount of the congregation, in the sides of the north: I will ascend above the heights of the clouds; I will be like the most High. Yet thou shalt be brought down to hell, to the sides of the pit." Isaiah 14:12–15.

18. "And there was a war in heaven: Michael and his angels fought against the dragon; and the dragon fought and his angels, and prevailed not; neither was their place found any more in heaven. And the great dragon was cast out, that old serpent, called the Devil, and Satan, which deceiveth the whole world: he was cast out into the earth, and his angels were cast out with him. And I heard a loud voice saying in heaven, Now is come salvation, and strength, and the kingdom of our God, and the power of his Christ: for the accuser of our brethren is cast down, which accused them before our God day and night. And they overcame him by the blood of the Lamb, and by the word of their testimony; and they loved not their lives unto the death. Therefore rejoice, ye heavens, and ye that dwell in them. Woe to the inhabiters of the earth and of the sea! For the devil is come down unto you, having great wrath, because he knoweth that he hath but a short time. And when the dragon saw that he was cast unto the earth, he persecuted the woman which brought forth the man child." Revelation 12: 7–13.

19. Anselm of Canterbury, "On the Fall of the Devil," in *Anselm of Canterbury: The Major Works*, ed. Brian Davies and Gil Evans (New York: Oxford University Press, 1998), 193–232.

20. "Pride goeth before destruction, and an haughty spirit before a fall." Proverbs 16: 18.

21. Maximilian Rudwin, *The Devil in Legend and Literature* (New York: AMS Press, 1931), 7–8; and Jeffrey Burton Russell, *Lucifer: The Devil in the Middle Ages* (Ithaca: Cornell University Press, 1984), 55. "So (when He inspired into him His revelation) the angels submitted one and all. But Iblis did not, he behaved arrogantly for he was of the disbelievers. God said, 'O, Iblis! What prevented you from submitting to him whom I have created with My own special powers (bestowing him with the maximum attributes). Is it that you seek to be great or is it that you are (really) of the highly proud ones (above obeying My command)?' Iblis said, 'I am better than he. You created me from fire while him you created from clay.' God said, 'Then get out of this (state); you are surly driven away (from My mercy). And surely upon you shall be My disapproval till the Day of Judgment.'" Qur'an 38: 73–78.

22. Jeffrey Burton Russell, *Satan: The Early Christian Tradition* (Ithaca: Cornell University Press, 1981), 16–17.

23. (Augustine 380–411; Russell, "The Historical Satan" 45). Augustine, *The City of God* (New York: Modern Library, 1950), 380–411; and Jeffrey Burton Russell,

"The Historical Satan," in *The Satanism Scare*, eds. James T. Richardson, Joel Best, David G. Bromley (New York: Atdine de Gruyter, 1991), 45.

24. Jeffrey Burton Russell, *Mephistopheles: The Devil in the Modern World* (Ithaca: Cornell University Press, 1986), 23. Of course, theologians have also gone the opposite way, positing the Devil as an aspect of God himself, but that sort of dualism does little to exacerbate the theological analysis of "It's Raining Men."

25. Along with the literary manifestations of the Lucifer myth cataloged below, it is also of no small significance that corollaries of the story have appeared in a variety of other ancient religious/mythological contexts. As Maximilian Rudwin has noted, "The opposition of Lucifer to the Lord has an analogy in that of Vrita to Indra in Hindu mythology, of Ahriman to Ormuzd in Persian mythology, of Set to Horus in Egyptian mythology, of Prometheus to Zeus in Greek mythology and of Loki to the gods of Asgardh in Scandinavian mythology." Rudwin, *The Devil in Legend and Literature*, 2.

26. Rudwin, *The Devil in Legend and Literature*, 9, 15; and "Revolt of the Angels," *New York Times*, 18 October 1914, BR445. For more examples, see Mildred McCollum and Betty Flora, "Arts and the Devil," *The English Journal* 49 (October 1960): 464–468.

27. John Milton, *Asimov's Annotated Paradise Lost*, ed. Isaac Asimov (New York: Doubleday & Co., 1974), 10.

28. Stella Revard, "Milton's Critique of Heroic Warfare in Paradise Lost V and VI," *Studies in English Literature, 1500–1900* 7 (Winter 1967): 131–135, 138; and Milton, *Asimov's Annotated Paradise Lost*, 597.

29. Of course, there are other problematic consequences of this type of imagery, completely unrelated to its theological implications. What would the survival rate of the falling men be? If they were more likely to survive when hitting bodies of water, would there be a run on river banks and beaches? What would such a run do to the economy? The roads? Would the catastrophic horror of having dead men splattered all over the ground kill the libidos of these ravenous women? If not, does that prove that Mother Nature was, in fact, evil all along? It is important, perhaps above all else, that in these endeavors to parse meaning and significance from the broader popular culture, we scholars not take ourselves so seriously. Imagining a group of confused men falling from the sky and a group of expectant women waiting below is funny. The song presents stark theological consequences and takes its place in a long literary line, but it's still funny.

30. For more on the Mother Nature and the amalgamation of goddesses and natural life, see Monica Sjoo and Barbara Mor, *The Great Cosmic Mother: Rediscovering the Religion of the Earth* (New York: Harper, 1987); and *The New Larousse Encyclopedia of Mythology* (New York: Crown Publishers, 1987).

31. As Peter Shapiro—a staunch defender of disco's musical viability and importance—has argued, "Disco is all shiny, glittery surfaces; high heels and luscious lipstick; jam-packed jeans and cut pecs; lush, soaring, swooping strings and Latin razzmatazz; cocaine rush and quaalude wobble. It was the humble peon suddenly beamed up to the cosmic firmament by virtue of his threads and dance moves." Shapiro, *Turn the Beat Around*, 3.

32. The executive Joe quotes remains anonymous, cited only as "the head of one disco-oriented record label." Joe, *This Business of Disco*, 23–24.

33. "Fly, Robin, Fly," in *The Billboard Book of Number One Hits*, 5th edition, by Fred Bronson (New York: Billboard, 2003), 421.

The Anhedonic Among the Camellias

Woody Allen and Reflective Love

coauthor Brent Riffel

R oland Barthes's analysis of Alexandre Dumas's *The Lady of the Camellias* (*La Dame aux Camélias*) describes the play's central character, Marguerite, who "loves in order to achieve recognition, and this is why her passion (in the etymological, not the libidinal sense) has its source entirely in other people ... Marguerite is aware of her alienation, that is to say, she sees reality as an alienation ... [she] is never anything more than an alienated awareness: she sees that she suffers, but imagines no remedy which is not parasitic to her own suffering."[1] Woody Allen's analysis of his fictional Alvy Singer describes the film's central character, who "would never belong to a club that would have me for a member."[2]

Alvy, in fact, serves as a makeshift Marguerite. If the clauses of Barthes's aforementioned analysis serve as topographical pinpoints on a map to anhedonia, the central protagonist of *Annie Hall* follows the blazed path. As the film opens, Alvy recounts himself as a character in relation to his estranged girlfriend (or perhaps he finds his source entirely in other people). His chronicled childhood memories are dominated by a classroom scene where he catalogs the future exploits of his classmates. ("I run a profitable dress company," says one. "I'm into leather," concedes another.) Even the film's title belies this insecurity, as a film ostensibly about Annie Hall's boyfriend retains *her* name on the poster—implying that any accurate definition of Alvy must principally include Annie.

Certainly, Alvy is aware of his alienation (that is to say, he sees reality as engendering alienation). "The rest of the country looks upon New York like we're left-wing Communist Jewish homosexual pornographers," he laments. "I think of us that way sometimes, and I live here." This situation, like Marguerite's, is the dual state of suffering and awareness of suffering. And Alvy, like Marguerite, imagines no remedy which is not parasitic to his condition. Of course, the remedy he tries is love, fulfilling the self-defeating cycle described by Dumas. In his relationship with Annie, Alvy's actions appear less like those of *The Lady of the Camellias* and more like *Pygmalion*. His projection of himself onto the object of his affection manifests itself in the form of teaching the girl from Chippewa Falls, Wisconsin, how to be New York-proper.

But Alvy's attempts at palliative love are unsuccessful. "Why did I turn off Allison Porchnick?" he asks in a narrative aside. "She was beautiful, she was willing, she was real intelligent." Fulfillment, however—the removal of that awareness of alienation—never happened. Just before this awakening, Alvy spends his time alone in the bedroom with his wife, contemplating the Kennedy assassination. This is not to say that attempts at love are not worthwhile. As Alvy and Annie sit in a deli ordering sandwiches, he recounts a second unsuccessful attempt at marriage.

Allen's cinematic treatment of love (in marriage or otherwise) argues that the experience is an ineffective but ultimately worthwhile palliative for anhedonia—the inability to experience pleasure or romantic fulfillment. Love, for Allen, is essentially unattainable, or at least incapable of bringing happiness, but it remains the best coping strategy at our disposal, and thus remains a worthwhile endeavor. Herein lies Allen's (like Dumas's) backhanded endorsement of love: *You might as well*, he tells us, *because, if nothing else, love will lead to sex, which makes you forget death and loneliness until the next morning*. While Marguerite copes through servile behavior, making herself a social object, Woody Allen chooses mild narcissism—brooding over his alienation and functioning as an object of the recognition he seeks through his original conception of love.

Perhaps Allen's most effective presentation of that narcissism-as-escape comes in *Crimes and Misdemeanors*.[3] Clifford Stern, a documentary filmmaker, is trapped in a frustrating marriage devoid of that necessary reflective love. The situation leaves him brooding over his own inadequacies and spending his time trying to instill his values in his niece. It is no coincidence that the woman who captures his affection is a film producer, in whom he can find the reflection that can help him forget his lifeless, loveless marriage. Together, the two dissect the philosophy of one of Clifford's documentary subjects, professor Louis Levy. "What we are aiming at when we fall in love is a very strange paradox," declares Levy. "The paradox consists of the fact that when we fall in love, we are seeking to re-find all or some of the people to whom we were attached as children. On the other hand, we ask our beloved to correct all of the wrongs that these early parents or siblings inflicted on us. So love contains within it the contradiction—the attempt to return to the past, and the attempt to undo the past." For Levy, that attempt at love was necessarily reflective and, in its role as reflector, necessarily impossible.

It is also no coincidence that the philosopher commits suicide before the film's conclusion. Paradoxes by their very definition are unsolvable. Love cannot be a verdict; it can only be a recess. Its presence as palliative, however, and its fundamentally selfish nature, make it neither wrong nor unnecessary. Though Clifford experiences the closing credits alone, Allen's prototypical protagonist continues to appear, expanding on similar fears about death, loneliness, and a general existential abyss. His solution every time is another attempt at reflective love—a love in which he can see himself as the object of the affection of someone who will be the intellectual, emotional, and sexual embodiment of all his preordained ideals. His attempts are necessarily ineffective, but more importantly, they never abate. Love, presented in each film and in the collective Allen oeuvre, is the best option for staving off the harsh realities of life, even if, in the end, it is no option at all. So Allen presents a protagonist whose inability to be happy is postponed through fumbling attempts at reflective love, finding recognition in his passion (both in the etymological *and* the libidinal sense), its source entirely in other people. The director's ambivalence toward love, his trenchant observations about it, and the reasons for his sustained devotion to the grand ideal lies somewhat hidden but ever present—like Dumas's lady, somewhere among the camellias.

For Allen, love thus becomes a strategy for survival, or what anthropologist James Scott calls a "weapon of the weak."[4] That is, faced with existential crisis at every turn, Allen's characters construct a way out through the idealization of the notion of love—rather than, say, the idealization of a particular person. His 1979 film *Manhattan* illustrates this in several respects.[5] For one, the recurring motif of existential dread is expressed in several scenes, but perhaps most cogently in the sequence in which Allen and Diane Keaton, seeking escape from a downpour, tour the Hayden Planetarium. The metaphor is almost overbearing but still resonates: we are adrift in the universe, just as is Allen's Isaac Davis, *Manhattan*'s protagonist. Indeed, love seems to be the only viable antidote to nothingness. Clearly, Isaac's affair with the adolescent Tracy (Mariel Hemingway) signals his wish to recapture his youth, when love was all-encompassing. The pivotal break-up scene—set to brilliant effect in an old-fashioned ice cream parlor—reveals how absurd Isaac's efforts have been. Indeed, in *Manhattan*, all of the characters career from one failed attempt at love to another.

The city itself represents a major character, but Allen consciously idealizes this as well. In the same year that Mick Jagger described the city as rife with vermin and disease, Allen offered an ode to the island.[6] Carlo Di Palma's lush camera work, set to Gershwin's music, underscores Allen's conceit that Manhattan is a city of romance and dreams. It thus becomes significant to note that his 1985 *Hannah and Her Sisters* takes a more cynical, yet more realistic, view.[7] In the latter film, the characters once again pursue doomed relationships (leaving romantic wreckage in their paths), but this time the sets—designed by Santo Loquasto—are bleaker and more desolate. Michael Caine's feverish confession of his adoration for Barbara Hershey (his wife's sister) is framed against a backdrop of graffiti and urban decay. Moreover, Allen's date with Diane Wiest takes place in the Bowery, at the punk club CBGB. Although both films recognize love as the only means of coping with the world, *Hannah* presents a more sanguine view. *Manhattan* ultimately represents the stronger work, if only because Allen refuses to compromise his ontological position. In *Hannah*, the plot lines are neatly wrapped up: Allen escapes cancer and suicide, and even manages to find love. In *Manhattan*, he insists that his characters stare into the abyss, that they face their own hypocrisy.

Allen's most trenchant criticism is reserved for the character Yale, played by the often-brilliant character actor, Michael Murphy.[8] Yale seeks renewal and meaning in extramarital affairs, while longing to express himself creatively (he halfheartedly attempts to craft a biography of Eugene O'Neill). But ultimately, he chooses to buy a Porsche, and for Allen this marks his slide into decadence. In siding with the material, Yale has admitted defeat in the larger struggle to find meaning and fulfillment. In one of *Manhattan*'s pivotal scenes, Isaac and Yale argue beside a Cro-Magnon skeleton. The symbolism is clear: death is inescapable.[9] One's only recourse is to have character and integrity. Referring to the skeleton as he berates Yale for betraying his friendship, Isaac puts it succinctly: "I'll be hanging in a classroom one day and I want to make sure when I thin out that I'm well thought of."[10] Of course, Allen stops just short of making his own character, Isaac, possess integrity. Instead, he ignores his own moral code and begs his young lover to stay with him in the film's closing moments. (And this despite his earlier insistence that she leave him in order to improve herself.) Thus in *Manhattan*, love does not serve as a mechanism for finding deeper meaning in life, but rather as a tool for deluding ourselves.

Allen spent much of the 1980s exploring new techniques, often with astounding, if under-appreciated, success. His mock-documentary *Zelig* further advanced the motif of man's inexhaustible quest to find acceptance, but critics and audiences tended to ignore the film's ideas in favor of praising its skillful mixture of genre: the seamless blending of newsreel footage, interviews (with real figures such as Susan Sontag), and still shots. All served to obscure its thematic nuances.[11] His other work of the decade returned again and again to the notion of love as an escape hatch. And if love proved unworkable, popular culture would have to suffice, as films such as *The Purple Rose of Cairo* and *Radio Days* suggest, which idealize bygone forms of entertainment. And both, significantly, allow Allen to stop time, as he continues to search for a stay of his own existential execution—a death by a thousand small cuts.[12]

Allen's 1992 *Husbands and Wives* marks a more potent expression of the anhedonic crisis that has gripped Allen's characters as far back as his portrayal of Virgil Starkwell in 1969's *Take the Money and Run*.[13] Evoking Bergman's *Scenes from a Marriage*, *Husbands and Wives* opens with the unraveling of a marriage. This opening sequence, once again shot by Di Palma, is done with handheld cameras, injecting the film with a sense of realism, which is further enhanced by the documentary-style testimonials each character gives to an off-screen interviewer. Jack (Sydney Pollack) and Sally (Judy Davis) casually announce to Gabe and Judy (Allen and Farrow, whose off-screen relationship famously collapsed during the postproduction of this project) that they are getting a divorce.[14] The subsequent plot hinges on these four characters reacting to this revelation. All of them proceed to pursue their own respective relationships, with varying degrees of success. Jack, much like *Manhattan*'s Yale, seeks sexual renewal in a youthful, if intellectually bereft, aerobics instructor. Tellingly, she foolishly attempts to explain the prescience of astrology to skeptical academics at a dinner party—Allen has been steadfast throughout his career in deriding New Age escapism. Jack's estranged wife Sally struggles to overcome her bitter resentment at the male species—the film's funniest scenes trace her attempts to reenter the dating scene. Critic Vincent Canby rightly called her one of Allen's most "endearingly impossible characters," and her seething rage nicely contrasts with Farrow's "submerged anger."[15]

Meanwhile, Allen and Farrow engage in affairs of their own. Gabe quickly falls for Rain, a young creative writing student played by Juliette Lewis, and Gabe is wary from the outset, wondering if this affair isn't like "$59,000 of psychotherapy dialing 911."[15] Unbeknownst to Gabe, Judy tentatively pursues Michael (Liam Neeson), who works in her office, but whom she initially introduces to Sally, only to fall for him herself. Described by her ex-husband as passive-aggressive, Farrow's Judy is, as Canby pointed out, a "waif with claws." Indeed, she represents a remarkable, significant turn in Allen's work. In *Husbands and Wives*, the idea of love ultimately comes unhinged. Jack and Sally reconcile, and in doing so openly concede that love is imperfect, if not unattainable. The portrayal of love as expressed by Judy is revealed to be full of cunning—a strategy of conquest. Finally, Gabe laments at the film's close that he is susceptible to "kamikaze women," who crash into him, leaving him in ruins. But as if to complete the circle begun by *Annie Hall*, he admits that he must continue to seek out new relationships. In the cold world of Allen's films (a world ironically stuffed with one-liners and sight gags), love is all there is. That the endless search for it fails to bring fulfillment ultimately proves irrelevant.

Barthes reads this love as problematic. He describes the "mythological content of this love, which is the archetype of petit-bourgeois sentimentality. It is a very particular state of myth, defined by a semi-awareness, or to be more precise, a parasitic awareness."[16] Allen depicts the same parasitic component of love, but understands it as inevitable. After all, the character he chooses for himself is generally the parasitic lover. Love among the camellias, for Allen, is better than the abject absence of flowers. Or perhaps his characters belong among chickens rather than flowers—animals rather than vegetables. "This guy goes to a psychiatrist and says, 'Doc, my brother's crazy. He thinks he's a chicken.' And the doctor says, 'Why don't you turn him in?' Guy says, 'I would, but I need the eggs.'" As the voice-over continues, Alvy leaves the street corner.

"I guess that's how I pretty much feel about relationships," he concludes. "They're totally irrational and crazy and absurd, but I guess we keep going through it because most of us need the eggs." Would that Marguerite would have felt the same about the flowering of her romantic entanglements. And would that she could have somehow crept into a club that would patiently have her as a member.

Notes

1. Roland Barthes, "The Lady of the Camellias," in *A Barthes Reader*, ed. Susan Sontag, 89–92 (New York: Hill and Wang, 2001), 91.

2. *Annie Hall*, directed by Woody Allen, 1977.

3. *Crimes and Misdemeanors*, directed by Woody Allen, 1989.

4. James Scott, *Weapons of the Weak: Everyday Forms of Peasant Resistance* (New Haven: Yale University Press, 1987).

5. *Manhattan*, directed by Woody Allen, 1979.

6. Rolling Stones, "Shattered," from the album *Some Girls*, Virgin Records, 1978.

7. *Hannah and Her Sisters*, directed by Woody Allen, 1985.

8. See, for example, Murphy's performance in Robert Altman's 1973 *McCabe & Mrs. Miller*.

9. Allen makes a similar point in *Annie Hall*, when he insists on buying for Annie a copy a of the 1973 pop psychology book, *The Denial of Death*, by Ernest Becker (New York: The Free Press, 1974). In interviews, Allen has cited this book as a major influence on his thinking during the mid 1970s; indeed, the attempt to escape death informs the work of this period, if not his entire oeuvre.

10. The subtext of this line suggests Allen's own sense of his legacy as a filmmaker, a point he will return to in, among other films, *Stardust Memories* (1980) and *Shadows and Fog* (1992).

11. *Zelig*, directed by Woody Allen, 1982.

12. *The Purple Rose of Cairo*, directed by Woody Allen, 1985; and *Radio Days*, ibid., 1987.

13. *Husbands and Wives*, directed by Woody Allen, 1992; *Take the Money and Run*, ibid., 1969.

14. For speculation on the parallels between Allen's personal life and *Husbands and Wives*, see John Baxter, *Woody Allen: A Biography* (New York: Carroll & Graf Publishers, 2000), 259.

15. Vincent Canby, "Husbands and Wives; Fact? Fiction? It Doesn't Matter," *New York Times*, 18 September 1992.

16. Barthes, "The Lady of the Camellias," 91.

Denmark Vesey and
Historical Context

C ontext is the business of historians, but it is not always necessary, and when misapplied, can actually be detrimental to the practice of history. Same for *mise en scène, zeitgeist,* and the rest. In historical debates about specific facts or instances, context should never trump systematic reason—or, the application of logical analysis to a specific set of data. Bertrand Russell best enunciated this principle in his "Knowledge by Acquaintance and Knowledge by Description," in which he evaluates his own acquaintance with the historical Bismarck.[1] To evaluate a claim such as "Bismarck is mortal," he applied symbolic logic to produce a truth statement: $(\exists x)(Bx$ & $(y)(By\prod y=x)$ & $Mx).$[2] While arguments against this formula abound (for example, other symbolic systems or Christian belief in life after death[3]), descriptions of German unification, diplomacy, or even historical examples of stress as a detriment to health *cannot act as arguments against it.* Their truth or falsity bears no weight on the presented truth statement. *Modus ponens* offers a similar example:

If p, then q
p
Therefore, q

While an involved treatment of the historical context of the relationship between p and q can aid an argument using *modus ponens*, it could never go the other way and somehow warp the structural integrity of the formula itself.

Historians, however, sometimes assume that context is the one true historical constant—that it is the lens through which all historical activity should be examined. And, in a sense, they are correct; a broader understanding of Bismarck beyond truth statements about his existence requires the very context historians provide. In historical debates about specific facts or instances, however, context only clouds the evaluation of value in historical claims. Context can hinder a historian's ability to judge truth statements, and therefore *cannot be considered a constant by historians.*

In the October 2001 *William & Mary Quarterly*, Michael P. Johnson argued that historians had placed unwarranted faith in the official trial transcript of the 1822 Charleston Court of Magistrates and Freeholders' proceedings against the free black Denmark Vesey and his alleged accomplices.[4] He compared the two surviving manuscript transcripts and the official report to find many discrepancies, additions, and omissions. He concluded that the grand insurrection planned by Vesey and others was neither grand nor an organized insurrectionist plot, and formulated theories about possible alternative scenarios, principal among them a conspiracy by white magistrates to convict slaves as a warning to an unprepared white population. He also criticized three authors of 1999 books on Vesey and his conspiracy—Edward A. Pearson, Douglas R. Egerton, and David Robertson[5]—for misusing the manuscript versions of the trial transcripts and failing to question the conspiracy's existence.

Johnson argues that his analysis of the manuscript transcripts proves that the wrong version has been given preference, thereby leading many historians to false conclusions about the Vesey trial. Johnson then offers an alternative scenario based largely on the doubts about the proceedings held by South Carolina Governor Thomas Bennett and US Supreme Court Justice William Johnson. Here Johnson offers his own interpretation of what transpired in the sequence of events commonly called the Vesey conspiracy. The description is an acknowledged speculation and does not in any way help or hinder his argument about the transcripts. If Johnson's evaluation of the transcripts is correct, the work of Pearson, Egerton, and Robertson immediately becomes—if not invalid—at least suspect in its historical accuracy. But none of these authors choose to confront Johnson on his transcript evaluation. Johnson's treatment of what actually transpired could be met with an alternative treatment, but that new story *cannot be an argument against Johnson's transcript analysis.* Johnson's evaluation of the trial transcripts stands alone as an argument against the conspiracy. It is a closed system—like Russell's Theory of Acquaintance or *modus ponens*—and textual analysis of other documents unrelated to those transcripts, while helpful for providing historical context, cannot penetrate the original evaluation. In responses published in the next edition of the *William & Mary Quarterly*, however, the criticized authors call upon alternative peripheral sources to engage Johnson's speculation about an alternative scenario—alternatives that do not bear upon Johnson's foundational transcript case.

Pearson's *Designs Against Charleston* bears the brunt of Johnson's criticism, an evaluation that ultimately led the University of North Carolina Press to pull the book from its list of titles.[6] *Designs Against Charleston* presents an edited version of the manuscript copies of the trial record, along with a lengthy historical introduction. Johnson points out numerous errors in Pearson's transcription, including additions and omissions that fundamentally change the meaning of statements made by interviewed slaves. Johnson demonstrates that Pearson mistakenly superimposed one version of the record over the other. Accordingly, Pearson concedes this error.

"I plead guilty to his charge that my transcription of the trial record is deeply flawed," writes Pearson, though he claims that his lengthy introductory article, "based on my reading and consideration of the evidence," still merits attention. His defense begins in the opening paragraph of his "Trials and Errors: Denmark Vesey and His Historians," Pearson lists a number of historians before him who have acknowledged the existence of the Charleston conspiracy.[7] William W. Freehling, Eugene Genovese, and Sterling Stuckey "regard this episode as genuine," he writes, grounding his argument with the weight of revered names in the field. Those names, however, do nothing to disprove Johnson's argument. Eugene Genovese's 1974 description of the 1822 conspiracy has no bearing on Johnson's 2001 reexamination of the evidence Genovese and others have used. This is the equivalent of placing Johnson's article on one side of a see-saw, then—in lieu of removing it—placing a bevy of books on the other side, hoping to negate the article's weight by default. But this tactic does even more damage. It deflects the reader (who more than likely is not turning back to the prior article in the journal's previous issue at every paragraph break) from Johnson's argument. It gives the reader a false reason to accept the pronunciations of Pearson.

Egerton does the same thing, citing Norrence T. Jones, Margaret Washington, Stanley Harrold, and Marcus Rediker.[8] David Robertson, not a historian by trade, doesn't use a list of well-known historians, but makes the same kind of lateral move: "Revisionists," he writes, "are terrible simplifiers."[9] Since each makes the case, this line of argument would seem to be considered valid historical rebuttal. But what each is actually doing is making a variation on the schoolyard claim, "Everyone else is doing it, so why can't I?" While "everyone else" are certainly important historiographical names, neither Norrence Jones nor Eugene Genovese wrote meaningful commentary on the status of manuscript trial transcript validity in the case of the Vesey conspiracy. They described the conspiracy. They used the trial record and other sources to examine the meaning of the Vesey conspiracy for historical understanding of slave life and resistance. But they never dealt directly with the transcript discrepancy. Their research, in fact, was the product of the same error Johnson is attempting to correct. Using their work as tools of argument moves that argument away from its target. It makes the debate historiographical rather than historical—about accepted dogma rather than document validity.

Another problematic tactic is the association of less revered historians with the work of an opponent. Pearson begins by describing not the argument of Michael Johnson, but of Richard C. Wade, who argued for the possibility of the Vesey conspiracy's nonexistence in 1964. It was "probably never more than loose talk by aggrieved and embittered men," wrote Wade. But his argument quickly fell out of favor.[10] "After many years in the interpretive wilderness," writes Pearson, "Richard Wade has now found an ally in Michael Johnson."[11] Johnson certainly sympathizes with Wade, and cites his argument in the body of his article, but Pearson's critique is not used to describe that relationship. It is used at the end of the opening paragraph of Pearson's ten-paragraph response. Just as he attempted to tie his own opinion to that of Freehling, Genovese, and Stuckey, Pearson attempts to tie his opposition's argument to a name red-flagged by the historiographical forethought of most slave rebellion historians. Egerton goes even farther, subtitling his article, "Or, Oliver Stone Meets Richard Wade." He describes Johnson's as "not so much an update as an extension of Richard C. Wade's much-battered 1964 thesis." He then follows by denigrating Wade's article, at no point describing any aspect of the work that bore on Johnson's thesis.[12] This is a blatant attempt at character assassination of Johnson through character assassination of Wade. If the attempt of Pearson and Egerton is not to intentionally malign Johnson by artificially applying negative (and invalid) connotations to his name, then the historians must consider this valid argument. It is not valid argument.

"Bring us the head of Denmark Vesey," writes David Robertson, "and we'll bid it sing." He denies that Johnson's is a "fresh view of the records," but claims in the next sentence that "Johnson privileges one archival manuscript of the Vesey investigation over the printed text." Indeed, Johnson's "privileging" of one manuscript is in fact the "fresh" view. It carries the entire thrust of Johnson's view. He "is a contextualist when such a practice supports his thesis and not a contextualist when the historical documents might compromise his authority."[13] Robertson has misread Johnson's argument, which—again—is about the necessary precedence of certain principal historical documents.

"Historical scholarship," explains Pearson, "is an intellectual endeavor that stands on the twin pillars of proof and persuasion." Again, this statement is misleading. Pearson uses it to defend his introductory essay to his flawed translation of the Vesey trial transcripts. But if his source material is admittedly interpreted in error, then his ability to persuade is hindered— his argument has fallacy built into its base. The false assumption that proof and persuasion are "twin pillars" leads to the aforementioned misdirection, which places persuasion (character assassination, historiographical name-dropping, etc.) as a substitute for proof. In fact, if history is anything more than an intellectual exercise, then proof should be the foundation upon which all pillars of persuasion are built.

To that point, Pearson cites various ledges in Johnson's exposition where specific reasons for the white court's obfuscation go lacking. Though he acknowledges Johnson's plan to produce a book-length manuscript on the subject, and he acknowledges Johnson's "ingenious reconstruct[ion]" of the white court's actions, he expresses his frustration that "he never explicitly states why [the court would so conspire]."[14] Here again Pearson attempts to steer the reader away from Johnson's critique. A book-length project is forthcoming. Johnson's article was intended to demonstrate the primacy of the original trial transcript and problems with the Official Report. But Pearson still grasps at straws, secure in the knowledge that readers' heads will be turned by the inimitable words "why" and "explain"—even in a situation that does not call for them. "It may ultimately turn out that Johnson has exchanged one conspiracy for another," writes Pearson, referring to Johnson's alternative scenario. Maybe so. Johnson devotes the second half of his article to describing the culture of revolution in the antebellum period and the resulting culture of fear in the white community. This part of his article is not a debate about a specific fact or instance. It is context—the business of history—but does not bear on his original claim that the transcript discrepancies preclude the likelihood of a slave conspiracy.

In each of these instances, commentators use historiographical and historical context in arguments that do not call for either. The authors seem to have assumed them as constants—applying them to the Vesey debate because they apply them to everything. But there can be no rehearsed questions pulled out of any available hat as substitutes for learned responses. Otherwise, historical analysis becomes a Talmudic reading of those who have come before. This might produce books, but it does not help us to understand the past. In this case, a reliance on standard forms of historical argument caused historians to miss the true critique of their work.

In Johnson's counter-response, he paraphrases an argument by Hayden White that proclaims the uselessness of attending the archives at all, as they are just slates upon which historians impose their own presuppositions. Johnson disagrees. "The historiography of the Vesey conspiracy suggests instead that the path to writing history should run through, not around, the archives," writes Johnson.[15] Johnson's choice of one trial transcript as the superior of others demonstrates his devotion to archival research. The Official

Transcript, cited by William Freehling and Eugene Genovese, is published and available outside of the archives. Implicit in Johnson's statement is the assertion that other historians are not doing the proper legwork. Pearson and Egerton never confront Johnson on this point, though it is certainly not infallible. (Johnson's evaluation of the transcripts, for example, uses the absence of certain names from the document Johnson assumes to be the "original." His analysis is—and must be—speculation and is therefore susceptible to counter-speculation. But it never comes.) But historians might do well to listen to White on another point. "Narrative," he writes in his *The Content of the Form*, "far from being merely a form of discourse that can be filled with different contents, real or imaginary as the case may be, already possesses a content prior to any given actualization of it in speech or writing."[16] Form, by its very recognizability, has content. It appears in the above examples of the misapplication of context that historical discourse itself has assumed a content-laden form—conventions that act as shorthand for reason.

"If historians had to rely only on statements willingly made to officials in open, democratic courts that lacked any racial or class bias—as if such a venue has ever existed in *any* society," writes Egerton, "the available scholarship on the law and popular resistance to it would be thin indeed." He describes all slavery documents as "problematical." But this is precisely the point Johnson is making. Egerton is simply attempting to co-opt it for himself. Some of the magistrates' additions in the Official Report come from memory, he tells us, not from notes. He then uses this fact (which only seems to argue the opposite position) to make the case that Pearson's flawed transcription is the best possible solution to the varied accounts.[17]

Egerton also argues that Johnson's use of the original transcript took precedence over other available documents, which could validate the Vesey story. For example, Archibald Grimke's 1901 narrative of the event should have been consulted. The memoirs of a white planter, Samuel Wragg Ferguson, in which he remembered that black drivers in the country were recruiting men for an insurrection, could have proven the conspiracy. The letters of "Charleston socialite" Mary Lamboll Beach recount that she heard from the minister that visited Vesey in his cell that his was a "glorious" cause.[18] While these and other mentioned primary sources may be important, they have nothing to do with the validity of the trial transcript.

What Grimke remembered years later about Vesey, what Ferguson heard out in the lowcountry, and what Beach heard from the minister do not bear on Johnson's argument that *his* transcript is the correct transcript, and that it suggests there was no conspiracy.

Like Egerton, Robert L. Paquette follows this faulty line of argument, citing similar sources of peripheral connections to the trial, hiding the tree by throwing a forest around it. One of Paquette's explanations for why the white court would not have promulgated this conspiracy, for example, comes from Stephen Elliot, "president of the Bank of South Carolina, [who] observed in 1822 that Charleston's lawyers were 'frequently men of talent and generally of integrity.'" This does not address the question at hand. Similarly, at the end of his response, Paquette quotes a conversation in which a slave admits to his intention to kill his master.[19] It is a powerful rhetorical statement—demonstrating the anger and frustration bred by the South Carolina slave system—but it appears in a letter written by someone other than the slaveholder or slave.[20] Egerton, Pearson, and Paquette all create powerful portrayals of the personal difficulties of slave life and slave insurrection, but they never engage Johnson's trial transcript distinction, which is the foundation of his argument against them.

In a 2004 article, Paquette continues the same project after two years of reflection. "From Rebellion to Revisionism" produces more "evidence" that does nothing to refute Johnson's argument. The final four pages of this second article deal almost exclusively with Morris Brown and the African Methodist Episcopal Church.[21] Again, this discussion may be relevant in other contexts, but not as a refutation of Johnson. Nor is Paquette's chiding of the media and historians who uncritically took Johnson's side. In a letter he wrote with Egerton to the editor of *The Nation*, Paquette insinuated that Jon Wiener's endorsement of Johnson's thesis stemmed in part from his time spent teaching in the same department with Johnson at the University of California, Irvine.[22] His 2004 critique does the same for Philip Morgan, chair of the Johns Hopkins history department.[23] Morgan's defense of Johnson appeared in the same *William & Mary Quarterly* issue as did Paquette's original critique. He argued that Johnson's skepticism about the trial record should be applied to all supposed conspiracies. His exuberance could easily draw criticism, but Paquette instead chooses to question Morgan's motives. Scholarly debate should have no room for such assertions.

Thomas J. Davis criticizes Johnson more reasonably in his *William & Mary Quarterly* response, arguing that black speech against whites, whether that group was arming itself or not, was still illegal, and could have merited the verdicts rendered under South Carolina law. In other words, the conspiracy was there whether the transcript is accurate or not. "Speech was not free in the 1700s and 1800s," remarks Davis. The point is valuable, and Johnson will likely consider it in his book-length examination. His paper, however, also avoids the issue of transcript validity.[24]

If validity is what historians are after, then the rules of engagement need to be more firmly established—if not through a written code, then by a general refusal to accept arguments (particularly those critical of fellow historians) not grounded in elementary logic. Historians cannot lean on the tactics of historical presentation to debate validity amongst themselves. They must attack arguments, not their accoutrements. And never assume context as a constant. Michael Johnson argues in his "Denmark Vesey and His Co-Conspirators" that historiography (or its historians) has conspired to keep us from history. Edward Pearson, Douglas Egerton, Robert Paquette, and David Robertson admirably prove his point in their critical responses to his work.

Notes

1. Bertrand Russell, "Knowledge by Acquaintance and Knowledge by Description," in *Mysticism and Logic* (Mineola, NY: Dover Publications Inc., 2004), 170.

2. Where B stands for Bismarck, M for his mortality. There exists an x, for all instances of Bismarck, Bismarck is mortal.

3. This formula adheres to Russell's Theory of Acquaintance, but even his prior Theory of Descriptions finds a different representative form: $(\forall x)(Bx \prod Mx)$. For all x, Bismarck is mortal. Christians could challenge Russell because they could offer different definitions of "mortal." Even the author has attempted a challenge of Russell's Theory of Acquaintance based on historical precepts. See Thomas Aiello, "Russell's Bismarck," unpublished manuscript, in the possession of the author.

4. Michael P. Johnson, "Denmark Vesey and His Co-Conspirators," The William and Mary Quarterly October 2001 http://www.historycooperative.org/journals/wm/58.4/johnson.html (6 October 2005).

5. The three books are Edward A. Pearson, ed. *Designs Against Charleston: The Trial Record of the Denmark Vesey Slave Conspiracy of 1822* (Chapel Hill: University of North Carolina Press, 1999); Douglas R. Egerton, *He Shall Go Out Free: The Lives of Denmark Vesey* (Madison, WI: Madison House, 1999); David Robertson, *Denmark Vesey: The Buried History of America's Largest Slave Rebellion and the Man Who Led It* (New York: Knopf, 1999).

6. *New York Times*, 23 February 2002, B11.

7. Edward A. Pearson, "Trials and Errors: Denmark Vesey and His Historians," The William and Mary Quarterly January 2002 http://www.historycooperative.org/journals/wm/59.1/pearson.html (6 October 2005).

8. Douglas R. Egerton, "Forgetting Denmark Vesey; Or, Oliver Stone Meets Richard Wade," The William and Mary Quarterly January 2002 http://www.historycooperative.org/journals/wm/59.1/egerton.html (6 October 2005).

9. David Robertson, "Inconsistent Contextualism: The Hermeneutics of Michael Johnson," The William and Mary Quarterly January 2002 http://www.historycooperative.org/journals/wm/59.1/robertson.html (6 October 2005).

10. William W. Freehling was probably most influential in his denunciation of Wade, calling the new interpretation "a step backward in understanding Vesey's antipaternalistic *reality*." Richard C. Wade, "The Vesey Plot: A Reconsideration," *Journal of Southern History* 30 (May 1964): 160; and William W. Freehling, "Denmark Vesey's Antipaternalistic Reality," in *The Reintegration of American History*, 34–58 (New York: Oxford University Press, 1994), 45.

11. Pearson, "Trials and Errors," paragraph 1. [Though "paragraph" will be removed, the numbers following abbreviated article titles for the three responders will be paragraph number. *The William & Mary Quarterly* articles were retrieved from the History Cooperative (www.historycooperative.org), which numbers its reprints by paragraph rather than page.]

12. Egerton, "Forgetting Denmark Vesey," 3–4.

13. David Robertson, "Inconsistent Contextualism: The Hermeneutics of Michael Johnson," The William and Mary Quarterly January 2002 http://www.historycooperative.org/journals/wm/59.1/robertson.html (6 October 2005), 1, 4, 6–7.

14. Pearson, "Trials and Errors," 8.

15. Michael P. Johnson, "Reading Evidence," The William and Mary Quarterly January 2002 http://www.historycooperative.org/journals/wm/59.1/johnson.html (6 October 2005).

16. Hayden White, *The Content of the Form: Narrative Discourse and Historical Representation* (Baltimore: The Johns Hopkins University Press, 1987), xi.

17. Egerton, "Forgetting Denmark Vesey," 6–7.

18. The article continues similarly through its conclusion. He discusses Vesey's children. He discusses Fredrick Douglass's exhortation to black Civil War soldiers to "Remember Denmark Vesey." Again, while these instances might be relevant in a book about Vesey or the memory of Vesey or in any other broader treatment, they are irrelevant here. Egerton, "Forgetting Denmark Vesey," 10–11.

19. Paquette also united with Egerton to write the letter to the editor of *The Nation*. Robert L. Paquette, "Jacobins of the Lowcountry: The Vesey Plot on Trial," The William and Mary Quarterly January 2002 http://www.historycooperative.org/journals/wm/59.1/paquette.html (6 October 2005), 12, 15.

20. The full citation is Martha Proctor Richardson to James Screven, Aug. 7, 1822, Arnold and Screven Family Papers, Southern Historical Collection, University of North Carolina Library. Paquette, "Jacobins of the Lowcountry."

21. Robert L. Paquette, "From Rebellion to Revisionism: The Continuing Debate About the Denmark Vesey Affair," *The Journal of the Historical Society* 4 (Fall 2004), 323–326.

22. "Denmark Vesey's Slave Rebellion—Letters," *The Nation*, 29 April 2002, 2.

23. Also, instead of going to Johnson's academic work to cull a portrait of the author's view of Vesey, Paquette instead pulls a quote from an interview Johnson did with the student newspaper of Johns Hopkins University. While there is nothing strictly wrong with this, Paquette uses the quote as a "more concise" version of Johnson's opinion of Vesey: "A guy who thinks slavery is wrong, he hates white people, he thinks blacks should be equal to whites, and he won't shut up about it. He's endangering the black people and scaring the pants off the white people. And so made himself a target." Paquette, "From Rebellion to Revisionism," 293, 310; and Glenn Small Homewood, "Sleuthing Prof Debunks Slave Plot," *The Gazette Online*, http://www.jhu.edu/~gazette/2001/22oct01/22sleuth.html, accessed 8 October 2005. Egerton and Paquette also produced one more article, to similar

effect. See "Of Facts and Fables: New Light on the Denmark Vesey Affair," *South Carolina Historical Magazine* 105 (January 2004): 8–35.

24. Thomas J. Davis, "Conspiracy and Credibility: Look Who's Talking, about What—Law Talk and Loose Talk," The William and Mary Quarterly January 2002 http://www.historycooperative.org/journals/wm/59.1/davis.html (6 October 2005), 5.

The Linguistics of Taste

C oors Light does not taste colder than Miller Lite or Bud Light because the universe won't allow it. The universe or Mr. Webster.

Miller Lite does not have more taste than Coors Light or Bud Light because we do not live in an alternate world where everything that means absolutely nothing automatically becomes real.

Through the spring and summer of 2005, two of the three major American brands of light beer created television marketing campaigns touting superior aspects of their products' taste. In so doing, the companies entered a unique place in the pantheon of dishonesty.

Advertising is inherently deceptive. The necessity of its presence contradicts its claim that the product or service it peddles is necessary. The deception, however, usually takes place within the realm of possibility. For example: Without Bud Light, your ears will stop working. This is a lie, but the disparity between cause and effect does not disallow the fact that ears can stop working. We will call this category of dishonesty the Full Lie.

But what about this: Bud Light tastes better than Miller Lite. Let us assume for the sake of the example that the qualitative differences between the two are minimal, or that you as the receiver of the message disagree with the claim. Bud Light may even comply with your standard of "better."

Either way, the implication of the statement is that the better taste of Bud Light is established fact—that taste is not a matter of taste. While around half of the recipients of that message will agree, or while some may be persuaded by the message that their own whims match its claims, Bud Light's better taste can never be a fact because taste is not quantifiable, and no mean measurement exists to judge aspirants to the title of "better." Still, people can either agree or disagree with the statement. "Betterness" exists, as do beers and opinions. The personal truths within the blanket falsehood serve to redeem the claim—to make it acceptable to those receiving it. But we cannot label this category the Half Lie. There is no such thing. A lie does not have degrees. And so let's call it the Full-2 Lie.

It is, in fact, this grading of the un-gradable that has changed the message of the beer companies. Miller Lite's 2005 campaign claims that the beer has "more taste" than Bud Light. In the commercials, people reveal hurtful secrets about themselves to significant others, to a response of easy acceptance. When they pull back the veil on Miller Lite's larger amount of taste, however, their loved ones are visibly and comically dismayed. But what has Miller Lite promised? Taste does incorporate sweetness, sourness, and bitterness, and so the strength of the sensation, or its intensity in one of these categories, is not constant. One brand of beer could certainly be bitterer than another. But "taste" is a noun signifying the presence of those various elements. Both have taste, and Miller Lite can taste different from Bud Light. Neither, however, has more taste because taste, in its given context, is un-gradable.

In other contexts, more-and-less terminology is appropriate. A taste can also be "a small amount." Sitting across from that same significant other, a Miller Lite drinker could easily ask for "a little taste" of the companion's Bud Light. But when commercials claim to have "more taste," they imply the sensation provided by the receptors in the human mouth. Those receptors discern different tastes, they demonstrate the greater or smaller intensity of various elements of a final product, but the final product itself—taste—cannot be more or less. In making the claim, Miller Lite reformulates the presentation of advertising deception. Unlike better taste and non-functioning ears, "more taste" does not exist. By proclaiming the banner, the company does not just deceive, it creates a false category. This Creator Lie, if I may name the type, has also found favor with Coors.

"Coors Light is the coldest-tasting beer," proclaim television commercials for the product. It is brewed in the Rocky Mountains and shipped in refrigerated trucks and boxcars. It starts cold, and thus tastes colder than its competitors. But how can this be? The noun signifier described above is the register of existence for various sweet, sour, and bitter sensations received by the mouth—elements that are inherent in the taste-carrier itself. Cold, however, is imposed externally. The temperature of any bottle of beer will fall when prompted, as will that of the Webster's Dictionary. If a container of Coors Light and an advertising ethics manual are placed in a refrigerator set to forty-two degrees, both will eventually reach that temperature, irrespective of taste. "Taste," in its various definitions and its simple role as noun signifier, does not include temperature as a valid component. When Coors Light claims to taste colder than its competitors, it similarly imposes an alternate category of dishonesty. Whereas Miller creates a false measure of taste, Coors creates a false component of it.

Imagine a claim by one of the brewers that "Our beer is preferred three to one by spacemen." This seems pretty outrageous as well. But "spacemen" can be interpreted as "astronauts," and astronauts probably have opinions about beer. The claim would either be a Full Lie or a fact. Its structure eliminates the possibility of a Full-2 or Creator Lie. Unlike this seemingly absurd example, however, "more" and "colder" carry no possibility for alternate interpretation. Coors Light and Miller Lite create, and in so doing, destroy.

Both of the companies make impossible claims that, unlike Full or Full-2 Lies, serve to fundamentally harm the popular perception of language. The assumption of truth—or, for the more cynical, the assumption of a Full Lie—leads to either acceptance or misplaced frustration about the claims both the companies make. A lie is a lie. While claims of more taste and colder taste are not better or worse than other advertising deceptions, they are different, and that difference creates new consequences that we would all do "better" to acknowledge.

Meta-Interloping and the New Double Consciousness

Traducing the Interdisciplinary Veil

The School of Criticism and Theory (SCT) at Cornell University extends through six weeks in June and July. As I sat quietly at the orientation, I scanned down the participant research list looking for any other attending historians. Upon reaching the end, I felt a new guttural loneliness at not only coming from Arkansas to walk behind the ivied walls of Cornell, but at coming from the Department of History to the frontier of interdisciplinary humanities theory. That feeling of being the odd man out, however, wasn't alien. I have felt it in the History Department on more than one occasion, a consequence of being drawn to theoretical debates and their consequences in a department that largely finds those debates (to say nothing of their consequences) threatening. But despite that virtual consensus, and despite my lone name on the SCT roster, I was convinced that interdisciplinary dialogue between the sometimes-closed systems of literary theory and historical research could only benefit both endeavors.

Cornell looms over Ithaca in much the same way that the University of Arkansas looms over Fayetteville. It sits on a high hill, allowing the town that surrounds it to see it from all points. But there are differences, as well. Anyone who so chooses can take time out of his otherwise hurried

223

day, walk over to Cornell University's Schoellkopf football stadium, walk right through the open gate, and plant himself in the north end zone. At a Southeastern Conference university, attempt this at your peril.

The graffiti was variously baffling:

The first floor basement men's bathroom of the Olin Library of Cornell University, over the second urinal to the left, of a set of four:

I'm a fuckin
social misfit
a misogynistic
queer with no
respect for myself
or anyone else
I hate you too
give me a cigarette.

The first floor men's bathroom across from the HEC Auditorium, Goldwin Smith Hall of Cornell University, over the second of three urinals:

$$E=mc^2$$

Armed with these impressions, I embarked upon a remarkable six weeks. "The heroic protagonist requires the visionary," said Amanda Anderson, Chair of the Johns Hopkins English Department, in an early lecture, "actualization on the plane of social existence." 'Yes,' I thought, hopeful and self-absorbed. 'The visionary.' An hour-long question and answer session immediately followed each of these public lectures. At various points in the coming days, additional sessions allowed further time for discussion. I took my place in the back and observed.

The Joplin-Dubois Paradigm

Those among the theory minded speak loudly with their hands—that is, their hand gestures are far more demonstrative than their voices. The most consistent gesture, performed so regularly that the word "constant" might not necessarily be inappropriate, I took to calling, "The Take Another Piece of My Heart Now Baby." The move is performed by cupping the hand as if preparing to grip a baseball to throw a change-up, all five fingers circled around an imaginary orb. The gripping hand is turned toward the speaker, resting close to the sternum without making contact. Upon speaking, the hand then rotates upward approximately 115 degrees while the forearm extends from the body two to three inches. The gesture repeats upon each new sentence rather than with any timed consistency. It is a form of punctuation, and it is not hard to imagine that if there were gifts in those continuously giving hands, and people standing in a position to receive them, the room would have been far more joyous.

Along with a panoply of public lectures, colloquia, picnics, and mixers, participants attend one primary seminar throughout the duration of the school. Mine was titled "Black Intellectuals," taught by Brent Haynes Edwards of Rutgers University's English Department. An early seminar allowed a fresh reexamination of W.E.B. DuBois's *Souls of Black Folk*, but even though our discussion hinged—as the title of our course might suggest—on DuBois's role as a social theorist and representative black intellectual (with all that phrase's possible attendant meanings), there was still hovering over our discussion the author's inimitable veil.

A veil is an interesting artifact. It serves, we dutifully noted, as an obstruction to the way others see you, but also as an obstruction to your own vision. It is, in other words, a confession as much as it is a complaint. This ambiguity necessarily leads the reader to ask who, within the construct of this concept metaphor, sees better. This lack of surety about the upper hand in a vision contest (which is, in the end, a knowledge contest), leads DuBois into his internal split, his by-now-emblematic double consciousness. He is a Negro. He is an American. And the attendant meanings those words carried with them in 1903 disallowed the author from seeing himself as both. (This duality, and his framing of it, clearly borrows from William James, with whom DuBois studied at Harvard. An interesting question to ask here—to historians, critics, theorists, *et. al.*—would be as follows: If James's *The Double Self* help lay the intellectual groundwork for DuBois's notion of dual identity, and thus his inability to countenance himself as both Negro and American, was Jamesean psychology the impetus for DuBois's psychological identity crisis? *A Pluralistic Universe*, indeed!) His solution for sublimating, if not his own double consciousness, those double consciousnesses to come a generation later, is universalism. It is universalism, if anything, that will allow him to traduce the veil of identity.

On Speaking as if You Intend for Someone To Understand You

But back to his role as a black intellectual. DuBois spent the majority of his working life wrestling with sociology and its ability, as a science, to actually do any practical work for those for whom it advocates. And though he read his own effort as scientific, he was never squeamish about allowing history, fiction, and memoir into his conceptual framework. This was academic universalism, and its success is demonstrated by the fact that the preceding two paragraphs of this essay appear helplessly old hat. Interdisciplinarity made DuBois (to say nothing of James) effective, and left historians a potent example for meaningful scholarship.

History isn't just antiquated empiricism. Literary theory isn't just pie-in-the-sky rehearsals of post-structural linguistics. But historians often conceive their projects solely as empiricist praxis. And literary theorists often divorce their thought from context, using a complex application of jargon along the way that divorces the potential of their thought from 99.9 percent of the population. When students of history and students of literary theory meet in venues like SCT, these chasms between the two languages are bridged, slowly but surely, to the betterment of both.

That said, I still felt the difference between myself and my classmates during most of the day's seminar. We discussed the literary and logical consequences of DuBois's words rather than the historical force of his ideas. We spoke more about the conceptual and structural work of his pronouns than we did the intricacies of his critique of Booker T. Washington. While the seminar proved extraordinarily helpful for me in framing the text in a new way (or, perhaps, in an additional way), I sat quietly and listened. I couldn't bring myself to actively participate in the conversation because I didn't know how to talk like that.

In the larger group settings, including all the SCT participants, the speakers' presentations were likewise helpful. Eric Santner, Geoffrey Hartman, Dominick LaCapra, Judith Butler, and Stanley Fish (an unidentified emergency dental situation kept Alain Badiou, scheduled to speak, grounded in Paris) each presented informative and engaging lectures. They were followed, however, by an hour of thoroughly uninformative questions. To the groping rhythm of the "Take Another Little Piece of My Heart Now Baby," interlocutors spent anywhere from two to five minutes explaining "my own work" and its loose relation to *that-sentence-back-on-page-three-of-the-lecture* that sounded somewhat familiar, "and I was wondering if you could just comment on that." Throughout the question—throughout most of the questions—hallowed names of literary theory that the questioner used in an attempt to map out the space where he/she had pitched his/her critical tent only served to dominate the question. Agomben says this. Foucault says that. Zizek this. Derrida that. Again I watched in silence. I did know how to speak this way, but my conscience would never allow it.

(R)Evolution: Or, Distance from Home as the Arbiter of Academic Value

But then, on the last day of the fourth week, Friday, 14 July, just after 9:30 am, Joe Varghese Yeldo—a member of the "Black Intellectuals" seminar and a doctoral student at the Indian Institute of Technology, Kampur—pulled back the veil. The seminar was engaged in a litany of complaints about Stanley Fish's lecture two days prior—its illogic, certainly, but also the speaker's angry, inconsiderate refusal to countenance questions that seemed to oppose what he was saying. Can you blame him? Joe asked. He described his frustration with the highbrow grandstanding and name-dropping of questioners. It wasn't productive. Theory, he argued, must be something that is integrally linked with life as it is actually lived. It must be something that is both extracted and used as a tool of extraction from texts, then applied to something that actually matters. Otherwise it is pointless. Otherwise it becomes the sort of project that most historians find suspicious or intellectually irresponsible. "And you just have to think," said Joe, "this is what I hear at home. Did I come all this way just to hear the same things over and over again?" His hands remained on the table the whole time.

It was a manifesto. And it was a success. All around the table, the participants began to applaud. Any lingering feeling that I was crashing someone else's party all but disappeared.

A few days later, I presented a paper on the role of acquaintance in Bertrand Russell's theory of descriptions, and how the discipline of history had, for the most part, proved him wrong. The question and answer session demonstrated that literary critics have no problem siding with History in theoretical fights when its argument is reasonably presented. History, I think, should reciprocate by listening to literary theorists. Through the problematic jargon-laden lit-speak, there are Santner, Hartman, LaCapra, Butler, Anderson, and Brent Edwards. There is Joe. And the entire corpus of W.E.B. DuBois's writing is telling us that historical analysis cannot be limited to a standard subset. The world is larger and more interesting than that.

Conclusion

There are many histories that converge at, for example, a frustrated elevator ride up the insides of a building, where the doors that open unleash their passengers into a crucible of marginal scholarship and cliquish behavior. There were a handful of hydraulic freight elevators floating around the urban buildings of the mid-1800s when, in 1852, Elisha Otis created a passenger elevator with a safety mechanism that protected passengers in the event of a cable break. In 1880, Werner von Siemens built the first electric model. But any full history of the bank of elevators in my building would require a broad, full-spectrum history that takes many other factors into account. A corporate history of the Otis Elevator Company. A history of the building that housed the elevators. An institutional history of the university. A total history of the region and the city where the elevator bank resides, chronicling the economic, political, and cultural situation that allowed the university to exist and grow as it did, to the margins, where the building that houses the history department is located.

But even more would be required. A history of postmodern architecture, which dominated the design of the building and placed the elevators in their current location. A history of disability and the modern requirements for building access to those unable to walk. Then there would be the technological history, working backward to the Industrial Revolution, electricity, the Newtonian revolution, and metallurgy. Archimedes built an elevator more than two centuries before Christ. The Greeks were typically well-versed in the fulcrum, the lever, the pulley. Such would be the long, complete, near-cinematic history that brought those elevators to life, as I swiped my card, announced my difference from the other potential passengers glancing around for an opportunity to ride, then pushed the button and began the grand mechanical process that would ultimately dispense me on the fifth floor, where I would find Professor X, scowling as ever.

In the preceding essays, however, I am engaged in a fundamentally different project. There is no *longue durée* here. Instead, I have attempted to demonstrate the plot points along which such monumental histories turn. If language is not the core of all reality, it is the cope that surrounds every possible conception of it. Conflicts over its meaning provide the control system that spur the gears to spin.

Hilary Putnam argued that spoken, computational language and its mental, cerebral equivalent could not be adequately described by the sciences. The rules of nature, reference, meaning, and intent had to be flexible because such concepts are malleable, variously known and defined. They aren't set entities. For Richard Rorty, inheritor of the linguistic legacies of Putnam and others, that led truth to a state of functional temporality. Truths are contingent on sentences, he argued, which are contingent on languages, which are contingent on history. Understanding, in essence, is relative to a specific time and place, and the language of that time and place is so singular as to be fundamentally unknowable to later examiners. And we are, in our darker moments, left with incoherence.

I envision a world where every fact is contingent on language, too. But I think there is coherence here. By seeking out these moments of definitional difference, we can find coherence in the dialectical motion of historical evolution. Besides, that is how we discover the state of being of any society. By parsing out the definitive elements, the prime movers of a culture—both its broad movements (its relationship with ideas or religion) and its individual exemplary moments (its songs, its books)—we plot the points that constitute its topography. We push the buttons, load the algorithm, enter the doors, and ride.